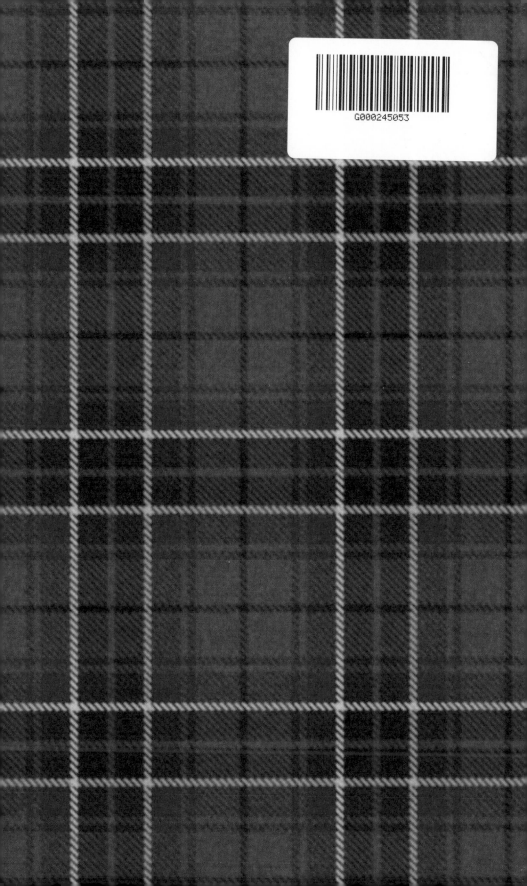

One Shot
at Life

One Shot
at Life

To Peter

All the very best

Bobby McAlpine

For Angela, Euan, Sara, Christopher and Emma

ISBN 978-1-899163-96-0
Copyright © 2012 Bobby McAlpine
First published 2012

Published by
JJG Publishing
Sparrow Hall
Hindringham
Norfolk NR21 0DP

Designed by Graham Hiles
Printed in China through Colorcraft Ltd, Hong Kong

Contents

Acknowledgements

I started this life story about three years ago and cannot say I have found writing a book remotely easy. The only thing I would say in my defence, is that I have written every word myself, whether for better or worse, I must let my readers be the judges.

In the early days, I received excellent secretarial assistance from Chester Racecourse, where Richard Thomas allowed me to call on the services of Alex Jarvis, who managed to translate my appalling handwriting. My current secretary, Sue Davies, had to carry on from there and as I have never learnt to use a computer, she also had to deal with my illegible script. I am most grateful to both ladies.

Roddy Bloomfield, a most distinguished editor himself and a director of a large publishing company, has been extremely helpful and introduced me to my publisher, Jeremy Greenwood, who founded Quiller Press. I cannot thank both of them sufficiently.

Meryl Evans has been extremely helpful in trying to make sure that I have not caused too much offence to others in the book.

Wendy Cousins has corrected me on some racing details in the Robert Sangster chapter and I thank all others who, learning I was writing a book, have given encouragement. I hope they are not too disappointed.

Illustrations

Thanks to:

Society Wedding Press – 12

C.B. Livingston – 7

Jim Meads, who has always taken the shooting photographs at Llanarmon – 42, 44, 45, 46, 47, and the back panel of the jacket

Fiona Vigors (now Marner) who took the photo of the mare and foal and myself – 34

Gary Talbot, who took the High Sheriff photograph – 21

Stuart Rayner, who photographed various pieces and pictures at Tilstone Lodge

David Langdon (front cover), who did the caricature for the Ladbrokes Racing Calendar

Julian Herbert/Getty Images for the shot of Inglis Drever – 35

... and to everyone else who has taken the photographs that I have used.

Chapter 1

Early Days

Between Chester in England and Wrexham in Wales there are two villages, Rossett and Gresford – both on the Welsh side of the border. All my first three childhood homes were in or near one of the two villages and the first of them 'Barnfeld' was the closest to the border, but still a mile into Wales. This was later to give me a qualification to play squash for Wales, a source of great amusement that with a name like mine I could represent Wales at anything.

In fact Barnfeld, hidden away down Barton Lane, is the only one of the three houses I have lived in as a child still standing much in its original form; it is a nice-looking substantial house with I suspect several major additions since my parents' time there. I have only one memory of Barnfeld – being taken downstairs by Nanny to meet a visitor of my mother's who wore a nurse uniform and was probably my maternity nurse.

Just before my third birthday we moved less than a mile up the road towards Llay to a house called 'Stoneleigh'. This was a much bigger Victorian house of three storeys and, though not classical, was well laid out and had all the comforts that a rich young married couple with children would look for. I remember the layout of the house well; through the front door was a room to the right which my parents used as a small drawing room. Now it would have been the television room. To the left a much larger drawing room for the grander occasion and next to it another room in which a bar with stools had been installed. Silver shakers were on the bar as it was very much the cocktail era and I have a particular memory of Kiora passion fruit which Father used to put into cocktails. The last main room at the front of the house was a large dining room used by my parents for their three main meals. Upstairs there was a master suite which involved a bathroom and Father's dressing room. There were several other main bedrooms and a self-contained nursery wing down a corridor to the right of the house and Nanny, I and brother Billy, who had been born just before the move, all had bedrooms down it. At the end of the corridor there was a large nursery where Nanny and the maids had a constant battle to get rid of mice which seemed attracted to that part of the house. From the nursery we had a good view of the garages and stables at the back of the house and the walls of an extensive kitchen garden.

What are my memories of Stoneleigh? Many and still clear must be the answer. The fleet of fast cars fascinated me from the start, particularly the Lagondas. I would peer into the interior and study the speedometer, 130 mph was mildly disappointing, 150mph much more exciting. Whereas Father would occasionally take us for a drive and get up to really fast speeds, my mother who also drove a Lagonda would slow down and deliberately get me used to slow speeds.

Like all little boys I was excited by trains and Nanny would walk us on most afternoons to Rossett station where I would watch with fascination as the trains either thundered through or stopped there. Once there was a major football match in Wrexham and train after train went through the station to much excitement.

It was the era of Cowboys and Indians and we would dress up in elaborate Indian headdresses or cowboy wide-brimmed hats and fire imitation six-shooters with caps or toy bows and arrows. My birthday in early May was the scene of children's parties carefully organised by my mother who had to cover up the fact she couldn't be there herself. The reason, it was always on the same day as the Chester May Festival race meeting and, although she genuinely tried to get back in time to see the end of the tea party, they always had such a good time at Chester that the best of intentions went by the board. Sixty years later when I was chairman of the racecourse and the screen above the weighing room flashed up the words 'Happy Birthday Chairman' I understood only too well the dilemma my mother had been in.

Nanny was, of course, an integral part of my and Billy's life and I was lucky – or unlucky as some would later tell me – in having a gentle middle-aged lady to look after my needs. She did make the occasional feeble effort to discipline us and the only serious time I can remember was when she strapped me in the pram and left me in the kitchen garden. A weekend guest came along and asked me what I was doing to which I replied there had been a terrible mistake and would she fetch help. Help was a long time coming!

Although I did not realise it, Nanny had no training and this was to cause major problems in one area, namely she did not teach me to be tidy and my mother and my prep school headmaster both blamed my appalling untidiness on lack of initial training in this department. I never did ask my mother why she hadn't done more because parents were simply not expected to supervise children in their formative years.

Apart from Nanny there was a veritable army of staff. Wages were low and domestic service was prized. I lost count of the maids. There was a butler, an under butler, at least three main gardeners, two chauffeurs and many others. One summer day when my parents were away they were all allowed their own sports day and I marvelled at the number who turned up. Billy and I were each allowed to win two races and after that, having taken part in one where we finished behind, we were led away.

Two of the big events of the year were Christmas and my birthday. The thrills of opening the stockings are forever etched in my mind. How did Santa get such amazing presents, all the ones I'd been hoping for months I would receive? Santa was indeed a genius and fortunately nobody told me the facts of life in this direction until I was eight or nine. Christmas lunch was one of the rare occasions when Billy and I were allowed at a grown-up meal, and a very grand affair it was with various other members of the family asked as well. I was allowed a small glass of champagne at an early age but my small brother was not. He looked longingly at my enjoyment and without a word grabbed my grandmother's glass and downed it in one go.

Two major family events that took place at Stoneleigh were the christening of Billy and the wedding of my mother's sister Jean to Bill Kington, whose family owned the local brewery – Border Breweries of Wrexham. Billy was over a year old when the christening took place and howled constantly through the service. I was next to my paternal grandmother who told me to sit still and behave. Not the most enjoyable of events.

My aunt's wedding was a very different affair. Everybody was in a party mood and my mother was obviously enjoying being the hostess. The bride looked radiant and Bill was for some reason in full army uniform. I was offered all sorts of goodies, particularly a great favourite, sausages on sticks. My blossoming love of champagne was given a great fillip by pretending to well meaning guests that I had been promised a glass and never received it. I was eventually rescued and taken to the nursery slightly tipsy, an event my mother would make sure would not reoccur until many years later.

The other wedding I attended in my early years was in London where I was a page. Either the bride or groom was a Topham, the family who owned Aintree Racecourse, and I was boarded with my mother's cousin Doreen McLaren and her husband. To my horror Nanny was not to accompany me and my two main memories were of Doreen putting me on the loo in the full view of the household and a terrified tearful little boy being coaxed up the aisle. Years later Peggy Hennessy, who was chief bridesmaid, told me how she had tried to get me to behave and that I was the worst pageboy she had ever come across.

There were of course frequent visits to my two sets of grandparents who both lived close by. It would be hard to imagine a greater contrast than the two homes my grandparents lived in. Mother's parents lived in the small house called Whitegates at the top of Marford Hill halfway between Rossett and Gresford. The house had been bought for them by my other grandparents as my maternal grandfather, who was originally a German national called Adolf Sauberg, had become an American citizen and settled in America in 1913. He lived there with his wife and two children until 1929 when a severe financial crisis forced him to bring the family to England and ask his wife's rich relations for help to get him on his feet again. As my mother hated talking about that period I learnt little about the true events but Stewart Kington did extensive family research and believes it was not just the Wall Street crash which brought my grandfather down, but bad debts and a failed lawsuit also.

Whatever the reasons, the strain brought about a premature attack of Parkinson's and he was sadly a wreck of a man by the late thirties.

Although Whitegates was a small house it had a pleasant garden and sufficient lawn to play all the children's games then current, 'Grandmother's Footsteps' being a particular favourite of mine.

Marchweil Hall, the home of my paternal grandparents, is a large attractive Georgian house which has extensive grounds which in the late thirties were exceptional even in those lavish times. Apart from a hard tennis court there was in summer at least two grass courts and country house tournaments were played there. The cricket ground in full view of the house was in existence before my grandparents bought Marchweil but had been enlarged after the Great War and a cricket pavilion erected dedicated to the memory of my grandmother's brother who had been killed in the war. Behind the cricket pavilion a wooded area lead to a lake which was stocked with trout and fished by my grandfather, a more than keen fisherman. It was a great treat to go in the boat with him. The cricket ground was used by the locals and although it was called a village side the excellence of the ground and wicket attracted many good cricketers who would normally have played elsewhere.

My early memories are being taken to the 'country house' matches where my grandfather's XI, captained by Father, would take on touring sides. Some very good Lancashire and even England cricketers had been recruited by my grandfather so the standards were very high. Father was also Captain of the Denbighshire side which played in the minor counties competition, the only Welsh county (apart from Glamorgan) to obtain such heights – although Father admitted they hardly won a match. He was a medium fast bowler and I followed every ball he bowled with the greatest of hero worship. He was indeed a dashing, glamorous figure in those days.

Marchweil had the usual number of staff expected in large country houses operated by rich owners. The principals were: 'Cousins', the butler, a kindly gentleman who once told me that his experience in the trenches in the 1914-18 war had been so terrible that he'd lost all interest in religion; Mrs McNance, an enormous genial Irish lady, ruled the kitchen with several assistants; Miln, the chauffeur, was not liked by Father who told me he was bone idle and when the Second World War started told everyone how pleased he was he didn't have to go to the shoots and race meetings any longer. There were, of course, several outdoor staff comprising gardeners, a cricket groundsman and a woodman.

No account of the first six years of my life would be complete without a memory of my dreams which were intense and very vivid. The two I remember most clearly were one where I eventually confronted a large animal, lion, tiger or wolf which was about to eat me when I woke up. The second much pleasanter dream was dropping into a river or pond and drifting along with the fish all around me.

In the summer of 1939 mother told us that we were to have a summer holiday on a small island on the mouth of the Clyde. This would be a change from holidays on the Isle of Wight, where my mother would take a house with Kay Lloyd who had three children a little younger than me. The island was called 'Little Cumbrae' and was owned by Ian and Diana Parker, great friends of my parents who had previously given memorable children's parties in their home at Bromborough in the Wirral.

The island only had two buildings: a large comfortable house which I later learned was supposed to be haunted, and a lighthouse. The only means of getting to nearby Great Cumbrae Island was by boat and the Parkers had quite a large one with a reasonably reliable outboard motor. Little Cubrae was a walker's or a wildfowler's paradise. The beaches were perfect and the bays abounded with fish which could be seen in very clear water. There were other friends of the Parkers on the island with children and for a time we were a jolly happy group. But the grown-ups were looking increasingly sombre and after two months there was talk of war being declared. The children were despatched to look for U Boats and, as one side of the island looked directly up the Clyde, there was plenty to see with the river traffic.

In fact what was to be a normal seaside holiday lasted for four months and, although I did not know it, my parents were getting divorced and my mother was searching for a house to live in. As the winter of 1939 set in she found one and we left Little Cumbrae, sadly never to return, and moved in to Glan Alyn near the bottom of Gresford Hill, owned by a Mrs Clayton whose son Michael was one of my main playmates at that time.

Glan Alyn was an attractive, large to medium sized house with a decent area of lawn and garden and – very important to two small boys – a nice fast flowing river, the River Alyn, at the end of the garden. Our way of life became very different; the staff consisted of a cook-housekeeper and nanny, who had gone to Little Cumbrae with us and was to stay until my brother went to boarding school when she moved a few miles away to look after my cousins, Miles and Stewart Kington.

There were three main things I remember about the first eighteen months of the war. Food rationing caused my mother all sorts of problems. The lavish meals were replaced by austerity and the orchard and kitchen garden really came into their own. Worse still was petrol rationing. The shiny black Lagonda was put into the garage until the war ended and was replaced by an Austin which did a substantial mileage per gallon. Nevertheless we were always short of petrol. Mother used to drive us as slowly as possible and freewheel down the hills; although whether the turning off and on of the engine really saved any petrol I am not sure.

As a result of petrol rationing a number of parents got together and arranged for their children to be taught by a Miss Dutton at one of the parent's houses. Glan Alyn was quite central and often chosen. The class was not demanding and there were none of the pressures children face now. The one department I was well ahead of the game was reading. I was then as I am now an avid reader. At the age of five I could read an Arthur Ransome book and was later fascinated by the Wizard of Oz and desperately tried to get mother to buy all the 'Oz' books. It was a shame that after the first four they became impossible to get in wartime Britain.

The third major memory of that period was the blitz. Many people think of it as mainly affecting London but Liverpool, only 25 miles away from us, was also an important target. Although we were far enough away not to be in the frontline, there were frequent times when German bombers dropped their load close by. Mother came to an arrangement with the Duckworth family who lived at Gresford Lodge next door, a large house with a deep cellar, that when the blitz got really intensive we would walk from Glan Alyn up the kitchen garden through a door which separated the two properties and join the Duckworths in their cellar. In practice we only did this on one night. It was all very exciting for us children, the sky was ablaze with activities, fighters attacking the German bombers and Ack Ack guns blasting into the sky from Liverpool and its surrounds.

In 1941 I was informed by my mother that she had arranged for me to go to a preparatory school, Selwyn House, which had been evacuated from Broadstairs to a large house in the small Welsh village of Llanfyllin, virtually in the middle of nowhere. I would normally have gone to the family prep school, Sandroyd in Dorset, but the relatively short distance from Gresford to Llanfyllin made Selwyn House much more practical. Mr and Mrs Green, the headmaster and his wife, had visited Glan Alyn and had seemed pleasant enough – so one day at the beginning of May my mother took me by train from Gresford to Gobowen where the London train decamped the Greens and a large number of boys. Mother bade me a tearful farewell and said rather dramatically, 'He's in your care now, John.' We all boarded a local train to Oswestry and then another which took us to the last station on the line, Llanfyllin. Selwyn House had not gone to Llanfyllin by accident. Llwyn, the house the school moved to, was owned by Mrs Green's father, John Dugdale, a former headmaster who in turn moved to a farmhouse about half a mile away. I was later to discover that the same thing had happened in the 1914-18 war, when Selwyn House was first evacuated to North Wales.

In many ways it was ideal for a school. The rooms fitted nicely into classrooms and dormitories and there were comfortable living rooms for the Greens at the front of the house. The problem, as I was to discover, was the lack of outdoor facilities and the shortage of similar schools to play games against. Hawtreys, evacuated to a Williams Wynn house nearby, and Packwood, now one of the best preparatory schools in the country, were our only opposition, joined later by Ellesmere junior school.

I had arrived at Selwyn in good spirits but the following morning was one of the most dispiriting of my life. No nanny on hand to pamper me and some very rough boys around. The captain of the dormitory was Patrick Cliff, the only non-new boy, and next to him was John Merrison, an outstanding school boxer, who eventually boxed and played rugby for the navy. Two others were Michael Fitzroy, the younger son of the Duke of Grafton, who sadly died in the South Seas in his late twenties, almost certainly taken by sharks, and Donald MacPherson, who I met again at Winchester during school rackets matches and occasionally in the city in later life. Also Hugh Cantlie, who I had lunch with in Whites only weeks before writing this.

Strangely several in the dormitories seemed fascinated by corporal punishment. They did not have to wait long. On only the second night of term three of them were taken to the headmaster and smacked with a slipper for talking after lights out. They came back laughing and giggling and for several nights the process was repeated until the headmaster got fed up and sent the whole dormitory to bed on one fine Saturday summer afternoon.

Whilst the slipper was used frequently the headmaster had a stick which was only used for serious transgressions. I was twice caned with it. The first time a boy called Peake and I both received it for not working hard enough. When I protested that I was far from bottom of the form I was told I should be much nearer the top.

The second occasion was during my last term when Mrs Green decided to go around the dormitories and catch a number of us reading on a light summer evening. When I arrived outside the drawing room door I found John Merison, the head of school, I was the deputy and there were a few other senior boys. The first miscreant, a boy called Milner, endured the only two serious strokes as on the third the stick broke and John Green was forced to use a baton from the school concert and, scared of breaking it, the rest of us received light slaps.

I can't say I look back on Selwyn with a great deal of affection. Because of the lack of facilities we were taken on a lot of organised walks and runs. The focal point was always a lone pine tree which stood out at the top of the small hill some distance in front of the school. Whilst the countryside was glorious it was largely wasted on me. I was good at the two main games, cricket and football, and longed for more organised matches.

My first term was however more than just eventful. On one of the first Saturdays I was allowed to go out with both my parents. It was a glorious hot afternoon, and although I did not know it enjoying a delicious picnic lunch on the side of a hill, it was to be one of only two school visits Father ever made to my two schools, his second to watch me play rackets in my penultimate term at Harrow.*

About halfway through the summer term I was really struggling with the lessons, particularly Latin, never my favourite. When one afternoon I suddenly felt really ill, went to the matron and was put to bed, the local doctor was called for and scarlet fever was diagnosed. Nowadays scarlet fever has been nearly eliminated in Britain, but then it was more common and easily the worst of the common children's illnesses – measles, mumps, etc.

Three others had also gone down and the situation was really serious. A qualified nurse from London was sent for. When she arrived my temperature had gone up to 105 degrees and she said aloud, 'Any higher and it's hospital for you.' Fortunately it got no higher, though I was to stay in bed at school until halfway through the summer holidays and suffered severe complications with my ears and eyes. My ear problems caused a surgeon from Chester to come out and perform, under anaesthetic, a small operation, which was successful, although my first experience of ether was very unpleasant.

Obviously my parents and grandparents were very concerned and I received regular parcels from Marchweil of fruits from the garden –

---

*He did though give my mother and I lunch during one Eton and Harrow event. After lunch he took us to the Cavendish Hotel in which the famous Courtesan was still living. He bought a bottle of Ayala champagne and asked if Madame was well enough for him to go and talk to her. After an interval the housekeeper came back and said that Father and I could follow her, and we went upstairs, where an old lady was in bed. The one sentence I do remember was, looking benignly at me and saying to Father, 'I wish I could look after him the way I looked after you Jimmy.'

particularly grapes from the greenhouse, a great treat during times of austerity.

When I eventually got home I was allowed a few days of peace and enjoyment before being told that my tonsils were in terrible condition and had to come out, and Billy was told his were to come out too. We were taken to hospital in Chester to be treated by the same surgeon who had operated on me in Llanfyllin. We were both given tablets and told they should send us to sleep. Billy, always more relaxed than me, duly went to sleep and only woke up after the operation. I, who had a foreboding after my previous anaesthetic, arrived awake in the operating theatre and endured a horrendous anaesthetic, impossible to fully describe. It gave me nightmares for years to come and a terror of anaesthetics which only receded a couple of years ago after a hip operation at the King Edward hospital in London, where the anaesthetist who came to see me the night before the operation said, 'I'm the best anaesthetist in England; you will be well when you wake up and feel no effects' – I didn't.

After the tonsils I was allowed a proper holiday which went well until halfway through the winter term when I was returned to Selwyn where everyone must have been told to treat me with 'kid gloves' – staff and boys were particularly kind until the end of term. The following year saw me for the first time spending some of the summer holidays with Father. I went straight from school to the train, disembarked at Shrewsbury only to find no one there to meet me. Father, notorious for his unpunctuality, arrived ten minutes later with Billy in his cream Lagonda and the three of us drove to his Shropshire home, Tickwood Hall. We were greeted by my stepmother Mary, who did everything to make us feel welcome and happy. She was a particularly attractive lady with a warm kind disposition, and even then I could see why Father was so attracted by her.

Tickwood was another perfect family house. Built in the William and Mary period it had about three hundred acres of pleasant wooded areas overlooking what is now Telford and Ironbridge power station, then a very small station.

When two or three years later I was given a small light shotgun, it was the perfect estate to learn to shoot on as it has every form of wild game birds, not in large numbers but sufficient to be able to fire several shots on any walk. Its previous owner had a small booklet privately published listing all the flowers and fauna to be found when walking at Tickwood.

Father was to me in those days an immensely glamorous larger-than-life figure and he undoubtedly had a major influence on my development. In many ways he was extremely unconventional. He was almost certainly partly dyslexic and had absolutely no time for the academic side of life. Even in the days of Common Entrance being almost a formality, he barely passed the exam to Repton where he spent the first two years in the bottom form. Sent by my grandfather to Pembroke College, Cambridge, who took him mainly on his cricketing ability as a prominent member of a good Repton XI, he not only failed his end of first year exam, but in fact never put pen to paper. He often told with great amusement the story of my grandfather sending the family butler, Cousins, to collect him and taking several days to get back to Marchweil.

The holidays were from now on spent almost equally between Tickwood and Glan Alyn. My mother always had a boyfriend in tow, the first being a genial 'Bulldog Drummond' type of man called Jack Elliot, who sadly had a brain tumour which eventually killed him. He was followed by several others whose names I don't remember. When she reached the stage when things got more serious she would ask Billy and I what we thought, and thoroughly jealous at the encroachment onto our territory we would always give a low opinion of the intruder.

School also progressed steadily. I was good at games and was the youngest boy to get in the school cricket XI of that era. After the one painful warning on the academic front I was bright enough to keep out of trouble. I neither particularly liked nor hated Selwyn House. I found the Headmaster small minded and fussy, remembering his endless lectures on how not to use too much loo paper and make sure all sides were properly used. Mrs Green was unpopular and supposed to be a sadist. Wonderful stories circulated, probably grossly untrue, about her hiding behind the curtains whilst boys were being beaten. The one amazing character was the senior master Mr Meade-King known as MK. He took all the games and his whole life was wrapped up in the school. He hated the holidays and every year he put together a booklet to be sent to old boys and parents chronicling the activities at the school. A prolific smoker he had the grubbiest fingernails I've ever seen but his heart was in the right place and I remember him with affection. He did however have one weakness. In a period when John Green was seriously ill he was acting headmaster and took over the discipline. He liked smacking boys on their bare bottoms with his hands which lingered rather too long before the smacks came. We all used to be highly amused but whether our mothers would have felt the same is debatable.

In 1944 a sad event occurred when Billy and I were asked to see the headmaster after breakfast to be told that our grandfather, Sir Alfred, had died. He had been in poor health for a long time and had frequent visits to health spas, particularly one locally at Ruthin Castle. When my mother first came into contact with her in-laws she named them 'Pops' and 'Sugar' which were amusing Americanisms. Whilst Pops suited my grandfather well, the opposite was true with my grandmother. She had good points but Sugar she was definitely not and unfortunately her husband's death affected her dramatically and any balance she had rather departed from then on.

His will left Marchweil to my grandmother, the company – Sir Alfred McAlpine and Son – equally to Father and his two sisters, and Llanarmon, the shooting estate he had bought from Bendor Duke of Westminster, was put in a strange trust called the Scottish Trust with Father the first named trustee. It was eventually to cause all sorts of problems but my mother was particularly angry that he had left no money in trust for myself and Billy as she felt he had promised to do so and with good reason she totally mistrusted Father on the financial front.

She was very short of money herself and was frequently behind with the rent for Glan Alyn. Like most divorced wives of the time she had nothing like the alimony which would have been awarded these days, but as I was to discover in later life she did tend to spend quickly whatever she had.

I was due to finish preparatory school in the end of 1945 and go to Harrow, a school which Father had decided for me through a number of Harrovian friends, particularly Eric Lloyd whose old house The Grove I was put down for.

My last term at Selwyn was also the one the war in Europe ended and the school embarked on a series of celebrations which included a trip to the Welsh beaches, never my favourite scene. My cricket continued to progress and I captained the side in my last year in the XI. Perhaps I got a little carried away by being easily the best player in the side because none of the others made their public school XIs afterwards. Common entrance was duly taken and I passed into the top shell form at Harrow – designed for the better than average academically.

The last event of the term was the leaving lecture when John Green walked us individually down the drive and gave us 'The facts of Life'. We had all prepared for a breathtaking 'grown up' talk but in fact it went completely over my head. I remember snatches of it: 'rubbing produces a very pleasant sensation', 'doing it' will make you very tired at work, and the headmaster asking if I understood it all. I kept answering 'yes sir' without understanding anything and amazingly at the age of thirteen none of us knew what sex was about. Television was certainly going to change all that.

Mother had arranged that we would stay for a month on the Isle of Wight in a house she had taken with the Lloyd and McLintock families. I had not seen the Lloyds since pre-war days in their house in Hampshire and holidays also in the Isle of Wight. I had never met the McLintocks whose mother Jean was a sister of Kay Lloyd, both being Canadian by birth and related to Lord Beaverbrook, owner of the *Daily Express*. William McLintock had already had a term at The Grove at Harrow and his comments did nothing to allay my fears about going to public school. The holiday was not a success. Whilst Robert Lloyd, a year younger than me, liked to play cricket, the two McLintock boys did not and there were constant arguments.

I was relieved to get home to Glan Alyn, but the day soon came when we packed up and went to London where we were to spend two days before boarding the tube from Baker Street to Harrow-on-the-Hill station. As the new boys arrived early to be interviewed by their housemaster, mother and I walked up the hill and rang the bell at The Grove and the butler Harry ushered us in to see Lance Gorse the housemaster. Lance Gorse was a genial, slightly overweight parson and was certainly very welcoming on this occasion, reminding my mother that he had started his teaching career at Repton and that Father was at the school his first term there. He took us through to the room I was to share with John Stancliffe who seemed nice enough and the first evening passed pleasantly. The next day we were given a lecture by the head of house and allocated 'fagging duties' to one of the prefects who would bellow 'fag' loud and long. You had to know his voice and rush to get inline, the last ones to do so being given whichever job was needed.

The first day was also given over to a rugby trial. Although I didn't consider it my best game I must have fallen on the ball at the right time and shown some aptitude because I was put into the top junior game. Whether I would have made the junior XV was debatable, but in fact I had a mishap in the gym where I never showed much ability and fell awkwardly. Nobody showed much concern and I played rugby the next day but my arm was very painful and the master in charge took me out of the scrum and sent me to see the house matron, who arranged for an x-ray which showed my arm was broken and needed setting under anaesthetic.

My terror of anaesthetics immediately took over and I rang my mother who did her best to persuade Lance Gorse that I should be given a new drug Pentathol which sent you to sleep by injection. Although I wasn't told until just before the operation, I was given the injection which made all the difference and I returned to The Grove with my arm in plaster and off games for most of the term.

About three weeks into the term John and I, who had the room below the head of house, had gone to sleep only to be woken by the sound of a savage beating being administered to some wretched small boy in the presence of the other prefects. Although house beatings did not happen regularly there were about three or four a term in my first years. They followed an elaborate ritual and were very frightening. After lights out a boy in the room next to the head of house was told to go and fetch the miscreant who was lying quaking usually knowing what was in store for him. He was brought to the head of house's room to be told why he was being beaten and then made to wait outside whilst some furniture was changed. He then had to knock, enter the room, hand his dressing gown to one prefect and slippers to another and was made to bend down for the beating. Although you were allowed to cry, any movement was severely frowned on. The beating left severe bruising which lasted for weeks and I always felt it was too severe a punishment. In fact the beatings declined considerably over the five years I was at Harrow as a more enlightened era began to emerge.

I was probably lucky to go the term I did as the previous head of house was a sadist whose beatings became legends in the house. One particularly savage one was administered to the younger brother of a boy he disliked. The boy concerned had made the grave mistake, when he knew he was going to be beaten, of going to the housemaster who agreed he should not. The head of house, later known as 'The Beast of Belsen', bided his time, got permission eventually from Lance Gorse and administered a beating which severely scarred his victim. Even his fellow prefects expressed disgust afterwards.

I must not get this side of life out of perspective. Of the six new boys my first term, only one was ever beaten.

A little later in the term a more pleasant event took place: a visit to the school, which became an annual event, by Winston Churchill who had Harrow songs sung to him. One song 'Five Hundred Faces' required a verse to be sung solo by a new boy. My roommate was selected and sang it beautifully and without a trace of nerves. Later that evening Lance Gorse visited our room, congratulated John and said he'd given pleasure to one of the greatest men that ever lived.

At the end of term I had assumed John Stancliffe and I would be sharing a room again but he surprised me by saying he'd asked to share with Richard Parkes. A few years later I learned the true reason was that pressure had been put on him by senior boys to make the switch. He kept the room and I moved to one at the top of the house to share with two others.

The Easter term was a short one and we played a game called Harrow Football. I enjoyed it but sadly no other schools played it and it was useless to me after I left. I did start to play rackets, a wonderful game a little like squash but played in a bigger court with hard walls, a hard ball and stronger rackets. The professional, Fred Crosby, was a lovely man and an excellent teacher and his room behind the court was a great place to sit and gossip. Unlike The Grove, boys of all ages mixed freely there and the school pair, Geoffrey Simmonds and Robin Treherne Thomas, talked openly in front of all of us. At the beginning of the summer term there was great excitement because a popular boy who had just got into the cricket XI was caught in another house where Treherne Thomas was the head boy. He had in fact been reported to the house master by a junior prefect and Treherne Thomas had a lot of explaining to do including a grilling from the headmaster. It transpired that a small boy was the target and his name was soon known by the whole school. The older boy was duly expelled but the prefect who reported him was vilified and booed and jostled when he appeared in the schoolyard and the headmaster was forced to call the whole school together, but excluded boys in their first year, so I never heard his lecture on the pursuit of small boys.

During the Easter holidays I was taken to my first point-to-point in Cheshire on an unusually warm day and felt most peculiar and almost fainted. That night Billy and I went to Tickwood and the next day I came out in spots having caught Chicken Pox and Billy came out with them soon afterwards. We were in strict quarantine for three weeks and I persuaded my mother to extend the holidays by a few days so that I could go to the Chester May meeting. This was the first meeting there since 1939 and an immense crowd of over 100,000 attended over the three days. We went only the first day and I then returned to Harrow.

I was told to attend a trial for the Junior Colts, the senior game for under fifteens, and duly turned up. All the others had at least two days of net practice and I had to go into the game having not bowled a ball or held a bat for nine months. Not surprisingly although I got a wicket in my three overs I did not do myself justice, nor did I shine with the bat. Whilst I was put into the reserve eleven I was not selected for the Junior Colts. When it came to nets I was much more impressive and the head coach, Patsy Hendren who had played for England, was very encouraging and did make a couple of attempts to get more recognition of my bowling.

During the summer holidays an event happened which, although it seemed sad to me at the time, helped my progress on the rackets court. An outstanding junior cricketer and rackets player, who was certain to be in the junior pair, had stolen an expensive camera from an American exchange scholar in his house. When he attempted to sell it he was reported to the police and expelled during the holidays. The competition for the junior pair was now less intense and Dick Bridgeman and I were selected for the first match against Eton. I was quite small and Dick even smaller and the two Etonians who met us looked enormous and unsurprisingly hammered us in two straight games. We did far better in three more matches and my progress on the rackets and squash courts was well ahead of that on the cricket field.

After two years at Harrow we were no longer 'fagging' and were allowed our own rooms.

It was whilst three or four of us were larking around when something happened which was to change my outlook on life. A boy slightly younger than me touched me over my private parts and a sensation not unlike a pleasant electric shock swept through me. Amazed to see my reaction and surprise he asked me if I really didn't understand what was happening, took me to his room and in the space of a few minutes told me all about sex including the act of buggery which he said was too advanced for us. Looking back it seems incredible that at nearly sixteen I did not have the slightest idea what sex was about. It could not happen nowadays.

Another major event also occurred that year at home. I had a particularly difficult Easter holidays with my mother who was bad tempered throughout. In the first couple of weeks of the summer term she wrote a long letter apologising but also delivering the devastating news that she was getting married again and that by the time I received the letter she would be Mrs Dennis Hickman. My new step-father was the assistant manager of the Grosvenor Hotel in Chester, and was several years younger than mama. I had got so used to a series of her boyfriends usually older than her, that I had not taken the budding romance too seriously. A further letter brought the additional news that Dennis was leaving the Grosvenor Hotel and was to become manager of the Rougemont Hotel, Exeter, Devon, a far cry from Cheshire and North Wales. The summer holidays were to be spent between Father in Shropshire and my mother and Dennis in Exeter. I was amazed to find how badly Exeter had been blitzed, and quite large parts of the city had not been rebuilt in 1947.

The holiday part spent in Exeter went pleasantly enough. Mama had already made several friends and I found myself asked to tennis parties in nice houses with children my age or a little older, as fortunately my tennis was well above average. We swam quite a lot in the sea, and being used to swimming in the rivers Alyn and Dee (when we left Glan Alyn I knew every pool between Gresford and Rossett) I found the sea reasonably warm. A couple who were friendly with Dennis and mother had a daughter also fifteen and, after swimming together a few times, it was suggested the two of us should bicycle to Budleigh Salterton about nine miles away. Jane's parents provided a picnic and the two of us both used to long bicycle rides conversed happily, found a secluded spot, had an excellent picnic but then some-how the afternoon seemed to go downhill, and by the time we put our bikes into a local train to go home the atmosphere was distinctly frosty. I could not work out what I had done wrong and it was a year or two later that I realised that it was what I had not done which was the problem. What Harrow had not taught me was that girls also expected a little passion, and a soft kiss with my cycling companion might have made all the difference. Sadly I was never to get the opportunity again.

The part of the holiday spent at Tickwood was not quite as tran-quil as of old either. My father and stepmother were beginning to quarrel and whist I mentally sided with my stepmother as I could begin to see my father's desire to dominate everybody, I also began to realise that Mary, charming and relaxed when sober, could be quite aggressive after drinking. Billy and I had gradually been introduced to regular wine drinking diluted with soda or water for a few years. By the time I was sixteen I was allowed a couple of glasses and half a glass of port. Father was a great expert on port and Bordeaux in particular and I knew all the great port years from '08 to '45 with '27 and '34 as the best inbetween.

The after dinner conversations at Tickwood were amazing. Apart from the rallying against academic learning we were given frequent lectures that if we ever caught anything from a woman we were to see a doctor immediately. Father who seemed very proud to have caught something once or twice in his philandering youth unfortunately gave us no advice on what we were supposed to be looking for. Father's attitude to sex was simple: get as much as you can as often as possible. When I later confessed I found dancing very difficult I was told you simply must learn; dancing is an essential prelude to bed.

Back at Harrow I was beginning to find my relationship with my housemaster a little difficult. At sixteen we took a test called school certificate, and although I gained respectable grades they were not as good as his expectation and I had slipped behind one or two contemporaries in the house. There was little doubt about the reasons. Father had made it clear he was totally disinterested in any academic progress. He never read a report and was not going to let me go to university. Whereas all my friends had to work to get into university I was going to go straight into the family company when leaving Harrow.

Lance Gorse had also changed. He had always been a heavy drinker but we all sensed he was drinking more and becoming moody and unpredictable. Charles Lillingstone was to tell me later that Gorse had applied for the headmaster's vacant position at Haileybury and although he expected to get it somebody else was chosen. He felt Gorse never really got over that reverse.

Charles Lillingstone was a remarkable character who had been to Eton and revelled in being a total snob. Passionate about shooting, he had once taken a holiday job as tutor to the next Lord Howard de Walden at Chirk Castle close to Llanarmon. As in my last three years I was in the squash team, where he was master in charge, I got to know him well and transferred out of the army section of the corps which I hated to the RAF section which he was also in charge of. Charles had no more interest in the RAF than I had and on a visit to a local aerodrome we were met by a very senior RAF officer who said to Charles, 'Squadron Leader' (a courtesy title) 'your boys are going up in the Tiger Moths and I hope you will lead them.' Charles replied,

'Nothing would induce me to go up in one of those contraptions, but the boys have no option.'

These eccentricities did not appeal to Doctor Moore, the headmaster, and Charles was passed over in his attempts to become a housemaster. But after Moore's death Charles became close to the successor Mr James who gave him Druries as a house which he happily ruled over for fourteen years. If he liked you he could go out of his way to help. In my last two years he came to my rescue at least twice when I was in major trouble with Gorse and gave me excellent advice on how to cope with his mood swings.

My progress in the rackets court continued and I played for the first pair in the public schools competition just before my sixteenth birthday. We were drawn against Eton and lost in the first round to Ian Sales de la Terriere, the best player in the competition, and Colin Ingleby-Mackenzie, a year younger than myself and a schoolboy prodigy. Dick Bridgeman and I played three years running as the first pair and although we did not do very well the second year we should have probably won in the third year as we had beaten Winchester, the finalists in both home and away school matches the previous term All went well for a time and we won the first two games convincingly and had a good lead to win the fourth but I was aware that Dick, who was very small and smoked a prodigious amount of cigarettes for a schoolboy, was beginning to run out of puff. We lost the fourth game by one point and were never in the hunt thereafter. The match had one long term benefit for me as my subconscious told me that cigarettes were bad for fitness and I never smoked one again. Dick had his first heart attack aged twenty-four on a rackets court and died also of a heart attack, aged fifty, an absurdly young age. Cigarettes have a lot to answer for!

My two close friends at Harrow could not have been more different. John MacMullen came from a family of Herefordshire brewers and was a typical countryman who, like myself, loved shooting and country pursuits. Christopher Cruise, the son of King George V's eye surgeon, was an immensely talented scholar who could play the piano by ear and was confident and extrovert. I stayed every holiday with one or the other and became very attached to their families. Although Christopher and John were very different as individuals, holiday life followed the same patterns. I used to take a gun to stay with both and would shoot rabbits or pigeons and go to point-to-points in the vicinity. Staying with Christopher in Buckinghamshire we would often go and visit Evelyn Rothschild at Wing and I well remember being taken around the gardens by his father, frantically trying to make some sense of knowing about the plants he was very proud of. Evelyn's mother, who was presumably French, had a habit of trying to talk to us sometimes in French, which Christopher naturally handled rather better than myself.

My last year at Harrow was more akin to university life than an English public school. We had begun to drink substantial amounts of alcohol, largely provided by the cleaner of the rackets and squash courts who for a moderate tip brought us in whatever we could afford. We drank strange mixtures, Pimms mixed with cheap sherry and very cheap wine. The last term quality improved as parties were held in Evelyn Rothschild's study in his house, Elmfield. Evelyn was head of house with Christopher Cruise and Dick Bridgeman, both prefects. He brought in champagne from his Buckingham mansion and I have been a supporter of Rothschild's wines ever since. Christopher and I made the occasional journey to London where we found a nightclub called The Sunset which was owned and populated with West Indian workers in London. We would leave Harrow at about eleven at night and return on the first underground just after four in the morning. We daren't use Harrow-on-the-Hill station and would walk down the fields to South Kenton, the next station down the line.

We obviously took big risks but the only time we got into trouble was due to carelessness and stupidity. Both Christopher and I got sent to the headmaster having been discovered coming back from Harrow town which was out of bounds. Permission to go there could have easily been obtained from our housemaster had we bothered to ask it. Doctor Moore was an austere academic man who was not popular although I found him more than fair and we were set a milder punishment than we expected, much to Gorse's annoyance.

An even bigger disaster was narrowly avoided at the end of my penultimate term. The house team which I was in had just won the house final at Harrow football and a celebration was called for. Richard Parkes and I volunteered to go to a pub we knew and buy some booze. Mission accomplished we were met with a flashing red light upon our return and knew there was a problem. The booze was left outside the communal basement lavatories and we quickly realised an assembly was being called by the matron who had been searching for Richard whose mother had put a phone call through to him. Arriving breathless at the end of the assembly we said we had been in the loos and they must have missed us. This cut no ice with the matron who announced she was going straight to the housemaster. Richard who was leaving anyway had little to lose but it might well have been the end for me as I waited for the wrath of Gorse to descend. I later discovered from Charles Lillingstone that Gorse also celebrating his first house victory had gone on a two day bender and was nowhere to be found either that night or in the morning, and I never heard anything further. Sometimes you have a lucky break when you really need it!

Richard Parkes was due to do national service but his father, who had made a fortune from greyhound stadiums, was having none of it and decided to buy a house in Ireland so the family could live beyond English jurisdiction. The house Strancally Castle was near the mouth of the Blackwater River and Richard was sent out to unpack the family furniture and keep out of harm's way until the main family arrived. Christopher Cruise and I had both agreed with Richard that we would come and stay with him during the spring holidays but when Christopher told his mother in my presence she asked not unnaturally if Mrs Parkes had been informed. We discovered that she hadn't but was quite happy for us to go out and we spent an enchanting time in this enormous, mainly unfurnished house, on as lovely a stretch of river as I have ever seen. Richard met us at Cork with a car; I don't think he had a licence but nobody seemed to worry. We explored the local pubs and the wonderful Cork countryside and had as good a week as I can remember.

My mother and stepfather had moved to London where Dennis had been appointed manager in Fenwick's restaurant in their Bond Street store. He also started a restaurant of his own at 49 Elizabeth Street which he called House 49. Later, when he sold it, it was renamed Le Matelot and became an upmarket popular restaurant in that part of the world. Despite having little money he managed to buy a house in Victoria Road, Kensington – now a street with some of the most expensive houses in London. I still pass it sometimes and wonder how many millions it would fetch now, particularly as it had a garden where Dennis got planning permission to build a studio for his hobby, painting. The studio is now another house also worth millions.

At Tickwood it was more obvious that Father's marriage was deteriorating and the rows became bitterer. Father, who had two or three Labradors, used to send them to Llanarmon, where the Scottish head keeper Beaton trained them. My stepmother felt he was far too severe on them and got the response 'good gamekeepers are difficult to find, lousy wives are two a penny'. I felt very sorry for my stepmother as Father was spending more and more time with his latest mistress, an attractive lady who had the good sense to get Billy and I to like her and gave Father a good time without putting too much pressure on him.

I set off for my last term at Harrow determined to enjoy myself. Although I was to take higher certificate, which had I been going to university would have been very important, I had no pressure on that front and Gorse had relaxed trying to pressurise me to work.

Although I had narrowly failed to be in the winning public school rackets pair and was captain of the school squash side, my cricket continued to be in the doldrums and I played for a side run by Charles Lillingstone called The Outcasts. We had some very exciting venues, including two guards' brigade grounds, and there were usually opportunities to consume alcohol. Not that there was any lack at the school itself where we partied in various houses every Saturday and often other nights of the week as well.

Inevitably the term drew to an end and the last night featured the traditional house supper where the guest of honour was Terence Rattigan, a leading playwright of that era. I had met him at Queen's during the public school rackets competition. He introduced himself to Dick and myself as a former old Harrovian player who loved watching the game and suggested that we all had dinner one evening. When I told my mother how nice he was and that he had discussed the play he was writing, *The Deep Blue Sea*, with me and wanted Dick and I to have dinner with him, she nearly had a fit. 'Don't think it's your mind he's after,' she said darkly, 'and just tell him I'm coming with you.' It made me chuckle to think of all the shenanigans going on at school which some men took on to life afterwards.

The housemaster spoke at the end of the dinner and I'd hoped that when he came to the leavers he would be reasonably pleasant where I was concerned. However he was thoroughly sarcastic, and although he raised some cheap laughs at my failings, it was another nail in the coffin as far as I was concerned.

We had arranged a last party at Elmfield and close to midnight a number of us had assembled in Evelyn Rothschild's room. After two or three hours the wonderful 'Wing' champagne had run out and we went back to our houses. I found everyone including my brother still up and the festivities continued and an hour later a very inebriated Christopher arrived up the fire escape and staggered into my room. I got virtually no sleep at all and remembered the next morning that we were committed to play in a cricket match that Evelyn Rothschild had generously arranged at his private ground at Wing in Buckinghamshire. As this was near the Cruise family house where I was to stay the night, his sister Patsy having volunteered to collect both of us.

I arrived at Elmfield to find her desperately clearing up an appalling mess in Christopher's room and trying to persuade him to get dressed so that we could all proceed to Wing. I don't think I've ever seen him in worse shape but somehow we got him to the car and set off. Patsy looked increasingly nervous as her brother was now sound asleep as we neared one of the great English country estates.

The match should have been great fun. We were divided into two elevens and everybody was allocated three overs and the match proceeded. We both survived a difficult two hours in the field before an excellent lunch with either beer or wine. The problem arose when our XI started to bat. Christopher's mother had arrived by now and sat in a deckchair next to Evelyn's mother. Christopher and I who had made several visits to the Rothschilds previously were summoned over and sat in two deckchairs alongside. It was a swelteringly hot afternoon and both of us started to doze off. Lady Cruise was by now looking as anxious as her daughter had done earlier. Falling asleep next to Mrs Rothschild would definitely have been classed one of the social gaffes of the year.

I excused myself by saying I had to put my pads on and somehow kept awake until I had to bat. My innings did not last long but at least jolted me awake sufficiently till close of play when Patsy again drove us back to their house and we could have an early dinner and the best night's sleep I had had for many days.

So ended my Harrow career. As the headmaster wrote in his final report, more in sorrow than in anger, I had not taken advantage of all the opportunities the school offered. I had a lot of fun in the closing stages and not being allowed to go to university, it was a little compensation. I had made some very good friends and certainly had a lot more affection for Harrow than Selwyn House. My one great mistake was not to change houses when I had the opportunity. When I arrived at Harrow three houses were occupied by boys from Malvern College which had been requisitioned by the authorities.

After my first year the Malvern boys went back to Malvern and the three houses were reopened. My rackets master, Johnny Greenstock, was allotted one of them, 'Newlands', as housemaster and dropped a hint that he would welcome anyone who wanted to transfer to his house. At the time I was still getting on reasonably well with Gorse and was too young and immature to realise I would do much better in a new house without the competition which existed in The Grove. Not the only major decision in life I was to get wrong!

Chapter 2

The Learning Curve

I returned to Shropshire expecting to do the dreaded two years National Service, though I was not eligible until late September so had a couple of months to relax. Father's marriage was deteriorating by the day and my immediate future was not his foremost priority. I had a contact with two people in the Irish Guards who I had met playing cricket and were prepared to facilitate my entry to that illustrious regiment provided I passed the officers training course. Father kept muttering that the Royal Engineers would be far better for my future career in construction, but about a month before the date I would have had to take my medical he announced that he was arranging for National Service to be deferred so that I could take a course in engineering – which would entail a day a week at Wolverhampton Technical College. I would work the rest of the week in the company and would be on a salary which would cancel the small allowance which I was currently receiving from a family trust.

The family company, Alfred McAlpine and Son, was much the smaller of the two McAlpine construction companies and had in fact been 'hived' off from Sir Robert McAlpine by my grandfather who had reached an agreement with his brothers that he could take over the area that he was already looking after, i.e. North Wales, Lancashire, Cheshire and the North Midlands. I later discovered that my grandfather, having made a lot of money and in poor health, was seeking a quiet life where he could continue to earn an income but not exert himself too much. He regarded Father as a lightweight and encouraged his playboy lifestyle. His number two, Willie Shaw, was devoted to my grandfather and had recruited a number of other staff, two of whom had been promoted by my father when my grandfather died; they were effectively joint managing-directors. One, Alistair Kennedy, running the Cheshire, Lancashire and North Wales area; the other, Edmund Jones, looking after the Midland area from the

Wolverhampton office. The Cheshire head office had originally been in Liverpool but the blitz put paid to that and Willie Shaw had literally forty-eight hours to find alternative accommodation. He managed to find an empty house called The Oaks at Hooton, a leafy upmarket village between Chester and Birkenhead. As Alfred McAlpine expanded, Willie Shaw bought the house next door and joined the two together, forming a reasonably substantial office.

Father had intended to live near the head office but his parting from my mother and subsequent divorce had persuaded him to put a little distance between him and her as a number of their friends were more than sympathetic towards mama. Another factor was that his new wife, Mary, had also lived near my parents.

Tickwood Hall was about half an hour from the Wolverhampton office and Father spent a lot more time there than at Hooton. He played cricket for Wolverhampton and rented jointly, with Norman Partridge, a shoot on the outskirts of Newport, a small Shropshire town close by.

Edmund Jones, who was the director in charge of the area where I was to spend the first three years of my working life, was a genial, slightly overweight, football loving civil engineer who had great charm and a very kindly nature. He bonded exceptionally well with Father and I could not have asked for a more ideal person to watch over me in the first formative working years. Alistair Kennedy, effectively the senior managing-director of the two, was a very different character. Much more austere he had a rigid outlook on life but was a very clever engineer who ran his area very effectively. Whilst I never liked him as much as Edmund Jones I always admired him greatly.

The increased turnover that the war years had generated made an enormous difference to the company. The turnover in 1936, the year of the breakaway, was just over a million pounds. By 1950, the year I joined the company, it was at least thirty times greater.

There was one major problem in that I had no driving licence and the first site chosen for me to work at was a large contract at Walsall Power Station. Father devised a ludicrous arrangement that I was to be taken by a member of the household to Bridgenorth. There I would catch a bus to Wolverhampton, walk to another bus stop to catch a bus to Walsall and walk to the site. The whole operation took two hours and, worse still, because the household routine could not be disturbed I couldn't leave home until nine o'clock, which got me to the site about eleven in the mid morning.

The site itself was a hive of activity and I was to accompany one of the three engineers to learn how to use a level and a theodolite to set out the drainage and foundations. During my first hour on site I met the works manager, a small wiry Irishman called Billy Veitch who was screaming like a banshee that none of the pegs he had asked for had been set out. I soon learned that there was a war between the engineers and works management; the engineers claiming that the pegs they had carefully prepared had been ripped out by the heavy site machinery and Billy Veitch claiming they had never been set in the first place.

My first day at Wolverhampton Technical College was another shock. I was literally the only boy who had been to a major public school and my classmates treated me like someone from another planet. The course itself entailed a lot of drawing which I was hopeless at and Harrow's History Sixth had certainly not prepared me for my new undertaking.

Fortunately after three weeks I was transferred to a much smaller site on the outskirts of Wolverhampton but close to a bus stop on the Bridgenorth to Wolverhampton bus route. This cut the journey from home in half and I found a site where roads and sewers were being constructed far more to my liking. The man in charge, known as a site agent, was Owen Rich, who was destined to finish his career as effectively chief executive of the company, though we did not use that title. He had what was known as a 'good war' finishing up in Burma with the rank of captain. The engineer – Bill Walker – was extremely clever and the works manager, Bill Riley, was a lovely genial man who relied on his number two, known as a gangerman, to do most of the work under his direction. Unlike the previous site, all three were pleased to have the chairman's son amongst them and gradually they became good friends. The pace was a lot less frenetic than Walsall and I began to enjoy coming to work. Both Owen Rich and Bill Walker were excellent tutors and although the level and theodolite were never instruments I was totally happy with, I began to take some responsibility and my frequent mistakes with the level were met with tolerance.

The Technical College was not such a happy story. Although one or two of my classmates and most of the staff were showing some understanding, a lot of the curriculum was way beyond me and in the two years I attended I never had any aptitude for the work there. My only moment of glory came when a member of staff beginning the session made a quotation from a Keats poem and when he asked us if we knew where it had come from I was able to answer correctly. He looked at me in amazement and said that out of several hundred people I was the first to get it right.

As I still could not drive, my social life was severely restricted and was dependent upon those who had a car and could collect me. A friend who was very helpful was Dennis Partridge, the son of one of Father's great cricketing friends and brother of Susan Partridge, then one of the most promising young tennis players in the country. Although her career eventually fizzled out she was to marry Philippe Chartrier, the French tennis star.

Another who was very helpful was Martin Mander, the son of another great friend of Father's who was a director of a large family paint business in Wolverhampton. Things improved when Father embarked for his three month trip to South Africa, where the company had just established a base. The servants were all to be given a holiday and I would have to go into 'digs' and a suitable house run by a recently widowed lady was found for me by the company's Wolverhampton office.

Every Friday night the senior staff in the office would join the managing-director in the Conservative Club where prodigious amounts of beer were consumed. Everyone drank beer, either mild or bitter or bottled, and the great midland breweries of Mitchell and Butlers, Ansells and Ind Coope all had their devotees. Up to ten pints were consumed between five-thirty and eight, and it was after one of those sessions when I returned to my 'digs', virtually fell up the stairs and was extremely the worst for wear for most of the night. Although I frantically tried to clean up, the incident did not go unnoticed by my landlady, who had not had a boarder before, and it took a few weeks of much better behaviour to get back in her good books.

All the office and site staff were passionate supporters of Wolves football team, then captained by Billy Wright with a host of star players. I was taken to several memorable games, home and away, to Liverpool and Manchester. Billy Wright was the 'David Beckham' of his day and was hero-worshipped by the whole Wolverhampton area.

My great problem at this juncture was that I had no sex life and no girlfriend. My only two encounters with girls had both ended in disaster. The bicycle ride from Exeter and a day with a slightly older, highly prized, sister of a school friend who was supposed to have lunch with me and then go to the cinema. We never made the cinema.

My confidence was at its lowest ebb and it was not until the following winter when I joined the Wolverhampton Tennis and Squash Club that the situation improved.

I should at this juncture make two points. There was a rigid social order which is very difficult to understand today when everybody socialises and relaxes regardless of how many generations their forebears have been at the top of the tree. In the early fifties things were very different and it would be ten years before things began to change. Although Father himself was only two generations away from a grandfather who started life in abject poverty, he had been hauled right up the social scale and fully intended to stay there. In subtle ways it was made clear to me that although it was fine to mix with people from suburban Wolverhampton they would not be welcome at Tickwood.

Secondly, parents tended to guard their daughters' virginity with care and possessiveness. Girls were expected to go to their weddings as virgins and many did just that. It of course led to a spate of early marriages; many couples were frustrated and saw marriage as one way out of their problems. This became particularly evident when I later moved to Cheshire and, although a few couples lived happily ever after, many did not.

The Wolverhampton Tennis and Squash Club altered my social life in two respects. I found to my amazement that I was just about the best squash player there and began to play for Staffordshire with considerable success. As my other two recreations, cricket and shooting, saw me performing very poorly this was a great boost to my confidence which further improved when I discovered that some girls I was to meet at the club were actually keen to go out with me. My first real girlfriend was one of these – the eldest daughter of a couple with a thriving engineering business in the heart of the Black Country. She had been to a good private school and I found her very exciting. On our fourth or fifth date I parked my car on the edge of Perton Aerodrome, a disused runway and ideal spot for courting couples. At some point I said that one day I would have to teach her about sex and her reply was, 'Why not start now?' Two years of sexual frustration were over although because of the terror of pregnancy we never went the full distance.

She had a good-looking friend who had been at school with her who I introduced to my first Harrow rackets partner, Tom Pigott, and we went to the Eton and Harrow Ball as a foursome. Sadly it was the

Eton and Harrow cricket match the following year which finished this romance and a budding one with another sweet girl, also a member of the tennis and squash club.

I had briefly met Annabel, the daughter of one of Father's shooting friends, who owned an estate just outside Shifnal. She had been a major girlfriend of Dennis Partridge and had been dumped by him for his sister's doubles tennis partner, an attractive French lady. Annabel was also an aspiring actress who had played bit parts in a local repertory company and was hoping to play a minor role in a comedy in London where Billy Whitehead was to be the star. She had rented a room in London while they waited for a theatre to become available and out of the blue I asked her to go to the cricket match with me. Again I stayed with Tom Pigott at his mother's house and we all had a convivial evening after the first day, finishing at our favourite nightclub 'The Carousel'. At three or four in the morning I took Annabel back to her digs and was asked in for a drink to be told that it was too late to mess about and I could either get into bed or leave. It will be no surprise I took the first option, had several ecstatic minutes and drifted into a deep sleep. I awoke after nine the following morning to find the landlady berating Annabel for having a man in her room. I left hastily having arranged to meet her later in the morning to receive an equally frigid greeting in the Pigott household, Mrs Pigott understandably not being used to her guests not appearing until after breakfast.

Annabel's theatre career never took off and she came home so I took her out more regularly, having passed my driving test at the second attempt, much to the relief of everybody.

On the work front we had finished the Wolverhampton roads and sewers contract and the same team moved onto a similar one at Pelsall about ten miles from Wolverhampton. I was given increased responsibility and was extremely well tutored by Owen Rich and Bill Walker. I was also discovering the importance that the supervisory team made to site profitability. On the Wolverhampton site the resident engineer employed by Wolverhampton Council and Owen Rich had a bad relationship with constant rows and arguments and his Clerk of Works and Bill Riley were on similar terms.

At Pelsall things were very different. The resident engineer was underpaid and very amenable to being wined and dined and asked few questions on the measurements we submitted as a result. Pelsall was a very happy site and we made a decent profit, which, as I was to learn, was not always the case.

At home Father's marriage finally came to an end when he discovered that my stepmother was having an affair with a shooting friend of Norman Partridge. Father's rage was terrible, although he had a number of affairs himself and a very passionate one with Anne, who Billy and I liked a lot.

Father was about to embark on his three months in South Africa when the storm broke and he went alone on the understanding that Anne would follow him, and she duly arranged to go three weeks later. It was also arranged that Mary would find a home in the south of England and take my half-sister Valerie with her, and would not be at Tickwood when he got back.

What was not expected was that Father would be introduced to a lady in South Africa who'd been married three times, once to one of his great friends, and that this would develop into a relationship before Anne got there. Father jokingly described Anne's flight out there and back, after three days, as the most expensive poke he had ever had in his life.

His new love, who was born Rosemary Gregory Hood, was not introduced to me until mid summer at a cricket match in Leicestershire, but Father waxed enthusiastically about her and her connections, and to my amazement I realised how much the social side mattered to him and that he had a real complex about it. I found Rosemary perfectly friendly but I never developed the close relationship I had with Mary and I always felt that she lacked Mary's warmth. Father continued ecstatically on his way and they were married at the end of the summer. Billy, who had been taken away from Harrow two years earlier than was usual, and I both went to the registry office and celebrations at the Dorchester afterwards.

The next day I was expected to work as usual but got to the Pelsall site with a terrible hangover and eventually Owen Rich told me to go home. Billy had been put into the plant depot of the Wolverhampton office, where he stayed until his eighteenth birthday, when he started National Service in the RAF. Whilst we had our ups and downs as children vying for our mother's affection, our relationship was now very good and he was a great shoulder to lean on when I needed to pour out my problems over Father's mood swings and controlling nature.

Strangely I had far more problems with Father over cricket and shooting than I ever did on the work front. Although my cricket was in the doldrums, he insisted on carting me around and making me play in some very high-class club games. I was always in last and rarely allowed to bowl and it wasn't until Gubby Allen, the former England Captain, told me I would never make a run holding the bat as I did and taking me into the net at Marchwiel, where he made me turn my left hand far further across the bat, that things improved. The fifteen minutes of instruction transformed my cricket career and to this day I am still bitter that in all those nets at Harrow with top-class professionals and cricket masters still playing county cricket nobody thought to get my hands correctly round the bat. When I went back to Harrow a few years later to play against the school and made a decent score, Lance Gorse came up to me and sounded astonished at my improvement. I had great pleasure in telling him that had anyone told me how to hold the bat in school I might have done really well there.

A little later the same sort of thing happened on the shooting front, although this time it was my own doing rather than advice. It had taken ages for me to shoot my first pheasant and although Father was in two shoots at Newport and another at Acton Burnall, I was usually put in the worst places and my self-esteem was at a very low level. When Father restarted shooting at Llanarmon I was taken on the 'rough' days around the boundaries but not invited to the big covert shoot days. Gradually I was allowed to double bank behind the main guns, and one day I was summoned to take the place of Gwyn Reid Walker who had a major hangover and needed to be physically sick behind a hedge. To my amazement halfway through the stand I started hitting everything and, although it took a year or two before I became really proficient, my shooting career was to take off.

Also it was becoming impossible for me to attend Wolverhampton Tech any longer. Father and Edmund Jones, who continued to keep a fatherly eye on me, decided that my National Service deferment should continue, but I was to take a course in quantity surveying under the Chief Surveyor at the Hooton office. I was to go once a week to the main Technical College in Liverpool and of course would have to live during the week in Cheshire. I managed to find some excellent digs in what would be called a small unlicensed hotel, catering for mostly retired couples.

My chief contact in Cheshire was David Stern, the son of another of Father's friends, who introduced me to a number of my age group. David and I were, in fact, born within ten days of each other and we have remained close friends to this day. He was taking accountancy exams with a number of amusing people of whom Michael Stoddart in particular was to come into my life in a big way.

I had acquired a girlfriend who lived near me in the Wirral; she was pretty and more importantly was far further down the sexual trail than I was. On our first date she made it clear that she couldn't wait to get into bed with me but that I had to get condoms so, acutely embarrassed, I ventured into a chemist and asked for a packet of Durex. As I looked at least two years younger than my real age, the assistant looked long and hard at me but eventually produced the packet.

Every night we went out we would end up in bed and although we were fond of each other the sex was depressingly unadventurous and I was never told whether my partner had been satisfied. In fact I was to enter married life without gaining any real advice from the few ladies I had managed to have sex with.

I had become a member of the Liverpool Racket Club, which sadly had converted its rackets courts into some silly hybrid game. It did have squash courts, indoor tennis courts, a number of bedrooms and a very good dining and social scene. It was there that I was having dinner with David Stern and Michael Stoddart one night when Michael said he was taking out a girl who lived in Tarporley and who had a great friend next door who would like to come too and would David or I make up the foursome. David and I duly played a cold hand of poker and I found myself the winner of a blind date. As I was much nearer Tarporley than Michael was, I agreed to pick up my date and then his. When I rang the doorbell I was met with a gorgeous girl called Ginny and received a warm welcome from her parents. When we went next door I ran into a tirade of abuse from Geraldine's mother who told me, 'You young men are all the same, I don't know you from Adam but you walk in and think you can take out, etc etc.' I attempted to say that I was acting for Michael Stoddart and was merely the chauffeur, all to little avail. The evening was a great success and when I returned Ginny in the early hours with a chaste kiss and a promise that we would go out the following week I felt things were really looking up.

The following night I was due to go to a dance at the Grosvenor Hotel having been asked by Colin and Pam Rae, two other friends of David Stern's. I took Jennifer there and all went well except for Pam, who was a leading light in the young Cheshire social set, telling me I could do a lot better for myself and why didn't I concentrate on Ginny who was a great friend of hers and would be perfect for me. When I took Jennifer home I told her I didn't feel like bed and thought we should cool things down. The following Monday David Stern rang me up to tell me that I should know that Ginny had got engaged and that our evening had spurred her regular boyfriend into proposing – a salutary lesson to not burn your boats until you have to!

My twenty-first birthday was celebrated in great style at Tickwood with a mixture of my friends from Shropshire and Cheshire, and Father and stepmother Rosemary also. I was forced to make a speech, mainly to introduce Arthur Riscoe, a friend of Father's, who would be unknown to most people today but in the thirties he was a great cabaret, radio, music hall star having had previous triumphs with the likes of Frances Day, also largely forgotten now. He had just made a triumphant comeback at the Café de Paris and did part of his act for us at Tickwood amidst loud and well deserved applause.

The dance was a very good party and led to a spate of invitations to other twenty-firsts and whilst I don't remember them all a very smart dance at Burwarton for Michael Boyne and one for Peter Thompson who was to marry my first wife's sister were certainly two, also David Stern's a couple of weeks after mine. The following weekend saw another large party in a marquee given by the company for the staff. I was presented with a brand new Purdey twelve-bore, the first expensive gun I had ever had and a great help to my shooting in times to come.

1953, the year of my twenty-first, was also the first year I was to visit South Africa. Father had always gone out by boat on the Union Castle Line and come back by plane, but for my first visit, ridiculously short anyway considering the cost, was on British Airways and I was allowed to go first class. It was the time of the ill-fated Comet and I can't remember whether it was that year or the year after that one of its crashes had just occurred. The Comet was of course the revolutionary jet transport plane of a new jet age. Not only was it twice as fast as piston-engine planes but it cut the number of stops, making the journey much shorter. The piston-engine plane I flew on had to stop at Paris, Rome, Cairo, Khartoum, Nairobi and Salisbury before the final leg to Johannesburg. Inevitably one of the four engines would cause problems during the journey, usually at the most inhospitable of the six stops – Khartoum.

The whole journey took thirty-six hours and, although the service was good, sleep was at a premium, and I arrived in Johannesburg utterly exhausted. Father was for once on time to meet me and, when I pleaded exhaustion to get out of the cocktail party everybody was going to, I was told that Dennis Compton, my boyhood cricketing hero, would be there so I gained my first introduction to Johannesburg social life.

Johannesburg then was very different to today. Although the centre of the South African business community, the way of life was very different from five or six days in the office. Parties, both lunch and evening, abounded and a number of those who had made up the 'white mischief' scenario in Kenya had drifted down to Johannesburg and continued their way of life there. It was difficult to work out whether Father's priorities were work or play – probably an equal mixture of both. He also played cricket at a county club at Inanda and like myself found exercise, in the shape of tennis and swimming, a good antidote to the prodigious amounts of alcohol we all consumed.

It was the following year that I went for a much longer visit, starting with my first experience visiting an African site, the Tunduma road contract partly in Northern Rhodesia and partly in Tanganyika (now Tanzania). In order to get there I flew to Entebee to find a chartered one-engine plane in which an ex-Luftwaffe pilot flew me across Lake Victoria to an airstrip near the site office. The road I was visiting stretched three hundred kilometres of the driest and dustiest country in Africa and the following day Father, Nicky Knoop the managing-director and I managed to see most of the road that had been opened up. That night there was a party for the staff, which was the first of many memorable site parties I was to attend in many African countries. Every week the Nidola brewery, which had been reconstructed by our company, sent ten tonnes of beer – a substantial amount of which was consumed that night.

The managing-director Nicky Knoop had a very colourful background. His family were originally wealthy white Russians with Dutch connections who had fought the Germans, then the Bolsheviks and escaped Russia in a French destroyer. Nicky was brought up by an English branch of his family and had joined Alfred McAlpine as a junior site engineer in 1939 and then served in the RAF during the war, mostly overseas where he became convinced there was a big future for British construction companies. When he rejoined the company after the war he persuaded Father to let him start a company based in South Africa. He also married and took with him a very rich wife who was Gwyn Reid Walker's only daughter. He was the ideal person for Father to relate to because, whilst able to enter the Johannesburg social scene, he took the work side very seriously and was clever enough to give Father an equal amount of both scenarios.

In Johannesburg life was as much fun as ever and I was able to take a couple of lively young ladies to a popular nightclub. It was at this club that I saw for the first time a couple of very attractive hookers 'flashing' to attract the attention of an immensely wealthy young South African magnate called John Slesinger. They certainly attracted my attention!

Father was a tremendous sunbather who applied massive amounts of sun lotions and got so brown that his friends said that he would be lucky to get back through South African immigration as a white man. Much later in life he did develop mild skin cancer and these days he would almost certainly have been in trouble.

Back in England I was still based in Cheshire, though had made more friends in Shropshire. Apart from Dennis Partridge and the two Mander brothers and their cousin Doug Graham, there were the Guy brothers, Robin and Trevor, whose father had founded a prosperous motor company, the various Thompsons who owned an enormous engineering company between Wolverhampton and Birmingham, Jim Carpenter whose family owned a carpet company, and Hugh Meynell, another Black Country engineering heir. Also two years younger than myself, Christopher Motley, the eldest of four brothers whose father Louis was married to the owner of Wenlock Abbey, a wonderful house in Much Wenlock, and Panton Corbett, whose father had an estate west of Shrewsbury.

In Cheshire, David Stern had become engaged to and then married an attractive, sweet girl, Penny Nowell. I was his best man, not my first experience of this task as some months earlier I had been best man to John MacMullen. He was married amidst much pomp and ceremony in St Margaret's, Westminster. This was a terrifying experience and I kept clutching the ring in my coat pocket as I had read stories of the dreadful embarrassment of failing to produce the ring. On neither occasion was I called on to speak, though years later when I was asked to do so at David and Penny's Silver Wedding Anniversary Party, I did make the point that I had to wait all that time to speak in public about them.

My deferment was also coming to an end and, knowing full well I had no chance of passing the quantity surveying exams I was obliged to take (like Father at Cambridge, I hardly put pen to paper), I told him I was going to have to do National Service.

Just before going to the medical, I gave a farewell party at my flat in Parkgate. I had obtained some special gin from the American airbase at Burtonwood where I frequently visited the large contract we were working on there. The gin was about twice the proof of normal English gin and I stupidly thought it was amusing to get everyone inebriated. In the event only one guest showed obvious signs (he was in fact carried out) but I went home to Shropshire the next day with a monumental hangover, which took the whole weekend to get over. The following week I came out with large red blotchy patches on my chest and arms and, having been sent to a site in Derbyshire for the interim period before the call up, I managed to find out from friends the name of a good skin specialist in Derby. I duly went to the medical and the doctor examining me seemed as astonished as I was by the patches. I told him I was going to a specialist and was asked to come back when he had reported on my problem.

I duly went to the specialist who told me I had a severe outbreak of psoriasis which would require treatment and that he could not allow me to be passed A1 and would I like him to recommend complete exemption. As usual I went for the soft option and to my amazement National Service, which I had assumed was a matter of course, was averted. I later discovered that two old friends from schooldays, Colin Cowdrey and Robin Marlar, had also both failed – Colin invalided out after a few weeks for flat feet and sore heels and Robin failed for a strained back. It certainly didn't stop Colin playing top-class cricket for England or Robin bowling innumerable overs for Sussex.

In fact psoriasis is a fairly common skin complaint and in many people its manifestations are slight. The most obvious places are the elbows where in chronic sufferers like myself it is always there. The two main treatments recommended by the specialist were various lotions and regular doses of sunray. The sun is very effective at masking psoriasis but of course the sunray treatment would be frowned on now because of the fear of skin cancer. The one place difficult to treat was the scalp, which gets badly affected and very itchy. Most people think it is bad dandruff. Psoriasis is also hereditary and my mother discovered she had very mild symptoms when she had trouble with her nails and her manicurist asked her if she had psoriasis. When she replied that her son had it very badly she was told she must have been the culprit to pass it on.

With National Service out of the way I was put back on contracts and rejoined Owen Rich who was agent on a large contract at Longbridge for the British Motor Company. After a short period there I was very unexpectedly given a roads and sewers contract to myself at Donnington. Owen wrote out all the duties of an agent and with considerable trepidation I took up my new responsibilities. I had no engineer so had to do all of the setting out myself and amazingly there were no major errors on that front. I was however very stupidly given an equally inexperienced works manager, the idea being that Pat Quinn, one of the most senior works managers in the company, would visit regularly. This did not work out and whilst Pat was very effective when he had a large site to concentrate on he was unable to give Danny, my works manager, much help. It all came to an end with a visit from Father and Edmund Jones. Danny was nearly having a nervous breakdown trying to sort out some collapsed earthworks and he was summarily removed and I was given an experienced replacement and the contract was satisfactorily finished.

My social life continued to meander along without any major involvement with the other sex. It was an age where 'playing the field' was very much in vogue. Few got engaged young and neither sex expected to have a 'steady' partner. You were able to take out as many different ladies as would go out with you and I took full advantage. One pleasant evening occurred when I persuaded Juliet Weld Forester to have dinner with me. Juliet was the second very pretty daughter of Lady Priscilla Weld Forester, the most fearsome snob I have ever encountered. She was determined to marry her children to peers of the realm, the higher up the social scale the better. Her eldest daughter had written to my second cousin Owen Lloyd George, heir to an Earldom, asking if he would take her to her first debutante dance. Owen politely declined but she was then safely betrothed to Lord Bolton and Juliet was next in line. We got on extremely well but as we approached the long drive leading to the Forester ancestral home at Wiley, Juliet asked me to drop her off a hundred yards short of the house. When I expressed surprise she explained that she had told her mother that she was getting a lift to a large dinner party and that she wouldn't approve at all with her going out with a builder.

When I rang Christopher Motley the next morning, he roared with laughter and said he was going to take Juliet out the following night and that he would be much more successful. He did in fact make the front door only to be told by Juliet that the lack of a title was a bar to anything in the way of a serious romance. Juliet duly married the future Marquis of Downshire and sadly died of cancer at a relatively young age. Her two charming sons sometimes come in a let team to Llanarmon and we have a laugh about the night I gave their mother dinner.

Billy had come back from his two years National Service, mainly done at an aerodrome in Warwickshire, close to my new step-mother's ancestral home – Loxley Hall. We had by now become extremely close but he was soon sent off for a spell in Rhodesia with the company, which he was to enjoy enormously, make new friends and coming back full of self-confidence and new maturity.

There were several ladies during this period. The most serious, Helen, lived in London and whilst I had developed a good relationship with her I rarely went to London and although I did invite her as often to Shropshire as I could the distance between us made life very difficult. I also had a very nice girlfriend in Cheshire and it was at her house that I met a young attractive girl cousin who was to stay with a family called Anton in Shropshire about half an hour from Tickwood and I said I would give her dinner during her stay there.

I duly arrived at Tudor House halfway between Bridgnorth and Kidderminster to take Magsie out to dinner, little realising that I was also meeting Jane Anton for the first time. I registered that Mrs Anton, a good looking but very cold woman, didn't seem to like me at all and perhaps she had a premonition that I was trouble in the offing. The Antons were, like Magsie, Catholic although Mary Anton was a convert and like many converts more passionate than those who had been born into Catholic families for generations.

The evening with Magsie passed pleasantly enough but she was due to return to Ireland and I made a mental note to give Jane Anton a ring the following week, a decision which was going to change my life.

Father's third marriage had already begun to deteriorate. After the birth of Sally, my second half-sister, from two different stepmothers, Rosemary's interests were centred on her first child. She was forty-one and to have a first child at that age completely changed her outlook. She moved into the spare room on the pretext that she wanted

Sally with her, and although they were to stay married for another ten years, the scene became progressively more unhappy. Father was becoming even more difficult, selfish and self-centred. In the summer he had gone back to captaining Marchweil, the Welsh side who used the family cricket ground. Although my cricket had improved considerably, I found having to go around North Wales on every Saturday playing on some terrible pitches with people, however nice, I had little in common with, depressing to say the least. Similarly every Saturday in October was spent rough shooting at Llanarmon and prior to that were the grouse shoots where Father and his close friends always had the best places. It was not so much what he did that was depressing it was the way Father controlled everything that was the problem. Even the meals ran to a rigid timetable. Dinner was always on the dot at seven-thirty and Sunday lunch one-thirty prompt, the excuse always being to give the staff as much time off as possible. Whereas Mary had to some extent been an ally, Rosemary was far too preoccupied with her own problems to start fighting any of mine.

The consolation was the increasing time they spent in South Africa, which at least allowed me a normal life for three or four months. I was beginning, too, to make new friends in Shropshire. It was about this time that Brian Jenks came into my life. He was easily the most successful businessman in the area and had taken a small family firm into the much bigger Delta Metal, where he was a senior director and had made a lot of money reputedly by betting on the New York metal exchange. Although his first marriage was breaking up he had bought a large house and the surrounding estate at Astbury, just outside Bridgnorth. Another new friend was Jeremy Vaughan, a larger-than-life character, whose sister was to become Brian's second wife and who was developing a keen interest as I was in horseracing.

But the most important relationship of all was my growing feelings for Jane Anton. We had had an ecstatic first night – when I returned her to her house at around 2 a.m., she also asked to be dropped at the end of the drive, as she didn't want to wake her parents up. However her father managed to arrive just as we were saying our final goodbyes and a blazing row ensued between him and Jane. This did not put me off and we began a regular series of dates, despite her parents obvious opposition to myself. We eventually decided to become engaged when I returned from South Africa, where I was going on a long February visit. Strangely the opposition, particularly from her mother, who disliked me intensely, never put me off; in fact, if anything, it aroused the competitive nature in me and I left aged 23 for South Africa, thoroughly looking forward to putting a ring on Jane's finger when I got back.

I went to South Africa for the February period, partly holiday, partly work, knowing that I would be officially engaged to Jane Anton on my return. I had told Father and my stepmother and also Nicky Knoop, who ran the company from South Africa. One thing I was able to do was buy a ring from a Johannesburg jeweller Father had patronised regularly and having carefully hidden it in my luggage I set off home to meet first Jane and then my future father-in-law. The journey back included an emergency stop because of bad weather and I wondered whether Jane would wait at the airport for the British Airways flight which was four hours late, but I need not have worried as she was at the airport and extremely welcoming.

She told me her father was in London and that she had arranged for me to see him at six that evening at the hotel he was in. Mr Anton was a mild, nice, slightly fussy man, completely dominated by the better looking ice maiden he was married to and the interview went according to the book, with all the usual questions being asked, although he was well aware that I was going to ask his permission to marry his daughter. He did make a feeble attempt to suggest a postponement but in the end bowed to the inevitable and gave his agreement. The following evening when we had dinner in their house he did at least propose a toast to our future happiness.

My memories of the months between February and our wedding at the end of September are frankly fairly hazy. I do know I played a lot less cricket than usual and followed Jane around the local show jumping events. I even got on a horse myself and made an attempt to enjoy riding. All went well until I attempted to upgrade to jumping and soon realised my limitations. I was still boarding with Douglas Graham at his small company house at Tattenhall, though our evening excursions to look for girls at the Wolverhampton Tennis Club did come to an end.

Jane and I had one great stroke of luck when two Shropshire friends, Keith and Annabel Darby, offered us the rental of a most attractive cottage they owned at a little Shropshire village called Badger. This had the effect of focusing everybody on a wedding, which my mother-in-law obviously dreaded, and we began to collect furniture for the cottage.

Because Jane was a Catholic I had to undergo a course in understanding my religious obligations and attend a number of services at the church their family went to in Bridgnorth. The first I went to was hilarious because the priest preached a long sermon on how the church needed expensive repairs, particularly to the roof, and how the parishioners could help. It took me a few minutes to realise I was directly in the firing line and the main person in the congregation he was addressing was myself.

Although there was no direct pressure from Jane or her family I did mildly think of becoming a Catholic. There seemed to be more discipline in the way they held their congregation together and to someone whose religious thinking was extremely undisciplined this seemed at the time to be a bonus.

Although Jane was a serious Catholic she had made it clear there was one rule she was not going to obey, namely to do without contraception, the pill not coming on to the market until well into the marriage. It is difficult for the young today to realise how formal life was then, even for an engaged couple. Whilst for a normal couple 'above the belt but not below' might have been usual, with us it was above the neck but not below. Jane's mother had a tremendous influence in this direction; she literally brainwashed her that sex involved a great deal of pain and discomfort with the result that her daughter was absolutely terrified of that side of marriage. I did try and persuade her it was actually great fun but Mary Anton had done too good a job of persuading her otherwise.

The wedding was set for a Saturday in late September and a prominent local Catholic priest was set to marry us. Jane had written to Monsignor Ronald Knox but he was unavailable. We went to dinner in Staffordshire to meet our priest and he seemed very pleasant. I had my bachelor party a few days before the wedding at a hostelry between Wolverhampton and Bridgnorth, attended by Billy and nine Shropshire and Staffordshire friends. Sadly of the eleven at the party only five are alive today – myself, Doug Graham, Hugh Meynell, Michael Mander and Christopher Motley.

My mother and stepfather had come over from the Bahamas and stayed with Father and Rosemary at Tickwood, the last time I was to sleep in that lovely Shropshire house. Father true to form tried to provoke me into a row a couple of days before the wedding, but I was having none of it and refused to rise to the bait. The thought of getting away from his selfish, controlling presence was a definite plus for the future.

The wedding itself took place in a Catholic church in Droitwich, which had Anton associations, and I had to stay for a week in the Raven Hotel to establish a residence. The wedding day was a pleasant sunny day and things went well enough, though both my parents were to tell me later that the priest was far too fiery in his address. Perhaps Mary Anton had nobbled him. I had asked Christopher Cruise to be my best man but he was doing late National Service and Dick Bridgeman, my old rackets partner, took his place. My speech at the wedding seemed to go down well and the department of Harrods who had organised the reception were efficient, although I felt they tried to rush things through somewhat.

We set off for our honeymoon that night after spending twenty minutes divesting the car of various attachments and trying to wash out the usual inscriptions. I thought I had managed to hide the car but Billy and the others still managed to find it. I had booked us in at the French Horn at Sonning, which remains to this day my favourite place to stay in the South of England. The next day we flew to Barcelona to spend a fortnight in a rather isolated hotel on the Costa Brava, full of other honeymoon couples and a rather nice couple of young men who were obviously gay and in the antiques business, though they had to be very careful not to advertise the fact too openly. They joined us for several meals and lightened the atmosphere considerably, introducing us to other couples they had befriended.

Chapter 3

Facing tragedy

Back in England, life continued much as before except that I was now married and living with Jane in a small cottage in Shropshire. This may sound a ridiculous statement but much genuinely remained the same. I still went to work in the same way, started the shooting season with enthusiasm, played squash hard at the same level and mixed with the same group of Shropshire friends.

Determined to make a success of married life I had gradually worn down Jane's terror of the physical side, though things were far from perfect in this department. We spent a difficult Christmas with Jane's parents and in early January I contracted one of only two serious illnesses I have ever had, Scarlet Fever being the other aged nine.

I had just played squash for Wales against England in London and had taken a game off Roy Wilson, the then amateur champion. This was no mean feat as the hot, fast courts in London did not suit my game. I have never been fitter, yet two days later I woke up in Shropshire feeling so ill I couldn't even get out of bed. I have to say that illness has never been either of my wives' strong suits and instead of ringing the Wolverhampton office, who would have immediately produced a decent doctor, who would probably have sent me to hospital for a period, Jane found a local GP who was about to retire. He did at least diagnose Jaundice but had no idea how to treat it and the second time he came he announced he was off to Ludlow races the next day and would leave 'the chapter in the book' with me, 'and then you will know as much about it as I do'. I was in bed for seven weeks and should probably have stayed a further three. Whilst Jaundice is difficult to treat I later learnt that light steamed food not fried food is essential and that alcohol is totally banned for up to a year. None of this advice was obtained and when I staggered to my feet after seven weeks I was a pale yellow and still felt terrible. Numerous people came to see me and only one, Cil Parkinson, actually contracted the disease though in a much milder form.

As nobody had told me not to drink I kept having the odd glass although it did not help at all and it was not until we moved to Cheshire later that year that I went to a consultant in Wrexham who, after a series of tests, told me that my liver was not functioning properly and that I would have to go without alcohol for up to two years. He did also say that the liver was an amazing organ which had great powers of recovery and that when I started drinking again I should start slowly and gradually each year I would be able to drink a little more. He proved absolutely right and if only I had gone to him in the first place I could have saved myself a lot of misery.

The move to Cheshire coincided with a change in my working life; I was now attached to Hooton, the main office, but first I had to find a house. The first house I looked at, Park House, belonged to the Cholmondeley Estate and was occupied by Anthony Cayzer, who lived in baronial style, employing a butler and numerous staff. It was really too big and I began what looked to be a difficult search when I had a major stroke of luck. Billy had met John Leche who was the heir to a large Cheshire estate. The estate was managed by Geoffrey Evans, who had succeeded his brother David as the agent in charge of Llanarmon. Through Billy, Jane and I received an invitation to meet John Leche and view Lower Carden Hall, where a famous show-jumper, Wilf White, was about to move out, having rented the house for a short while.

The house was an absolute gem and Jane and I fell in love with it immediately. The original Carden Hall was an enormous Jacobean, black-and-white house which had burnt down just before the 1914-18 war, and Lower Carden Hall was a smaller copy used by the Leche family as a dower house for senior elderly relatives.

Although John Leche's father was still alive he was extremely unwell and two nurses took turns to look after him. Geoffrey Evans seemed to have full powers to manage the estate and the house and several acres were sold to me for £8,500. A year later I was able to negotiate for Doug Francis the purchase of Carden Bank plus sixty acres for under £12,000. We were extremely lucky to take advantage of a market which would alter dramatically a decade later.

Billy had also moved to Cheshire to work at the main company plant depot at Ellesmere Port. He was in fact being sidelined to eventually follow my uncle, Peter Bell, who was in charge of plant and quarries. He had found an attractive cottage on the Leche estate and we saw even more of each other. We would go to one of the local pubs, the Cock Inn at Barton, two or three times a week. The Cock was owned by the Leche estate but the tenant, Leslie Nicholas, was a tremendous countryman. He actually bred fighting cocks and had been one of four people to be convicted of illegally attending cock fights. The local magistrate, Geoffrey Egerton Warburton, had fined the four and issued a stern warning that a repeat offence would entail a more severe outcome. Leslie certainly heeded the warning and if there were any further fights, none of his regulars were put in the picture. Every evening Leslie would bring up the jugs of foaming Worthington ale from the cellars which cooled the beer perfectly. We became very friendly with the regulars, many of them farmers or attached to local estates. Although there were strict laws on closing times, Leslie seemed able to flout them with impunity!

We would also, on summer evenings, often fish in the local stream which was unpolluted and full of trout. Unfortunately the building of a small sewage works at Tilston changed that and one particularly hot, dry summer was to kill off most of the trout in the stream. There were also a lot of eels and Billy built a trap in a lane by a former windmill. The trap – still there to this day – trapped the eels when there was a lot of water coming down and Billy and I would rush there to collect them. He had a large, sharp knife and was adept at dispatching them – something I was not good at.

Shortly after buying Lower Carden Hall, Euan was born. The day started with excitement as I woke up early to find a herd of cows had invaded the lawn and gardens and were creating havoc. I rang the police station at Broxton who contacted John Edwards, a prominent local farmer, who was responsible for settling disputes in the area. He managed to get the cows removed swiftly and I agreed a sum of damages far less than I should have claimed and I set off to see my first born in a maternity unit at Trevalyn, near Rossett. Jane had a very difficult birth not helped by the fact that we both were patients of Father's friend and doctor in Wrexham, Shirley Stephens, who had been the family doctor for many years. He did not believe in expensive gynaecologists but we did not make the same mistake when Sara and Christopher were born and Jane had a much easier time with them.

We had hired a maternity nurse who arrived a day or two after the birth and expected to be waited on hand and foot, and as our staff consisted of two part-time dailies and Jane did the cooking she did not last too long. We then found a lovely girl called Mary, who was with us on and off until the children grew up.

Jane did occasionally get temporary housekeepers and one was an amazing girl whose father was quite a famous author called J K Stanford, who wrote a book called *The Glorious Twelfth*. To call his daughter lively would have been a gross understatement and I suddenly found a number of young bloods, some of whom I hardly knew, calling in at all hours to have a drink with us. The climax came when we took her to Llanarmon for a shooting weekend. John Leche got so excited that in his rush to join us he completely failed to take a sharp turn over the bridge outside Ruabon crossing the River Dee and ended up in the river. The car was a write off and he was very lucky to survive as two passers by going to the pub on the edge of the river managed to pull him out.

Life in Cheshire was much the same as Shropshire except there were more wealthy people in range of Manchester and Liverpool. Whereas the Shropshire establishment had made their fortunes in Birmingham or Wolverhampton or for the Thompson family in between the two, so the Cheshire establishment had usually made theirs in one of the other two cities. Then as the two cities grew, families tended to drift to the Wirral from Liverpool or to Wilmslow, Prestbury or Alderley Edge from Manchester. I had first come into the area when the rich from both had started setting up their homes in mid Cheshire. Snobbery was still rife and invitations from aristocrats around were much prized. In Shropshire it had been the Boynes, in our part of Cheshire, Hugh and Lavinia Cholmondeley ruled the roost and Jane and I were fortunate to get an early invitation from them. In fact invitations flowed in from the Ferrantis, the Delves Broughtons, Peter Henriques, whose wife Sara became one of Jane's closest friends, the Barlows, Raes and many others. David Stern was very helpful to getting us settled in and has remained a close friend to the present day.

My sporting activities were also largely unchanged; I still played squash for Wolverhampton and Staffordshire, though I also played for the Liverpool Rackets Club. Because of the length of time it took to reach Wolverhampton, Liverpool or Manchester, where the best players were, I had to devise a regime to keep fit. I would run on the roads for between two and three miles, then I would go into our large kitchen and run from corner to corner two or three hundred times, skip for five hundred times and shadow box for a period. All this after a day's work. Then I would crawl up to the bathroom and have a bath – I have always hated showers.

In the winter I shot as many days as I could and in the summer played cricket for Marchwiel on the family-owned ground. I also played for a number of other clubs around the country.

Father's third marriage broke up just after our move to Cheshire. He had wanted to buy a large estate near Ruthin in North Wales with grouse moors and lovely surroundings but Rosemary had vetoed it on the grounds it was too remote and would not move to Llanarmon for the same reason. They settled on a much smaller, perfectly nice but in my view rather characterless house close to Bangor on Dee, named Gerwyn Hall. It did have excellent farmland with it where he could move his bailiff, Millington, from Tickwood.

Father and Rosemary had never really functioned as a couple since the birth of Sally, moving into separate bedrooms shortly afterwards. Of Father's five marriages it was the most miserable and he had soon sought solace elsewhere. This time he chose a particularly unsatisfactory girlfriend, who was a fiery, attractive lady of Polish descent, called Basha, who Father had picked up in a nightclub called the Astor. Unlike Anne, she was anything but docile and the more she led him a merry dance the more infatuated and desperate Father would become. This reached its climax at the Chester May racecourse meeting, where he took a table in a backroom next to his friends, the Sterns and Bournphreys. It was just before we moved to Cheshire and Father moved to Gerwyn and we all stayed at the Grosvenor Hotel. I had two Shropshire friends, Christopher Motley and his girlfriend, Liz Leighton, also staying there and having consumed umpteen drinks on the racecourse we had moved to the Grosvenor bar when the news came through that Father had swallowed some pills and been taken to hospital. I was not allowed to see him for some time but the doctor, who was a friend of mine, said he was in a serious condition but would probably recover. I had to ring Rosemary, who said she would be over first thing the following morning.

It later transpired the Father had a blazing row with Basha and then swallowed a number of pills from the extensive 'medicine chest' he carried around with him. He could not have been too serious as he immediately rang Basha to say he had taken them and she rang the hotel to make sure somebody went to check on him. A couple of hours later Basha arrived but was not allowed near Father and I tore a strip off her, saying she should either look after him or pack it in. I got no marks when she chose the latter.

The following morning Rosemary arrived and said that I should go and tell my grandmother, which I duly did. I perhaps rather stupidly also said that I was sorry Father had put her through this, which did not go down well as my grandmother adored Father and would not hear a word of criticism. Father himself recovered very quickly but was told by the doctors that he was to spend a week in Cheadle Royal, a hospital specialising in mental problems. I went to see him at the end of the week and he was in great form, watching cricket and joking about the 'nutcases' in with him.

When he came out he made strenuous attempts to resume the affair with Basha but she had been totally frightened off and his blood pressure rose alarmingly. Shirley Stephens, his doctor, came to see me and said I had to get him away. 'Jimmy needs at least three weeks abroad or I will not be answerable for the consequences,' he said.

I then had the brainwave of ringing my mother in the Bahamas, telling her the situation, and before she could protest I said I think I will be able to get Billy to come with him. My mother was so overjoyed at the thought of her much loved younger son coming that she readily agreed to look after Father as well. They went off for a couple of weeks and I relaxed for the first time.

A fortnight later I took a long-distance call from Billy – Father has just met an unsuitable lady and is already practically engaged to her. This two weeks after breaking from his supposed great love was too much to swallow and I didn't take it too seriously until they returned after a further ten days.

When Billy returned, we met as usual at the Cock Inn and the whole story came out. Father was introduced to Margaret by my mother; he gave her dinner the next night and then hired a boat and they went off for five days. Mama, who was delighted to get Billy to herself for a few days, thought the boat trip was a good idea, never dreaming that Father would return as infatuated with Margaret as he had been with Basha. She was later to tell me that although she had only had a few days to prepare for Father and Billy's arrival she had selected Margaret with great care as far too young for Jimmy but an easy-going lady who liked a good time herself, and would provide Jimmy with one for a couple of weeks to get him over his breakdown over Basha. What she did not realise, although she was married to him for seven years, was that Father could not be without a woman for five minutes and would latch on to the first one who seriously crossed his path and a repeat performance was to occur twelve years later.

Billy saw the situation clearly and had no doubt that Father and Margaret would get married although Rosemary was still on the scene, and he proved absolutely correct. Although Father and Rosemary moved into Gerwyn, the marriage only lasted a few months more before Rosemary consented to move to London with Sally, her only daughter, and Margaret arrived at Gerwyn. The staff all took it in their stride and Billy and I were faced with our third stepmother.

I have to be very careful what I write about Margaret because she is still alive and she was to have a very successful second marriage to a senior American Admiral, who got an obituary in the *Telegraph* which filled three-quarters of the page. Plainly there was a side to Margaret which I was never to see because Father brought out the very worst in her.

Her parents lived in Portugal and Margaret had been employed by British Airways as both an air hostess and latterly a ground hostess in Nassau. Her two close friends, both very pleasant, were also air hostesses and one, who I particularly liked called Jonas, was to lose her job by having an affair with a school friend of mine at a stopover in the Middle East, which caused her to miss her onward flight.

Margaret was in her late twenties and rather immature and completely infatuated with the glamour she thought becoming the wife of the chairman of a large and famous construction company would bring. What she did not realise – and who could blame her? – was that Father having got the ring on her finger would revert to being the controlling, selfish man he usually was rather than the charming, do anything you want person he became during courtship. Whereas Rosemary had a child and then led a rather miserable separate life, Margaret did her best to integrate with Father's wishes. Unfortunately she seemed to me to lack the presence and intellect to carry it off and the marriage slowly started to deteriorate.

1961 – a tragedy was about to happen, which was going to blight my life and put my problems with Father and Margaret in the shade. Billy and I had two successive yearly trips to Mauritius with Father, Margaret and Nicky Knoop, who ran the African companies; Jane was also with us on the second. The first was particularly tied up with trying to sort out the problems we had with a large contract to provide a new drainage scheme for the island. When I came to have my passport stamped the official said, 'Is that really your name?' I said, 'Yes of course,' and then he said, 'We have had a hurricane which killed about forty people and compared with the arrival of your company, we prefer the hurricane.' Such was my greeting at the main airport of Mauritius and when we toured the contract the next day I could see what the official meant. We had blasted trenches on several main roads which had filled with rainwater and our staff were having great trouble keeping the few decent roads open. Our senior staff were totally demoralised with the workforce. 'All they want is to earn enough to buy several bottles of cheap brandy for the week-end. They then meet up with a girl, drink the brandy and are totally unfit for work on Monday,' a senior works manager told me. It also never seemed to stop raining. Sunshine and showers is island weather and Mauritius certainly lived up to that, although the brochures of today only talk of sunshine.

I have two memories of that first trip. One was the Indian minister of public works trying to impress Father by spouting quotations from Kipling, while Father tried to keep a straight face. The second was Father's determination to have a meal in a restaurant in the main port on the island. We found a restaurant which looked promising and the cheerful proprietor said we have fresh chicken, the only problem is I have to kill them first but while you wait I have some nice girls for the men to play with. Billy and I looked enthusiastic but the only lady, Margaret, looked horrified and Father, seeing the look on her face, said, 'Certainly not.'

The second trip was far more dramatic as we were in one of the worst hurricanes to hit the island in the twentieth century. We had in fact booked in a small holiday hotel, the first on the island as there were none of the large ones found on Mauritius today. We all had our own rondaavals with thatched roofs and for some reason Billy's was selected to store the alcohol to enable any of us to have a drink when we felt like it. Today the weather forecasts would have tracked the hurricane but forecasts then were much vaguer and, though we were warned a strong gale might come, nobody expected a full blown hurricane. We had all decided on an early night and about half an hour after I had tried to sleep the noise outside intensified and I could see from the window purple flashes coming from the power line. I rang Billy on the internal phone and put my best elder brother voice on and said, 'Billy, just bring a bottle of whisky, two glasses and sodas across while we sit this out.' A laugh came across and Billy said, 'It would be better if you came here.' I opened the door and tried to go a few steps and realised I would be spending an alcohol free night, while Billy would be tucked up with a large whisky. The hurricane was quite terrifying and went on for most of the night, sleep being impossible. When it abated I was able to go out at first light and I could see that the thatched roof of the main dining room of the hotel had blown clean off. How our smaller roofs had survived I do not know. The next day became sunny and calm and as we had a meeting arranged for mid morning with a house builder who had a proposition for us we decided to keep the appointment. When we drove to where we had been told his office was there was no sign of it. We saw a local and asked him where the office was – 'Just drive down the road half a mile and you will find it strewn all over the place.' The hurricane had killed fifty-four people and when I came back for a holiday two decades later our taxi driver asked if it was our first visit to the island? 'I was here in a hurricane,' I said. 'Oh, we usually have one of those every year,' he said. 'This was in 1961.' 'That was the worst we ever had.'

The construction continued to go badly but Nicky managed to retrieve most of the loss by employing the two leading barristers on the island for the subsequent arbitration, which was conducted under code Napoleonic, and we had two successful contracts later including a new civil airport. We certainly made our mark with the residents. When a school quiz took place in all Mauritius schools, one of the questions was what name do you most associate with England? Instead of Queen Elizabeth or Churchill, 73% said McAlpine.

The hurricane had disrupted Father and Nicky's plans as their plane back to Johannesburg was delayed for several days, but Billy and I managed to get to Madagascar and connect with our booked Air France flight to Paris. We found ourselves on a particularly impressive new jet and the first class had its own bar. We took off in another violent storm with thunder and lightning all around us until we eventually reached a high enough altitude when we headed straight for the bar, where we spent most of the flight. Back in an English March we resumed our normal lives and it was at the beginning of May when disaster struck. Jane, myself and Billy had all spent Sunday in Shropshire, which culminated in a good early dinner party given by Brian Jenks. We had separate cars and I in my Jensen was overtaken by Billy in his E Type Jaguar. A cheery wave of the hand and he was off to his cottage. The next day I went to Hooton as usual and was having a ten o'clock coffee when the senior secretary, Miss Lamb, walked into my office and said, 'I'm afraid Mr Billy has had a car crash and is in hospital in Chester.' I rushed over and went to emergency treatment and found Billy unconscious with his head swathed in bandages. A rather gloomy man who was attending minor injuries said he has compound fractures of the skull, will need an operation and you have the right to choose a surgeon.

I immediately rang Father, who was still at home – he never got up early on a Monday and fortunately was having his weekly blood pressure check taken by Shirley Stephens. Father sounded fairly grumpy at his routine being disturbed and put Shirley on the phone, who said, 'It shouldn't be too serious unless he has a compound fracture of the skull.' 'That is exactly what he has!' I shouted into the phone. 'In that case we will both come over,' he said, and about an hour later they arrived. By this time the senior surgeon around, John Wakely, was also on the scene and he and Shirley conferred. 'I think we will be alright,' said Shirley to Father; 'he is very nearly conscious, you and Bobby have lunch at the Grosvenor and hopefully we'll have better news for you when you get back.' Neither Father nor I realised the total gravity of the situation until we got back and a much more sombre Shirley said, 'I'm afraid he's gone downhill but they are doing everything they can and there is still plenty of hope for a full recovery.'

I had to get hold of Mama, who, as luck would have it, had gone with Dennis to a remote island, but a very efficient lady at Dennis's hotel promised to try and locate them and eventually I was given a number to ring later in the day. I had to tell her how serious the situation was and she had to get back to Nassau and book herself on a flight to Manchester getting in on the Wednesday morning. She came through and looked at me. I simply said he is still alive.

Mama was horrified when she saw the state Billy was in – unconscious and wrapped in ice to keep his soaring temperature down. I have nothing but praise for the doctors and nurses who were magnificent. The three days of Tuesday, Wednesday and Thursday were the Chester May race meeting and our table where we had so much fun remained empty. It was the Friday when some encouraging signs emerged and John Wakely said, 'I think he is very nearly conscious.' He did indeed regain consciousness later in the day and although obviously horrified at the situation he found himself in, he managed the odd smile. My sister, Valerie, had joined the group around his bed and all seemed to be leading for a recovery. John Wakely had brought in a senior consultant and they decided to remove the tube he had to his lungs to assist his breathing. 'This is a very old hospital,' said John, 'and as there are bugs everywhere, I want to minimise the risk of infection.'

For a few days Billy seemed to be on the road to a slow recovery and there was talk of a rehabilitation course but one morning he was definitely not so well and the two consultants told us that he should go to Walton, a modern hospital with far more facilities. An ambulance was arranged for midday and to take my mind off it I decided to visit the M6 site we were constructing between Warrington and Preston. When I got back to the main site office at lunchtime I was told to go to the Chester Infirmary immediately as Billy's condition had worsened. When I got there John Wakely was waiting for me. 'Billy has had a blood clot which has gone from his leg to his brain. It hasn't killed him but he is far too ill to travel to Walton.' He died a couple of days later. The funeral was at Llanarmon and my mother and I both insisted that it was open to all, against Father's wishes, who wanted a private one. Margaret came on the phone to my mother, 'For Jimmy's sake, let it be private.' 'For once Jimmy shouldn't come first,' said my mother.

As the local paper said, the small church of Llanarmon D C was full to overflowing and his friends came from far and wide. He was immensely and deservedly popular and his death was the worst single thing that happened in my life.

The inquest criticised him for driving too fast and pointed out that he had nearly a hundred yards to brake before he hit the milk lorry, which had come out of a farm entrance and not seen him. What was not said was that the brakes of the Jaguar were markedly inferior to the Aston Martin he had before. The other driver was charged and fined ten pounds and his licence was not endorsed.

I have several times had to talk to people who have had similar tragedies and have always said (or written) that time is the great healer as indeed it is. I was devastated for a long time but now, fifty years on, it seems a distant blur.

Chapter 4

Marriage and Beyond

Cheshire was in the sixties a very social part of the world with a large number of successful, glamorous couples giving regular dinner parties. Sunday lunch did not become a popular event until much later in the twentieth century. The social scene was dominated by Hugh and Lavinia Cholmondeley with their magnificent estate but there were many in close attendance. Sebastian Ferranti, a dashing rich industrialist, was another leading figure, as was Evelyn Delves Broughton and his wife, Helen. Evelyn had restored the family estate at Doddington Park which his father Jock of 'white mischief' fame had decimated. Although the main house was a girl's school, they had a very comfortable house in the grounds and gave frequent and successful parties. Close by were Peter and Sarah Henriques, who became great friends. David and Penny Stern had tried to buy Stretton Hall, the main Leche house, when it came on the market but had been outbid by Peter Black, who worked for the Nall Cains in their family brewery in Warrington. David settled for a converted farmhouse near Tarporley and was joined by Tony Hanbury Williams whose wife, Diny, was a Hartley cousin of my childhood playmate Jane. Tony bought a farmhouse next to David and they jointly farmed the land adjacent to the two houses. David's brother-in-law, Anthony Johnson married to Penny's sister, Zandra, was another who became a good friend through a love of racing. Anthony and I had a mutual friend in the shape of John Phillipson, whom Jane and I had met at a beach party in Devon when we had gone down to watch my horse, Marieson, run at Newton Abbot. Johnny had a particularly nice and attractive wife, Felicity, and seemed to be an ideal person to have fun with and regularly came to stay with either Anthony or myself. We would all go racing together and I would stay with them at their nice mews house in London. Johnny was working for Victor Barclay as a salesman in the Jack Barclay showrooms selling Rolls Royces. One night we got a phone call at his flat to say that Victor had been arrested for drink driving after a day's golf at Sunningdale and would we go to Mill Hill police station to collect him. We made our way there to be told by the station sergeant that Victor had swung a fist at his constable but that as he was so drunk it had missed. 'Nevertheless, gentlemen, it could lead to a serious charge.' I had persuaded Johnny, who had a wad of notes in his pocket, not to attempt to use them and hastily said, I am sure it can be smoothed over, officer. Johnny then rattled on about Victor's father's lavish contributions to the police charities and we were allowed to take a subdued Victor home. No charge was ever brought!

The sixties were a very happy period. Three delightful children where brought into the world, Euan, Sara and Christopher, and if Jane and my marriage wasn't going particularly well, nor were many of our friends'. The swinging sixties was of course the era when a lot of taboos, which had existed until then, were either broken down or lessened. For those of us who had married in the fifties, many had married either to get away from home or to be able to lead a normal sex life. Unfortunately many who had married in haste began to repent in leisure and whilst some were very happy a large number were not.

I had always privately vowed I would not get in the same situation as Father and I was totally faithful to Jane for nine years. In today's era of the young being able to sow their wild oats before marriage to their hearts' content, nine years may not seem like a very long period. What brought that particular state to a close was a very eventful holiday in St Moritz.

I had never skied but Jane was a passionate skier and had tried to persuade me to go for ages and, as Anthony and Zandra Johnson and the Marchwoods were going at the same time, I was talked into going. Two days earlier I had obtained my first Bentley from Victor Barclay, who was talking to an attractive girl in his office as I walked in. He introduced me to Angela, who wanted to stay but Victor seeing a good customer was all business and shooed her out of the office. However she was on the plane and also the train to St Moritz and recognised me at once. I in turn introduced her to Anthony and when Zandra met the train and the two got off first she rushed to the wrong conclusion and gave Anthony a difficult time for a few days. The holiday got off to a bad start as I was paired for my first skiing lesson with Dudley Cunliffe Owen's fiancée, Jean. The two of us were taken to the top of the nursery slope and told by the instructor to ski down. Both of us fell at least twice but we reached the bottom and Jean then said something to the instructor after which he vanished leaving us together at the bottom of the slope. Jean then burst into tears, which cascaded down. To this day I have never seen anyone cry like it. I realised that somehow we had to get up the slope which, being completely unused to skis, was more than difficult. The more I pushed Jean the more she slid down and eventually abandoning all protocol I used her ample bottom as a lever and we made a little progress. It took us nearly an hour to get to the top and I arrived with sweat pouring off me and Jean still crying. I made straight for a hut selling drink and ordered half a bottle of brandy, a drink I hadn't touched since my bout of jaundice. Jean and I finished the half bottle and with the last gulp we both drank a toast to never putting a ski on again, and neither of us ever did.

I had to do something during the day and a group of us, which included John Sunley, an old school friend, and Martin Summers decided to try the Cresta Run. For the first time from a junction about half way down the run you are allowed to go as slow as you like and I braked with my feet hard a lot of the way, finding the ride terrifying but exhilarating. I did one run most days of the holiday getting faster and never ceasing to be terrified. The sensation of going so fast on a tiny sled and getting severely bumped is one I always find difficult to describe.

We all headed straight for the excellent bar also stationed about halfway down where I found Angela and some friends. She seemed to know everybody and we talked happily together even going for a walk in the woods below the Cresta. I could not help contrasting how attractive she looked compared to Jane, who skied all day and arrived back late looking totally dishevelled. Angela had also met Prince Michael of Kent, who she introduced me to one night when we were all in the local nightclub.

Absolutely nothing happened between us, although I made one effort after a good lunch to go to her hotel and ask her for a drink. I was just getting her room number when I looked round and saw David Marchwood reading the paper. I beat a hasty retreat without being seen and the nearest I came to any form of intimacy was getting her home telephone number.

On returning home there was gossip in the tabloid press about Angela's relationship with Prince Michael, as she was his first girlfriend. It was therefore with some trepidation that I phoned her but she seemed happy to agree to a dinner date, where we had an enjoyable evening and after a chaste kiss we fixed a further date where things did progress further than the chaste kiss of the week before.

I went the next day to the Lebanon for three weeks on a trip where we were to meet the elder son of the King of Saudi Arabia, who was friendly with a Lebanese banker, who in turn knew Jack Lundy, who was employed by my uncle Edwin as a freelance finder of contracts for Sir Robert McAlpine. They were not interested in work abroad and I brought with me John Goodall, the most senior of our directors who wanted overseas work. The three of us arrived in Beirut to be installed in the best hotel and told that the banker would give us dinner that evening in a club which was the Lebanese equivalent of Annabel's.

We were told how influential the prince was and how he could place a large programme of airfield and road contracts our way, and that the prince would arrive in two or three days after undergoing medical treatment in Switzerland. It was also impressed upon us that to have dealings with a senior member of the Saudi Arabian monarchy, time must be considered flexible and in fact it took two weeks before his highness arrived. Both John and I had major work commitments at home and whilst the hotel swimming pool, the lovely weather and the Beirut equivalent of Annabel's all had their attractions, by the time his highness arrived we were desperate to get back.

I had rung Angela twice with great difficulty, there of course being no mobiles and long distance calls were treated very differently from today. I can't say the conversations were very satisfactory and I remember on one receiving a long discourse on the unreliability of men in general. Nevertheless, when I got back she seemed keen to take up a further dinner date and so I embarked on a lengthy romance. She was utterly realistic about Prince Michael of Kent – it will never last, his mother will make him move on, and he did.

Angela was one of two major romances in the second half of my marriage to Jane – Anthea Marr, who was separated from her husband for a long time, being the other. As Anthea finally returned to her husband Brian and as Angela has been happily married to a second husband, who I sometimes play golf with, I am sure readers will understand that it would be unfair to go into further detail. I have fortunately remained friends with both ladies.

Di and Toddy Hanbury were great friends from the early days of my marriage to Jane. Di had been married three times before marrying Toddy and had been a very good lady golfer, winning the Berkshire championship several times. Both she and her brother, Dudley Cunliffe Owen, had inherited a lot of money off their father, Sir Hugo Cunliffe-Owen, a wealthy industrialist baronet, who lived in an enormous house at Sunninghill, now used for conferences, sometimes major government ones. Their father had been a prominent racehorse owner between the first and second world wars and Di inherited some of his love of racing, although she did not own horses. Toddy was between Father and myself in age and had become a friend of both of us when he was working for a mining house in South Africa. He was a good tennis player and golfer and enjoyed shooting, joining the several South Africans who were asked to Llanarmon. He too was married with two children but his marriage broke up when he met Di and for two decades they had an extremely happy and successful marriage, living in a large house about a mile from the centre of the small Surrey town of Chobham. Toddy had been recruited into Singer and Friedlander, the merchant bank, by Michael Stoddart and Di started up an extremely successful interior decorating business in Chobham using her network of contacts to get work. She was in fact very social and loved to mix with major social figures. Jane and I had stayed happily at Queen's Lodge for a number of years and always had the same bedroom. When Robert Sangster joined the Ascot house party she enlarged the house to provide an en suite apartment for Robert, who was more choosy than we were. We were staying with Di when she announced that an important guest was coming the next day and we would have to share a bathroom with him. The important guest was no less than the Earl of Carnarvon, always known as Porchy, who owned an immense estate, Highclere, near Newbury, now immortalised in *Downton Abbey*, and Toddy had been a shooting guest there. Porchy was then in his seventies and Di made a tremendous fuss of him. He, like Toddy and I, was a member of the Portland Club and although he did not play golf he used to go to some of the summer Portland outings to play bridge. At the dinner parties at Queen's Lodge, he used to amuse us by talking about some of his amorous exploits and referring to the most important part of his anatomy as 'Mr Mouse'. 'Mr Mouse used to be very active but now he is retired.'

He had not been married for some time and in his old age (he was in his early seventies when he first came to Queen's Lodge) he liked to be accompanied by much younger, attractive, socially acceptable ladies and it was at a Portland golf weekend at Deauville, which was always strictly men only, that he appeared with a tall, extremely elegant lady, who I gazed at with great admiration. The Portland gossips told me she was Porchy's latest companion and was married to a French baron. Nobody was more amazed than me when Porchy sidled up to me the next day and said, 'My friend wants to go to the casino for dinner tonight and I want to play bridge, will you take her? I do want her back for lunch on Sunday.' He then introduced me to the Baroness, who seemed delighted to be taken to the casino and we arranged to meet there. The meeting went so well that late into the night I took her back to her hotel, the best in Deauville where Porchy had booked her into a large suite, and fell asleep to wake up close to nine in the morning. My dinner jacket was alongside the settee but I couldn't. find my bow tie anywhere and went down in an open-necked shirt and dinner jacket to the foyer, where I found a queue waiting for taxis to go to church. I eventually got to the head of the queue and set off for the Hotel de Golf, where the Portland party were staying. In order to get to my room I had to get from the front door to the lift and not wanting to be seen by anyone in the golf party, I ran the fifteen yards across the hall where, to my amazement, Porchy's valet/minder, Misen (I have no idea of the right spelling and for *Downton* fans he was more Bates than Carson), appeared from nowhere, opened the lift door and said, 'I hope you had an enjoyable evening, sir!' At lunchtime the Baroness was back at Porchy's side but we did manage to exchange phone numbers and she whispered that Porchy and she were back at Deauville in two weeks time and she would get me an invitation. Three days later a letter arrived at the office starting, 'Mon Cher Robert', and going on for several pages and telling me that a room had been booked for me at Deauville in a fortnight's time. I duly returned to Deauville where, to my surprise, I found not only Porchy but the Baron also in attendance. Where I fitted in the ménage I was far from sure! The Baron and Porchy seemed to get on like a house on fire and I felt distinctly spare and we all went to a dinner the Baron had arranged at the French Jockey Club, where Porchy was the guest of honour. The Baron was not in a wheelchair but was obviously disabled and Porchy was at his very worst, picking an argument with a Frenchman and announcing that he was going back to the hotel unless the Frenchman left, which he eventually did. The next day, the Baroness managed to get away from both her husband and Porchy by driving me to the station, where I was to take a train to Paris. She had in fact got us close to the station well before the train took off and I remember the two of us on a river bridge throwing pebbles into the river before she waved me off at the station, the only time I have ever been on a French train.

Back in England, a stream of letters continued to arrive and whilst I didn't match them, I did my best to reply. We did manage a couple of days later that summer in Paris, where I was shown all the sights including the Eifel Tower and the brief romance sadly ended in Spain, where I was shooting partridges in October. I had booked her into the Ritz Hotel in Madrid, where I was due to return to after three days shooting about two-and-a-half hours journey south of Madrid. The shoot always finished early on the third day, with a light lunch in the open and I had expected to get away about one, but because the first day had been affected by rain we finished much later and it was nearly four when Anthony Speelman, who was with me, and I extricated ourselves from the shooting party. We hit Madrid at rush hour and with no mobiles in those days, I could not warn the Baroness that I was several hours late. The reception I got was extremely frigid and plainly my perfectly valid excuse was not acceptable. Sadly, I never saw her again.

Porchy and I continued to meet at the Portland and my last memory of him was as my guest at a private dinner I gave there, where I sat him on my right with David Stern my other side. Porchy was by then well into his eighties and looked very frail. Announcing he was very tired at the end of the dinner, the faithful Misen was summoned, gathered Porchy in his arms and literally carried him downstairs. He died a few months later. He was in many ways a rather sad and lonely figure. Although he wrote a bestselling novel called *No Regrets* and appeared on television, he obviously craved the love and affection he had never received from his father in particular, who behaved brutally to him. There was to be a comeback when his granddaughter Carolyn became Steve Cauthen's first English girlfriend. Steve brought her for a shooting weekend at Llanarmon and they both stayed with Angela and I in our small house at Llanarmon. On the Monday I received a phone call from Carolyn who said, 'I have never been frightened by my father until today, when he went ballistic and obviously hates you.' I said that I had never met her father but I did know her grandfather reasonably well. 'That must be it,' said Carolyn. 'What did you get up to with him?'

Toddy and Di continued to be good friends through two marriages and the intervening period when Nicky Spice was working for her. Dudley, her brother, was also a close friend and I often stayed with him and Jean in their house on the Isle of Man. Another friend to us all was Tim Holland, a larger than life character, who made and lost a lot of money. Tim and Dudley were particularly close and they cashed in very successfully when the casino bubble burst in England, founding a casino called Crockfords and employing the manager of the casino at Le Touquet. They were keen to expand in the Isle of Man and we were appointed the contractor and an eminent architect, Richard Seifert, was chosen to design the first major casino and hotel to be built in Britain. The contract duly started and all went well for a time until Crockfords, which had been making large profits, found that a number of their leading clients were not paying their debts, which under English law could not be legally enforced. The brains behind Crockfords was Dennis Poore, a competent and successful businessman, who later founded a business called Manganese Bronze and his son-in-law, who ran the business after Dennis, was Edwin McAlpine's eldest grandson. Dennis attended a meeting in the Isle of Man, which I asked Bob Clarke, our senior non executive director, to attend. Dennis started the meeting by apologising to Bob Clarke: 'I am appalled, Sir Robert, that my two colleagues could have started this contract without my agreement and without making sure the funding was in place.'

Tim and Dudley had the sense to keep silent, although we all knew Dennis was fully in the picture. The casino was drastically scaled down from the original lavish specifications, much to the fury of the eminent architect, and the bedroom floor sizes were halved – as I was to find out when I stayed in the hotel for Robert Sangster's fiftieth birthday party. The contract was finished and we were eventually paid by the company who took over from Crockfords and for whom Dudley worked for many years. The opening of the casino was memorable as Sean Connery, then at the height of his James Bond fame, performed the opening ceremony with the first spin of the roulette wheel, which was a fiasco, as the spinning ball ended up on the floor. After two attempts the great star succeeded in landing a first winning number for the casino. Sean Connery was staying, as Jane and I were, with Dudley and when he was advised to leave before the crowd outside got too restive, we said we would go with him. We all headed for the hired Rolls outside, to be met by the most frightening crowd I have been through. The stewards fought to get the three of us through and a small boy punched Connery in the stomach, shouting, 'Mummy I've hit James Bond.' He was literally thrown onto Jane's lap as she was first into the car and while normally she might have welcomed the close contact, we were all so shaken that a very stiff drink was needed when we got to the baronet's house.

Di was one of the few people who took my side when I split with Nicky and married Angela and we both continued to stay at Queen's Lodge for Ascot and other events. Di's two children by her first marriage had gone with their father to Canada but had returned to their mother where they were rapturously received and a blissful family scenario ensued. Di's son, Grey, was to marry Toddy's daughter and the newly weds lived in a house less than a mile away. For Royal Ascot Toddy and Di always gave a party on the Thursday night after the Gold Cup, and we would go for several years to have lunch with the Buchanans (their children's surname, after Di's first husband). All seemed idyllic but perhaps it was too good to last. In a terrible year for the family, Toddy and Di split up, each blaming the other for a shortage of money, which seemed to have suddenly threatened the tremendous lifestyle they had. On the same day Di went to her divorce hearing, her son Grey rang up his mother and told her he was going into bankruptcy and was leaving the stock broking company he was working for. Unfortunately their marriage was not to last either. Only the worst of the current soaps that invade our television screens could have made up the ghastly script and I, who was very fond of them all, was immensely saddened.

I was summoned a year later to a boardroom lunch at Singer and Friedlander, where another longstanding friend, Panton Corbett, was present. He had also originally been recruited by Michael Stoddart and had the sense to keep fairly quiet, when the chairman, Tony Solomons, pleaded with me to arbitrate between Toddy and Di. He paid me a compliment by saying I was the only person in the country who could do it and I countered by saying the position was impossible and that both parties were in totally entrenched positions. I did make a weak attempt to talk to Di but the mission was impossible and I abandoned it.

I went to her funeral, where the only one of her ex-husbands to turn up was Michael Stoop, who was probably (apart from Toddy) the last person she would have wanted to see there. Michael was best known for lending the car to Lord Lucan, which he used in his final drive. The Baroness Trumpington made an excellent address and the wake took place at Tim Holland's brother David's house, where he and Julia, his delightful wife, presided over the sorrowful friends who had gathered to pay their last respects. The end of a tremendous era!

Why does a marriage go downhill? One answer is that both parties need to take into account each other's wishes and neither Jane nor I were good at that. Sometimes it is small things that continuously infuriate. Jane seemed incapable of closing a door and as we were close to a busy minor road the dogs were in constant danger if allowed to stray. In fact I don't remember one dog dying of old age and in one week we lost two dogs, killed on the road. Another constant grouse of mine was that she would never go to bed if there was a party. Like me, she was a big party drinker but never seemed to get a hangover or need sleep. I was the opposite and have always needed an average of eight hours sleep from an early age. She was extremely good with children and towards the end would berate me for not doing more with them. My answer being that I was not encouraged to do so.

No doubt I had habits which infuriated her but Jane was very single-minded and not a good communicator. Whatever the reasons the last years were not happy and it was only our very busy lives which prevented open warfare. Jane hunted two or three days a week and horses were a big part of her life. I had a busy work life and shooting, cricket and racing for recreation.

One thing we both did together was visit the children at school. Euan was the first to go to boarding school and I had entered him for Ludgrove as the joint headmaster was my brother-in-law, Peter Shaw's, father. Ludgrove was one of three preparatory schools which were popular with my friends, Sunningdale and Heatherdown being the other two, and it was my old mentor, Charles Lillingstone, who said to me at a cricket match at Harrow, when I was playing against the school, that I must send Euan to Heatherdown. I told him that I was committed to Ludgrove but Charles said it is never too late to change and I will introduce you to James Edwards, the headmaster, who is watching the cricket. He duly did so and James promised to let me know if he could squeeze Euan in, as he was technically full for the term Euan should go, less than a year away. Although I did not realise it at the time, James's wife was Tony Hanbury Williams's sister and this probably helped as I got a letter shortly afterwards from James to say he would fit Euan in if I let him know straight away.

So I bailed out of Ludgrove, getting an extremely rude letter from Tim Shaw's partner in the process – Tim himself being very understanding. The arrival at Heatherdown was an ordeal for both children and parents. A lavish tea was provided for parents of new boys and the boys themselves all looked nervous and strained with the boys and their mothers all trying to keep tears out of their eyes. Euan took some time to enjoy Heatherdown but eventually did well there.

Christopher had a similar start to Euan and on the first day of his first school holiday he went to play with the Hanbury Williams children. 'How are you getting on, Christopher?' said Tony Hanbury Williams. 'Alright Uncle Tony, except for the headmistress, she's really scary.' 'You know she's my sister?' 'Uncle Tony, you couldn't possibly have a sister like that!' Christopher always claimed that his last year was ruined when Euan, by then at Harrow, joined us for lunch at the Heatherdown half term sports day and we tried to sneak out after lunch to go to the heath meeting at Ascot. Instead of taking the back drive we went past the front door where Mrs Edwards was waiting to meet the Queen and Prince Philip. Without saying a word (her glare was sufficient) she waved us to the back drive. Not a good moment.

Both Euan and Christopher did well at Harrow but Sara had a much less happy time at St Mary's, Ascot. This was a top Catholic girls boarding school and although Jane had agreed to the boys going to a non-Catholic boarding school (both Euan and Christopher attended Catholic services at Harrow) she insisted on Sara going to a Catholic school. St Mary's, Ascot was run by a very formidable nun called Mother Bridget. When I went to see the school I was met by her deputy who apologised for the Principal's absence and said that although the school was full I was welcome to look around. The school was certainly impressive and when we finished and I was about to say goodbye to the deputy an elderly nun came up and introduced herself as Mother Bridget. We got chatting and I told her I was coming to the Royal meeting the following week and had a horse called Precipice Wood in the Gold Cup, who would run very well. The Tuesday after the Gold Cup I got a letter from Mother Bridget congratulating me on my win and saying she would accept Sara after all.

To outward appearances when Jane and I visited the school, Sara appeared happy and she certainly had very nice friends, but in the holidays she told me how she disliked the nuns. 'Dad they are so two-faced and mean; if they represent religion I want nothing to do with it.' The least academic of all my children, she had no desire to go to university and left St Mary's at sixteen, just at the time her mother and I were about to break up.

Euan's final day at Harrow was certainly memorable as he was head of house and at that time their fathers had to reply to their speech at the house dinner. The day before, as chairman of the Export Group for the construction industry, I had made the introductory speech to Dennis Healy, the Chancellor of the Exchequer, in front of 300 guests at the Savoy. Not only had I not turned a hair, I had rather enjoyed it and public speaking held no terrors for me. Quite the opposite! Whether it was the sherry, which was the only drink offered before the dinner, or the sight of Lance Gorse glaring down from his photograph on the wall, I don't know, but after Euan had got up and made a very funny speech full of in-house jokes, as I got up to reply I could feel myself shaking, indeed for a moment I thought I was going to collapse. I had prepared the speech very carefully and got through it with the odd laugh. I did make an *ad hoc* reference to the sight of Lance Gorse's photograph unnerving me which drew a laugh from the boys but not the housemaster, who in his final speech was full of praise for Gorse. Fortunately, although Christopher did nearly as well as Euan, the house was evacuated to another for refurbishment so I didn't have to endure a repeat performance.

It was neither of my two main girl-friends but a third relationship which was to bring my first marriage to an end. Zandra Johnson, who had long been divorced from Anthony, knew I was unhappy and having been a friend and confidante for years she had said if you want a shoulder to cry on I will provide one. We were careful to start with but she had commitments at home and told me that if we were to continue we would have to use her house, only four miles from mine. Crazily I agreed and the inevitable happened when a hunting friend of Jane's saw us together in the car park of the Crewe Arms by Crewe station. Although she knew me she did not know Zandra's name and fed Jane with a description which could have fitted one or two people; Jane leapt to the wrong conclusion and singled out another friend of ours as the culprit. At this point our next-door neighbour, John Squire, who was a close friend of both of us, had to listen to Jane blaming the wrong lady and blurted out the truth. I was furious but he always claimed he could do nothing else.

I moved to Doug Francis's spare room and had of course got the use of the London flat. So a slightly strange, nomadic existence ensued. Jane told me later that she never intended to exclude me permanently but wanted to teach me a lesson and expected me to come back with my tail between my legs – life is, of course, not like that.

Unfortunately Father's fourth marriage was also breaking up. Margaret was very unhappy and it was at a dinner, when we had all drunk a lot, when she confided to me she was having an affair with, of all people, a senior director of the company – even more stupidly she blurted out the truth to Father. All hell broke loose as the one thing Father was not going to forgive was infidelity, however much he practised it himself. As it happened he had met a lady who was doing the catering for a function at the Wrexham Golf Club, where he was president. She had come from a very different background and the publicity Father got was immense both nationally and locally. Whereas I would have been devastated, he rather enjoyed it. He had made the great mistake, when he heard Margaret was being interviewed by a national newspaper, of rushing to his house, Gerwyn Hall, from the mobile home he was living in with Cindy and was photographed on the drawing room sofa looking, to anyone who knew him well, decidedly the worse for wear. Nigel Dempster was to make the comment that Father had removed the nineteenth hole – like many he was to make about both of us, neither accurate nor fair.

There was widespread disquiet in the company although Margaret's affair was hushed up and the man involved quickly found a job with another company. Although everybody was used to Father's marital disasters they were not used to the appalling publicity attached to his latest break up. Even Tony Scurr in South Africa, where Father was immensely popular, rang up to say that the press there had followed the British media and that it would be better for Father not to visit the country for a while.

For myself, setting off for what would turn out to be three years of 'between marriages' life, it had a major impact, though I could not see it at the time. In particular it drew the attention of Nigel Dempster's team to our side of the family, which I could have done without as I battled with my considerable domestic problems.

I started the three years with Zandra as my girl-friend and it was not until the spring of the following year that my weekend on the Isle of Man brought Nicky on to the scene. The three years represented a very strange period in my life. Like many in my position I had a naïve concept that the break up could be amicable, would not be too expensive and that a wonderful new era would begin, where I could be really happy. I was soon disillusioned on one part of this happy dream as Jane immediately found a lawyer suggested by an old school friend of mine on the dance floor at a Shropshire party, not the kindest act to me as I was to tell him later. The lawyer was a senior partner of a well-known specialist divorce team and was both competent and aggressive. I, who had talked to my cousin Alistair, who had an easy ride on the breakup of his marriage, had engaged the same lawyer as he had used, who, though a thoroughly nice man, was far from a top-class divorce lawyer. I should have gone to my bridge-playing friend, Isadore Kerman, and when I did eventually go to him for advice on my break up with Nicky, I regretted I had not done so earlier.

I had plunged into a relationship with Nicky thinking that at last I had found the ideal companion and it took eighteen months before I seriously questioned if I had been sensible. She had a perfectly adequate house in the middle of Windsor, two young boys and a nanny/housekeeper, Millie, who was essential as Nicky was working full time for Di Hanbury's interior decorating business. I now had three places open to me to spend nights – Nicky's Windsor house, the London flat and Doug Francis's spare room!

There was one major complication at Carden: daughter Sara had become engaged against my wishes but I was powerless to stop it. She was frankly far too young. Having left St Mary's, Ascot at sixteen she had spent time with Jane particularly on the horse front and eventing, where she was very talented. The idea was that she should spend a year abroad when she was nineteen and gain some experience of life. She had one boyfriend before Robin Cayzer but as Robin was the first serious one and several years older than Sara, I could see that he was likely to dominate the relationship. The news was given to me in the London office by Mary Tempest, a school friend of Sara's, who had been given a temporary job as a favour. She said the engagement was good news and I had to get enthusiastic about it and added that I was asked to stay that night at Cornbury, the family estate then owned by Lord Rotherwick, Robin's father.

It was with considerable apprehension that I went to Cornbury, close to Blenheim, a magnificent house in equally fine surroundings. I was greeted by the butler who showed me to my room and the layout of the house before I met the family for drinks and Jane and Sara would join us for a family dinner where Bunny Rotherwick proposed a toast. The following day Robin took me for a walk in the garden and deer park and I realised the full splendour of it all. For fans of *Downton Abbey* Cornbury would stand up well in comparison and it did feature prominently in two or three *Inspector Morse* episodes.

One thing was obvious to me – that Jane was completely bowled over by it all. She also knew that I was basically not in favour, which made her even keener on the engagement. As I was to learn, anything which annoyed me would always find favour with her. What I failed to realise was that her judgement was very suspect. Sara was now nineteen, though as far as maturity was concerned she was light years behind my then unborn next daughter Emma at the same age. Whilst everybody agreed that a long engagement was in order it was never going to happen and Robin's single-minded determination to get married would eventually carry the day.

The engagement did have one consolation in that I was asked to shoot at Cornbury. Stanley Cayzer, a cousin of Bunny Rotherwick, was a regular bridge player at the Portland Club and gave me some solemn advice. The one drawback, he said, is that very little alcohol is dispensed. When it comes to lunch I have an agreement with the butler that my drink is three times the strength of a normal one and I will do the same for you. Make it last because you will get one small glass of wine and an even smaller glass of port afterwards.

We had a lovely day for the shoot and although the country was magnificent the birds were not difficult. I was lucky at the big morning stand by having a lot of birds over me whilst my next door neighbour, the future Duke of Bedford, had hardly any over him. It came to lunch and I dutifully followed Stanley into the drawing room, saw him nod in my direction to the butler and duly received a beaker of vodka and tonic, which nearly blew my head off. I was most of the way through it when the butler came back into the room. His Lordship is in a lot of pain with his hips and is going to rest and will not be joining you, he announced. He then added you have time for another drink, with which he took my glass and proceeded to return with a similar beaker to the first. It was perhaps fortunate that Stanley was correct about the following drinks as I could barely stand by the time we reached the dining room.

My mother's marriage had sadly broken up a few years before Jane and I parted. It came as a major shock as we had both spent a very good holiday in their hotel in the centre of Nassau and they seemed very happy. Dennis had left her for a much younger lady and was to have three children with her, although he had refused to let my mother have another child on the basis he couldn't cope with children. She had stayed on in Nassau where she had two great friends, Annie Orr Lewis and a Canadian Babbie Holt; both looked after her and found her a cottage near them in Lyford Key. However she decided she wanted to live the last part of her life in England and I bought a nice small house for her about three miles from Lower Carden.

Tragically she was diagnosed with stomach cancer shortly after she came back to England and the next six years were to be a constant battle with the disease, during which she had good and bad periods. But she was a great fighter to the end and until her last week of life would never have wanted to give in to it.

However at the time of Sara's engagement she was relatively clear and, although obviously disappointed at our split up, was very careful not to take sides.

As I had expected, Robin began to put pressure on to get a wedding date in the early months of the engagement and Jane soon fell in with his wishes and a date was fixed for January, nine months ahead. Because I was living away from Carden I was never sure what Sara's real wishes were. I was certain she was being dominated by her fiancé and mother but because she kept her real feelings to herself I never received a cry for help or even knew if she wanted to make one. I had of course my own problems to contend with. For the year after meeting Nicky I tried desperately to make the relationship work. The trip to Australia had gone well and Nicky had insisted we spend Christmas in Barbados. In many ways that suited me well but unfortunately her younger child contracted mumps just before we were due to fly. Although I did not think he was fit to fly, Nicky insisted on continuing and we duly went, Nicky and I in the front and the two boys and Millie in the back. Christmas was strange with the temperature well over 100 degrees, very hot even for Barbados, and the radio blaring Christmas carols and talk of Santa Claus and snow. Although I did not know it until we got back to England, I was also going down with mumps. The first of two children's ailments which I had avoided previously but which I was to catch from Nicky's children. I was lucky with mumps in that it only affected my neck and face and not a lower part of my anatomy. My genial London G.P., Ted Bott, who had left the Grove before I arrived, thought it all quite funny, warned me to stay in bed and hope the swelling didn't spread. It didn't. The second illness, whooping cough, was far more serious and went on for weeks before being properly diagnosed. I at least had a base of my own in Cheshire, as at Robert Sangster's suggestion I had bought Swettenham Hall off him – though I declined his offer to buy the land and stud with it, a decision I was later to regret. The house had been let out to friends of Robert's for several years and no maintenance had been carried out, so Nicky set out with great enthusiasm to redecorate the house while we had a base in the outbuildings.

Sara's wedding was set for January 1980 and Jane informed me that she and Sara had been to a Boyne wedding at Burwarton, which they wanted to model Sara's on. The wedding had taken place in the late afternoon and a champagne reception with canapés preceded a dinner dance. Although this formula is commonplace now, it was unusual then as the previous format was to have an early afternoon wedding followed immediately with a reception with the happy pair leaving about six and no dinner.

Although I was to pay for everything I only got my way on the caterers, who I insisted should be the firm who did all the company catering and looked after cricket matches and our private parties at home.

I was subjected to two highly unpleasant pieces in the Dempster column in the *Daily Mail*, accusing me of being extremely selfish in wanting the wedding late in the day so I could go racing earlier in the day. They had got every single fact wrong saying I was a steward of the Jockey Club rather than an ordinary member, that I was a steward at Haydock Park, where I was a steward on the flat but not during the National Hunt season. Moreover the late-in-the-day wedding was entirely Jane and Sara's idea, as I would have preferred the earlier time, as would a few older Cheshire friends who boycotted the event.

Totally unused to this sort of publicity I could not have handled it worse, just putting my head in the sand and refusing to do anything, although the company public relations man begged me to write to Dempster. When I met him two years later he told me he had not written or approved the piece and that I should immediately have written to him explaining the facts. Once I got to know him he never wrote anything unpleasant and told me it was much easier to write about people he had never met. The last time I ever saw Nigel Dempster was at Charles Benson's funeral, where he gave me a lift from the church to the wake in Sue Sangster's Eaton Square flat. The *Daily Mail* had provided him with a driver as the illness which was to take his life a little later had already started to affect his limbs.

In fact on the day of the wedding the weather was so unpleasant that I never went to Haydock, had a quiet lunch and collected an extremely nervous Sara from Carden. I did say to her in the car that it was still not too late to call it off and thought for a moment she might take up the offer, but she merely laughed nervously. When we got to the church in Malpas we found a large number of people outside the church, most of which were guests who could not get in. Somebody produced an umbrella and I duly escorted my daughter down the aisle.

My mother had a close friend, Betty Kenwood, who had for years written the society column in the *Tatler* and had elected to stay with her. Later in the evening Betty came up to me and said she had never been to a worse organised wedding. Totally taken aback I asked her what was wrong and she gave me a catalogue of administrative errors. In fairness Jane was desperately unlucky with the day, where torrential rain had followed six weeks of dry weather. She was also unlucky that my half-sister Sally's husband, Bernard Argent, a leading professional photographer, was so inebriated that he took twice as long to take the pre-reception photographs as normal. Tim and Sally Kitson, whose eldest daughter, Michelle, was getting married two weeks later, took particular interest in the wedding. Sally having seen how easy it is to be taken in by a church which looks large from the outside told me she went to her church in Bedale and counted every seat.

The stress of all the dramas had got to me before Sara's wedding and the skin problem psoriasis came out worse than it had ever been. My skin specialist in London was quite famous and gave lectures around the world on the condition. He had a small ward at the Westminster Hospital reserved for his patients and he suggested I spent three weeks there. When I told him that I couldn't possibly spare three weeks he told me that it had to be a full three weeks for the treatment to work and reluctantly I agreed. The treatment consisted mainly of lotions being applied by nurses to all parts of the body and the lotions went very close to an extremely sensitive part of the anatomy. There was a very popular television series shortly after called *The Singing Detective*, with Michael Gabon as the leading man. The screen character also had chronic psoriasis and had similar treatment to myself and there was one memorable scene when stark naked he looked at the ceiling and 'thought of England' to no avail as the nurse told him he was disgusting and walked away. With iron willpower I managed to emerge with my dignity still intact, though there was a particularly attractive ward sister who discussed her love life or lack of it with me for nearly an hour while she applied lotions everywhere. I often regretted not getting her phone number. My two main former girlfriends both came to see me, as did my estranged wife and, of course, Nicky. I had carefully arranged for Jane to come mid morning so she didn't run into any of the others but, determined to annoy me as always, she came in the middle of the afternoon and the schedule had to be rearranged. Amazingly the treatment worked and the psoriasis cleared literally on the last day and I stayed clear for several months afterwards.

It is difficult to say when I realised the relationship with Nicky wasn't going to work. I had right at the start of spending time in her Windsor house been aware that there was a tennis professional who she had lessons from and he did visit the house one morning when I was in bed with mumps. In the last year of our relationship her interest in tennis seemed to increase and there were two instances where my suspicions were strongly aroused. Both occurred after we moved into Swettenham and on the first she had arranged to go on a four-day course at Bisham Abbey, a sports arena where later the British football team trained. I rang her up as arranged the first night and then unexpectedly rang on the fourth day to be told the course had finished the day before. The second time was an even bigger giveaway. She had told me a group from her tennis club had arranged a cheap long weekend at Easter in Spain and she was paying extra to take the two children. When I rang her room late in the weekend a male voice answered in English only to be followed by Nicholas, the elder son. When I asked him who had answered the phone the poor little boy was totally confused and eventually his mother came on frantically trying to retrieve the situation, but I was now certain she was having an affair. I can't say I was too upset. The glow of the early part of the relationship, when I was sure she was 'The One', had long gone and I had been looking for an alternative. Angela, who had married and was now divorced from David Johnson, seemed to have my welfare at heart and introduced me to a couple of ladies, one of whom I could have had a lot in common with. She was divorced from her husband, had no children and was trying to break a live-in relationship with somebody she was very fond of but she knew he had no money and was unlikely to make any. She was very keen on golf and had played at County level, and we played a couple of times at her old Leicestershire club. I even got to stay twice with her parents. Sadly neither of us were in a position to devote enough time to the relationship and to my regret she went back to her boyfriend, though she was to marry someone else a couple of years later.

It was in the spring of the third year of separation from Jane that one of the most eventful days of my life took place. I had gone to Haydock with David Stern to see my good hunter chaser, Compton Lad, run and Michael Dickenson, the trainer, and I had arranged to meet for lunch there. He brought with him his other owner that day, Angela Bell, who had recently separated from her husband and had a close relationship with Jonty Ramsden, a Cheshire establishment figure who owned a Yorkshire moor, Middlesmoor, next to Swinton. A great deal of alcohol was consumed and my horse won and Angela's didn't but ran well. At the end of the day David Stern said that Angela must come to one of their dinner parties and took her phone number. A couple of days later I rang David up and told him I would like the number and tried to get through, only to find that David had not written it down correctly. I then rang up Michael Dickenson, who was reluctant to give it but eventually yielded to the pressure. I had met Angela once before when she had come with Jonty to a Saturday night dinner party at John and Sue Barlow's. Having had two big days at Llanarmon I was not at my best but I did say to Jane on the way back, 'How did Jonty Ramsden get a beautiful girl like Angela?'

Anyway, I duly rang Angela up and managed to get a date for the following Saturday night at the local restaurant to Swettenham, the Yellow Broom. I was captaining a cricket side against Repton school and totally misjudged the time of the end of play and that I was expected to give my side a drink afterwards. To my horror this left me with thirty-five minutes to get from Repton to the restaurant and the fact that I was only twenty-five minutes late is a fine testimony to the Aston Martin I was driving. When I arrived the head waiter told me I was only just in time as my guest was about to leave and he felt that would have been a pity! In fact after the initial frost the date went extremely well and I even got her to have a final drink at Swettenham, where Nicky was not in residence, before she went home to a little house she had in Wilmslow.

So began a great relationship. The first date was followed by another at Haydock races again and we went afterwards to her local restaurant at Alderley Edge, where the proprietor, Patrick Guilbaud, was later to become famous as the finest restaurateur in Ireland with his Dublin restaurant. We were indeed lucky to have such a good 'local'.

The next few weeks saw our relationship intensify and I had little doubt that I was again genuinely in love, though I was wary as two years earlier I had thought the same.

I had of course a huge problem with Nicky, who had moved into Swettenham with the two small boys. Although I had no doubt that she was being just as unfaithful, she was being very careful as far as the outside world was concerned and I could see I would be portrayed as the villain and she the usurped innocent. I was also aware that Jonty Ramsden was not wholly out of the picture either, as although he had told Angela he was marrying a Dutch lady who he had been introduced to by the wife of a great friend and gun in Middlesmoor, his grouse moor, he still seemed to be ringing her up two or three nights a week.

The whole situation came to a head on Derby day, when as usual Nicky and I were Robert Sangster's guests. The day got off to a bad start as we had arranged to meet at a private airport where shared helicopter trips did a ten-minute journey into Epsom. Nicky had come from London, I from Swettenham, and whereas I was on time, she was half an hour late, despite my telling her she must allow an extra half hour for traffic. As a result we missed our slot and were very lucky to get another one.

When I got to Epsom I was immediately tackled by Penny Hills, who told me I was treating Nicky very unfairly and that I should make up my mind as to what I wanted out of life. I knew exactly what I wanted and told Penny that Nicky was behaving just as I was, but she was having none of it. As a result we did have it out that night and I told Nicky that it simply wasn't working and we should think about the best way of parting. It soon became apparent that Nicky was prepared to part but at a considerable price to compensate, as she put it, for the major disruption to her life. We agreed that I would go on holiday to the Spanish resort of Almeria that we were building, and that she would leave before the return date.

I took Angela and the two boys on holiday, which went relatively well, though the manager got a shock when Angela appeared instead of Nicky, who had been there twice. My long time secretary, who usually coped well with explaining everything, had not told him of the change of plan. Both Euan and Christopher got on well with Angela and I returned to Swettenham to find that Nicky had left the day before accompanied by a large pantechnicon paid for by me. I had agreed to pay for a rented house near Sunningdale and she was to get married again shortly afterwards, to the brother of a good friend of mine, Alan Elliot.

Events moved fairly swiftly: I was due to go to South Africa in October and Angela made it clear she was not accompanying me unless we were married. I had of course made clear that I wanted to marry her but although the divorce had come through, Jane was using every excuse not to sign the 'Nisi' part to finalise it. In the event her lawyer got fed up and pushed it through although Jane later maintained she had not meant to sign it.

Angela and I were married in the registry office at Macclesfield on October 26th 1981; Doug Francis was the best man and caused some excitement when he went into the office with Angela leaving me behind. We had a reception at Swettenham, attended by our various children, Father and Cindy and a number of close friends. We had to leave early to be flown down to Heathrow to catch a flight to Johannesburg. We gave sister Sally and Bernard, her husband, a lift on the way down and the flight was enlivened by Bernard, as usual fairly drunk, ranting on about how badly the family were treating him. I avoided telling him that the family disliked him just as much as he disliked them.

We settled into two first-class seats and started to play backgammon on a board I brought out; when Angela threw a six and a one I tried to persuade her to put the two counters in the bar point, with which she closed the board and said she wasn't going to play again and as far as I know she never has. It certainly set the tone for the marriage.

We arrived in Johannesburg in the early hours of the morning to find that, although we had that day to recover, we were off at crack of dawn the next day to a road opening in Botswana, which the president was to open and I was to make a speech in reply. It was a scorching hot day and what I was not told before was that the president was speaking in Swahili, to be translated by an interpreter into English, and that I was expected to do the same, i.e. speak a sentence and then wait for the translation.

The president started off and said that Father, the chairman, had not been able to make the journey but had sent his beloved son in his place. I managed to get out my speech of reply suitably amended to take in the president's comments and somehow managed to space out the sentences for interpretation, it all taking much longer than I had expected. The day was then enlivened by the dance of the tribal maidens, a large number of nubile fourteen-year-olds naked from the waist up, who performed an excellent dance routine. Later, following lunch, Angela and I were received by the president, an impressive and extremely nice man, who was very popular and ran his country most effectively. Botswana was always my favourite African country. With a small population of around two million and considerable wealth, it was a haven of peace and prosperity with none of the tensions of other African states. Angela and I were to return to Gaborone, the capital, the following year to start a week down the Okavango, the most wonderful swamp on earth, with every form of animal, bird and river life.

We returned to England to settle down at Swettenham, a lovely house in a glorious estate, which Robert still owned but I had the use of. The only problem was that my real friends lived the other side of Cheshire and although there were a number of very pleasant people nearby, it simply did not have the same feel as West Cheshire. It was also considerably further from Llanarmon.

We decided to have our first married Christmas at Swettenham and asked both Ex's and all the children. Only Sara failed to make it but a very lively Christmas lunch ensued, when Jane, true to form and full of Christmas cheer, told us how much better she would have handled it. Chris Bell, Angela's former husband, was a solid sensible soul, who behaved impeccably and at least the children all seemed to enjoy it.

Angela's early memories are of my going to innumerable company related functions at both Hooton and London. We aimed to have two holidays a year, one beginning in late January, which in those days meant Barbados, and the other in the summer. The Barbados holiday meant that Angela, for the first time, met the full force of the racing fraternity, who supported the Robert Sangster golf tournament. I leave out, for the moment, his partner John Magnier, as Robert's friends dominated the management of the tournament, particularly Charles Benson and Sally Hindley.

Angela enjoyed her first holiday in Barbados, having previously been to Antigua and mixed in well with Robert and Charles. She got on well with Penny Hills and began a friendship with Jane Robinson which was to blossom over the following years. From our first year of marriage we would, every winter, from late January to mid-February, share a Barbados beach house with Barry Hills, until Angela's accident, when a group of us went to South Africa and stayed at Cape Town and Plettenburg Bay. After that we regularly rented a house in Constantia, an up-market Cape Town suburb. The owners, Ian Overstone and his wife Linda, became firm friends with Angela and I, Barry and Penny and Dick Bonnycastle. In the early days we played a lot of golf and consumed prodigious quantities of Klein Constantia Sauvignon Blanc, the local white wine. The golf was fiercely competitive and Barry, one of the best losers on the racecourse, was very different on the golf course. On many occasions clubs were hurled in all directions. He also got very restive towards the end of each holiday and felt he should be with the horses. On one memorable morning he had played unusually well and we were going down the eighteenth, when Penny came running down the fairway. 'I've got the tickets,' she said, 'but we must go straight away.' 'Don't be stupid,' Barry said, 'you should know by now I didn't mean it,' and headed for the bar. Another time we played at Clovelly, our favourite course, Barry drove off the first into thick rough on the right and sent his caddy to find the ball. He shouted 'I've found the ball but there is a large snake over it.' 'What do you do now?' said Barry. 'Well,' I said, 'under the rules of golf, I am afraid you have to play the ball where it lies or take penalties.' A serious sense of humour failure followed. Unfortunately, the Overstone family house was not ideal for two married couples and a bachelor, and although he did improve Dick's bedroom, Barry and Penny got fed up with a secondary bedroom. Towards the end, safety became a major issue because Ian's back drive was open to anybody. A very nasty incident at the Cape Stall, on the main road half a mile away, made us very jittery. A gang ambushed the lady who ran the Cape Stall, early on a Sunday morning. Having taken several thousand rand from the till they saw a pail nearby, filled it with water and drowned the poor woman in it. Life is cheap to the unemployed in Cape Town! Only once did the Overstone's maid see an intruder and she immediately called security and the police. Security arrived in two minutes and the police in four – very impressive!

Barry and Penny decided to go to Mauritius, which I always considered ridiculously expensive and one holiday there did nothing to persuade me otherwise. So our run of winter holidays together ended. Amazingly for two strong characters, despite having twenty holidays together, Barry and I never ever had a row. Dick Bonnycastle still comes over for two weekends in November, where he takes Llanarmon for four days.

When we got back from the first Barbados holiday I plunged into the usual work routine and it was early March when Angela suddenly announced she thought she might be pregnant. I was delighted but she was far from pleased and I had to work overtime to calm her down.

The pregnancy went fairly normally, though there were some dramatic moments, particularly during a week in the summer when we went to a health farm, Forest Mere, instead of taking a summer holiday. The stay started with a health check and when we went in I stupidly told the principal, a pompous individual, that Angela was continuing to smoke. He was horrified and dealt out a major lecture also telling her she was overweight and put her on a Spartan diet. After three days she was obviously desperate to eat and I went into the village to get her a couple of sandwiches and Mars bars. The resident nurse also did not approve of the Spartan diet and encouraged her to eat more. The stay was memorable for two other reasons. Christopher Soames, who I played bridge with at the Portland Club, had the next room. Although I often found him difficult at the Portland, he was charm personified on this occasion. He did have a habit of ringing America in the early hours and his stentorian voice would keep us both awake. The week finished with a golf match with Nick Robinson at the excellent next door course, Liphook, which also gave Angela the company of Jane for a few hours. I started feeling marvellous and was well up when about five holes from the end I started to feel a little faint. I suggested to Nick we cut across to the clubhouse at the next hole which was close to it, but he was having none of it and won most of the remaining holes. Feeling desperate, I intended to break all the health farm rules and headed straight for the bar and was about to order a pint of larger when I looked around and saw Forest Mere's principal drinking one. Hastily changing my order to a large tonic water I had to watch him and Nick enjoying their pints. Never has beer looked more delicious. The experience finished Angela off health farms and she never went again but I usually go once a year, now finding Grayshott Hall the only one which acts like a traditional health farm.

Angela had a gynaecologist in Manchester, who had looked after the births of her other two girl children, and she booked into the Wythenshaw hospital where he was based. I made the momentous decision to be present at the birth, a first as far as I was concerned, and got to the hospital just in time. I remember staring at the ceiling for much of the time and hearing the nurse say, you have a lovely daughter. I was delighted and although Angela would have preferred a boy, she soon joined in the celebration. I also remember the head nurse saying, 'At least this child has been brought into the world for all the right reasons. We get so many girls who have them for the state benefits that go with them.' A statement made twenty-nine years ago!

To mark Emma's birth I had given Angela a racehorse named 'Next Week' and trained by Michael Dickenson. He was to win first time out but sadly never ran again. Fortunately our early married years coincided with my second 'golden' period on the racecourse and 1982 was the year that Cormorant Wood started racing. She had just two runs, winning a good maiden at Leicester in her second race.

Her jockey, Steve Cauthen, had become a great friend of us both; not only did he stay for the local meetings, Chester and Haydock, but he shot at Llanarmon and Angela would organise tennis for him with friends who lived near Swettenham. 1983 was of course the first of Cormorant Wood's two tremendous years but sadly Steve was not on board in her first Group 1, the Oaks, the only classic she ran in. I am sure his thoughts would have been a lot more useful than Lester Piggott's and the race is described in the racing chapter. Steve also brought his two lovely girlfriends to stay, Carolyn Herbert, now Lady Warren, and later Annabel Croft, England's leading lady tennis player. Whilst I played tennis several times with Steve I never made the court with Annabel as a partner, though I nearly produced her as a surprise weapon on a couple of occasions at Queen's.

After Cormorant Wood's great runs in '83 and '84 came her half brother, River Ceiriog, who won the Supreme Novice in 1986, giving Nicky Henderson his first Cheltenham Festival win at odds of forty to one and producing his famous comment to Peter O'Sullivan: when asked how he pronounced the Welsh name, Nicky replied, 'You won't have to call him, Peter, so I wouldn't bother.' Although River Ceiriog had a poorer season in 1987, there was still plenty to get excited about before the 'desert' of the nineties set in on the racing front. Angela went with me to virtually every race meeting at that time and it was not until her accident that she began to lose interest.

In 1985 came another major event which was to influence our lives – Tilstone Lodge came onto the market. I had been very friendly with John Bibby, the younger son of the owners, Sir Harold and Lady Bibby. John, who very sadly took his life in the 'Ha Ha' at the front of the house, had invited me to two drinks parties, both on dark winter evenings, held in the large hall, when I had failed to get a proper impression of either the house or surrounds.

It was Christopher Edwards, my finance director, who, knowing I wanted to move back to that area, said I really should look at the house and without much enthusiasm Angela and I made an appointment to view. The butler, in fact, showed us over the house and we were amazed at both it and the lovely surrounds. Lady Bibby was a famous gardener and although at one time she employed five gardeners, she was always supposed to do the work of two of them.

The house was very large and had seventeen bedrooms but it had been put together at the beginning of the nineteenth century, just before Victoriana, at a time when comfort and economy of space had become important. We were both captivated by it but knew there were major problems if we were to put in a serious bid. I went to the family trustee, Robert Clarke, who was enthusiastic and said he felt that Emma's two major trusts could take stakes and a lovely family house was in everyone's interest.

I then talked to Miles Denton Clarke, a good family friend who owned a local estate agency; he was unenthusiastic, thought the house was too big and that it would be difficult to find a buyer. Fortunately I was approached by Andrew Froude, the senior partner of Jackson Stops, who were the leading agents for large houses locally. We still needed to find the right price, as an auction was to take place with sealed bids to be delivered. Here I had one piece of good fortune because Lindsay Wallace, the senior partner of the Bibby's land agents, rang me and told me there was a lot of interest and one very rich man involved and if I really wanted the house I would have to get near to the million mark. Bob Clarke and I met, and agreed a price of £930,000, which was a great deal more than the locals thought it would fetch, but Lindsay Wallace was absolutely right. The very rich man, who was a senior partner of an immensely successful business which had sprung up locally, would have paid considerably more but his agent had persuaded him that £900,000 would easily win the day. He was so angry that he sacked his agent and rang up

Andrew to ask if he bid a lot more would the vendors consider a revised offer. With a straight face, Andrew told him that it would be totally unethical and that he would be very unpopular for doing it. In fact Derek Bibby would have taken his shoulder off, so we were very lucky.

So we bought one of the nicest large houses anywhere in Cheshire and have enjoyed 25 wonderful years living in it. We did quite a few alterations to the house, mainly the addition of several bathrooms which, like many old country houses, were deficient. Fiona Goodhart was the interior designer we chose to do the two main rooms. She did once say she couldn't meet me as she had to go to Jordan to work on King Hussein's palace. I replied that I thought she was getting the bills mixed up and I was only half joking!

The sale of Swettenham went far less well. Robert agreed to sell the land and large stable complex, which included substantial living accommodation for the stable staff, so we had a joint sale. We had forty-nine people to view it but at the end of the day only one serious offer, well below my and our agent's expectations. It would of course now be worth vastly more and the buyer got planning permission for the outbuildings and even for a golf club before he eventually sold it on. There were not so many rich footballers in the vicinity in those days.

When we moved into Tilstone Lodge one of the funniest letters I received was from Rudolf Agnew, who sent me a £10 note with the words 'anyone who moves from a hall to a lodge needs my support'.

Sadly my mother, who had fought cancer for the last ten years of her life, died shortly after we moved in. Although she had some bad periods it was only at the very end when she finally gave up. In the last two weeks she was given doses of heroin and in fact those two weeks were the happiest she had for months. The lady who lived next door, Anne Cosby, and I spent hours by her bedside as she babbled about her times as a teenager. As Anne said, she was having a much better party than we were! Whilst her specialists did a marvellous job, I cannot say the same for her G.P.; on one occasion she rang me in great distress on a Saturday evening, and I rushed across from Swettenham to find her G.P. so drunk he could hardly stand up, although he was on duty. The same practice was in my opinion also very remiss when Jane had her stroke a few years later.

However these were mostly good times at the beginning of married life for the second time and it was not until my major problems with the family company began to emerge in the late eighties that life began to go downhill.

Also an appalling event occurred which had a major effect on that period. We had a yearly holiday in Barbados, starting in late January, where I would play in the Robert Sangster and John Magnier golf tournament at Sandy Lane. I had started to share a house with Barry Hills at the far end of the island, almost at Speightstown. It had an attractive beach and a very good hotel, Cobblers Cove, at the other end. With Emma shortly to be five we decided to take a short summer holiday with her, Angela's two children by her first husband, Trini and Sara and Emma's nanny, Marie. We would start in Florida, do a couple of days in Disneyland and then go to the house in Barbados for a week. It all sounded like a wonderful time for the children, which was the main objective.

The Florida visit went extremely well; the hotel we stayed in had a train serving Disneyland literally coming through the hotel. We all enormously enjoyed that part and set off for Barbados, expecting to have an excellent week there. I had never been to Barbados in the summer and found it very different to January or February. It was considerably more humid and the mosquitoes, a minor inconvenience in February, became a nightmare in August. We were halfway through the week when we all accepted an invitation to have lunch with Anthony Johnson, who owned a house, Maddox, bought from Lord Snowdon, with its own beach. The lunch went well and the others either went to swim or go in a powerful motor boat, owned by a German guest of Anthony's, who was also a client of his small catering business. I had stayed in the house to play backgammon, as had Marie and Emma, who wanted to keep out of the sun. We were in the middle of our game when a tremendous commotion broke out on the beach and somebody shouted, 'Angela's been run over!' I sprinted down to the beach, where a terrible sight awaited us. Angela was lying in the water only ten to fifteen yards from the shore where the boat had driven into her. The German owner had been completely distracted by a young water skier, also a member of the lunch party, who he had attempted to land on the shore, failing to see that Angela was right in front of him. He had also not posted a lookout although, under Bajan law, he should have done.

Anthony's second son, aged sixteen, jumped out of the boat and attempted to carry Angela to shore. Although she has a very high pain threshold, she was in agony and Sam dropped her in shallow water instead of going the extra few yards to dry land, which would have saved some infection. Nobody blamed him for that.

The only lucky thing was that a neighbour, who had witnessed the disaster, called an ambulance immediately but, because it was carnival time, it took over half an hour to arrive. Angela had seen the boat coming from some distance and tried desperately to get out of the way; she did manage to get the upper half of her body out of the way and all the damage was below the waist – a severely broken right leg and massive damage to both knees. Angela never lost her composure and reckoning the men would be pretty useless asked Margie O'Sullivan to go with us.

When the ambulance arrived she and Margie got in and a number of us followed by car, a difficult journey through groups of revellers enjoying the carnival. I have to say we were a fairly motley crew, straight from the beach in shorts and bathing suits. I hadn't even got a comb on me. What I was not prepared for was the blatant anti-white prejudice in the hospital. The sister made no pretence of her views and tried to get Angela to walk. When I told her Angela had a broken leg, she shrugged her shoulders. I had managed to get through by phone to somebody who knew the hospital and he told me there were two surgeons, neither were brilliant but one was much better than the other and pray you get him.

We did and I managed to have a long talk with him after the X-rays came in which showed extensive damage in both legs. He promised to do what he could and started an operation which lasted for three-and-a-half hours. At the end he came to me and said he had done his best, had not tried any major surgery as that would best be done by specialists in England. He did, however, clean up and stitch the wounds and Angus Strover, who took over in England, had nothing but praise for the work he did in that respect.

I had rung up England and told my number two in the company, Tony Scurr, what had happened and he alerted our healthcare company, who sprang into action. To my amazement they sent over a nurse the following day and she was wonderful, standing no nonsense from a number of anti-white nurses in the hospital. The next major problem was to get Angela home. In order to get her on a stretcher at the back of the plane they needed to take out eight seats and, as every plane was fully booked, most refused to take her. Eventually we managed to get on to a British West Indian flight –

Trinidad, Barbados, Hamburg – four days later.

I had also contacted Susie Gilchrist, a great friend and physiotherapist, who told me the two best knee men were the Queen's knee surgeon or Angus Strover, who practised in Droitwich. Whilst the royal knee man would be booked solidly she thought she could fix things with Strover and Droitwich would be a lot nearer than London for all of us. We arranged, through the company healthcare, for an air ambulance to take us from Hamburg to Birmingham and a private ambulance from Birmingham to the knee clinic. However, although I did not know it, our troubles were only just beginning!

When we all got to Barbados Airport, we were told that the BWI flight was on time and it duly landed and I got ready to board the flight an hour later. However, after half-an-hour an airport official came up to us, looking rather grim, and said that there was a major fault with the plane and that there would be a long delay whilst another plane with a fresh crew was brought from Trinidad, where British West Indian had their headquarters. He suggested that Angela and her nurse should wait in the ambulance and that I should accompany him to the control tower, which was air conditioned. When we got to the control tower the official introduced me to the controller, who was very friendly and when we were alone said, 'You are going to see how an airline can be run on a piece of string.'

The next hours were truly amazing. The controller had to do everything. There were a few small planes coming in which he directed but in the main he was on the phone to Trinidad, trying to track down the reserve crew, who should have been on standby. He was ringing restaurants and clubs but it took ages for him to get a crew together. He also had the job of advising ground staff in Trinidad to place weights in the plane so it could take off. I learnt that a plane empty of passengers needs major trim adjustments before it can take off. It took nearly eight hours before the crew were able to take off and I breathed a sigh of relief when the plane was in the air. The drama was not over because as he was nearing the airport, the captain said that he did not think his crew were fit to continue. My controller friend simply said, 'There is not a spare bed on this island, you have to go on.'

You can imagine how I felt taking Angela and the nurse on to the plane, knowing what had been said. My one piece of good fortune was there was no room for me in the back and I was moved to first class, where I was almost on my own. The first thing I did was order a large drink and observe the crew, who seemed to be behaving normally. I went to the back, where Angela and the nurse were having to cope with passengers who had been drinking for hours, stumbling over seats. Without the nurse, Angela could never have coped.

All's well that ends well, and we got to Hamburg the following day. The air ambulance was waiting and although we were diverted, we reached Birmingham in the late afternoon and drove to Droitwich Knee Clinic, a unit in a large private hospital. I cannot speak too highly of both Droitwich and Angus Strover, then their senior consultant. Angus had originally lived in Rhodesia and then South Africa and was, at the time, one of the leaders in the field of knee surgery worldwide. His first operation took eight hours and he was to do five more over a four month period before Angela could come home. The worst problem was the broken leg, which wouldn't heal properly, but she had lost all the ligaments in one knee and all but one in the other.

It was obviously a very difficult period; Angela had to face the fact that her legs would never be quite the same again. Fortunately she did not play tennis or golf but she did try and get on a horse again some time later but gave up on that as well.

The company insurance had covered Angela's long and expensive treatment but I was anxious to get some compensation. The German had told me he was uninsured and was a resident of Venezuela. His father had apparently moved there in 1945, which sounded ominous. Although he appeared contrite and told me he would do anything to atone, he became very difficult to contact. Julian Byng, who owned a house, Laughing Water, which he sold to John Magnier, was a lawyer himself and gave me the name of his own lawyer, who he said was the best on the island. I did not want to take Angela back to Barbados and we had an excellent holiday in Cape Town the following year with Angela still on crutches, and it was eighteen months later when we went back to Barbados. The police had taken extensive statements from everyone involved but when I asked for copies I was told there weren't any. When we got to the solicitors, he kept us waiting for an hour and it was only when I said we were going that I got in to see him. His first statement was, 'Have you any proof the accident actually happened.' In fact it had been well written up in the local press but it became obvious that everybody had been got at.

When I got back to England, I contacted Isadore Kerman, a friend as well as my top-class solicitor. 'I will find you one, Bobby.' Three weeks later he came back to me, 'You are absolutely right, there isn't a decent one on the island.'

I have some wonderful memories of Barbados, particularly in the early days, when it was more unspoilt than it is now, but my advice to anyone going there would be: make sure you are fully insured and don't have a serious accident.

The eighties ended with a summer birthday party for Father on his eightieth birthday. I tactfully got Euan to make a short speech, which he did extremely well. It was a lovely summer day and many old friends were there, though sadly his closest friend, Jack Bissell, had died earlier. Father was to live another two years. The end came very swiftly after a short spell in hospital. I went to see him the night before and as usual he didn't miss a trick. 'You said you would be here at six,' looking at his watch, I was fifteen minutes late. There is no point in pretending we had a good relationship and it worsened as he became more dependent on Cindy. One of the few things my two wives had in common was an intense dislike of Father. They could both see what a difficult time I had. Some seven or eight weeks after his death, Cindy acted as a loader for Angela's former husband, Chris, on a shoot; eventually Chris moved in to Gerwyn and they have been together ever since.

Angela's severe leg injuries were followed a few years later by an even more terrible event befalling Jane. We were on holiday in Portugal with my sister, Valerie and Peter, at their holiday house on the Algarve. Euan rang me up to say that his mother had been found unconscious in bed on Monday morning. It was not known how long she had lain there and she had been taken to hospital in Chester, where, unhappy at the treatment she was receiving, Euan hired an ambulance and had her driven to the London clinic, calling in a surgeon he knew, who diagnosed a severe stroke. She had apparently been ill for a week before but because she had just come back from a trip to Egypt, she had considerable difficulty getting her G.P.s to take her seriously, although she had threatened to ask a hospital to admit her. Susie Gilchrist, who had been so helpful with Angela, went to see her and rang me from the London clinic. 'The good news is she is alive but that could also be bad news.' Susie, who never minced her words, could not have been more accurate.

When I went to see her, two or three days later, she was totally paralysed but recognised me and gave a look of total anguish. She was obviously in deep distress. After twenty minutes of talking to someone, who could not reply, I got in such a state that I said to the nurse with her, 'I am just going for a couple of minutes fresh air.' The nurse followed me and said, 'Are you alright?' I replied, 'With the problems you have with your patient, you shouldn't worry about me.' The reply was, 'I can do little for my patient but I can do something for you, you look terrible.' I went back into the room and stayed another twenty minutes.

A few days later I went back and there was some improvement. A television was on, playing cartoons, and there was a flicker of a smile on Jane's face; she certainly looked happier. Shortly after she went to a rehabilitation unit but the hope she would gain more bodily movement did not materialise and Euan made the decision to move her to a home in Malpas, where her friends could visit her and she was given a room overlooking the street the Wynnstay Hunt often came down. Sadly she showed little interest in either her friends or the hunt and after a short period she contracted a respiratory illness and died shortly afterwards. I went to see her the night before she died, where all her children were present. It was a terrible time and sadly men and women who live alone are obviously at risk, as the sooner a stroke victim gets to hospital, the better the chance of recovery.

Jane's funeral was held in Tilston and the children were very anxious that I went to the wake at Lower Carden Hall. I told Euan I would not go if Jane's mother, by now nearly ninety, was going to be there and was assured she would not be coming. Nevertheless, she duly appeared, found me and managed to hiss a few words of pure hatred at me before somebody led her away. Jane's end was tragic. She was by then on good terms with Angela and myself and we had been to a large Sunday lunch party at her house on the outskirts of Malpas. She was a very heavy smoker although she never smoked in front of me and I never realised that her cough, which got worse as she got older, was entirely due to smoking. I must have been very naïve.

Chapter 5

Starting with the Company

The company occupied the major part of my life for forty-four years. To understand it properly would require a book in itself and in order to make it readable I will have to leave out a lot of detail. Basically when I joined there were two main areas: one with Alistair Kennedy in charge at Hooton between Chester and Birkenhead. We had been bombed out of Liverpool during the war and Alistair's predecessor, Willie Shaw, found two houses at Little Sutton, which he converted into offices although they were in the green belt. Gradually as the company grew planning permissions were obtained for major extensions.

The Midland area run by Edmund Jones started from a modest office in Waterloo Road. When the company's expansion took off in the sixties he bought Wergs Hall, which was then owned by Bob Ansell, a senior member of the brewing family. He really went from one extreme to the other as Wergs, though Edmund's and Father's pride and joy, was too lavish and lacked the functional aspects that Hooton possessed.

Both men had tremendous abilities although they could not have been more different in character. Alistair was a dour Scotsman but a brilliant engineer with both determination and courage. More important he had mustered a first-class team under him with excellent systems to go with it. Edmund had tremendous charm and an ability to get the utmost out of the lesser team he had. He too was a first-class engineer but the area was much more a one man band and Edmund needed all his charm to get out of some problems his area got into.

As a company the big difference between us and our major competitors was that we allowed our works manager's equal status on site with the site agent who was an engineer. Most of our competitors had relegated their work management to a more junior status to the engineers. When the motorway programme took off our system really came into its own and in fairness Father spent most of his time working out the best works management for any particular contract. Although I am critical of other aspects he neglected he did an excellent job with the works management side and they revered him for it.

At this point I must mention another major factor in the equation: the role of my uncle by marriage, Peter Bell, and his relationship with Father. Peter was a strange man who never really enjoyed the job he was forced by his marriage to do and he would probably have had a happier life if he had not married a rich heiress.

My grandfather was no doubt pleased to find a respectable, competent son-in-law for his younger daughter Mary, in many ways a gentle, pleasant lady with a nicer nature than her two formidable siblings, who were ahead in looks and personality. Peter had not been allowed by his father-in-law to stay in the services during the war and was one of a number, which included Father, who was exempted from having to join up. He had been chosen to head the plant side of the company, a side which was to grow considerably when the road programme got into full swing. He also had the gravel extraction under him which, when I joined the company, was relatively small but which was also destined to expand a great deal.

Peter and Father had made an attempt to get on together although Father had little time for his younger sister. When I came on the scene he tolerated Peter rather than liked him. All that changed in the mid fifties when he and Rosemary and Peter and Mary found themselves in a group on holiday in Scotland. As usual the alcohol had flowed and in the early hours Father had turned on Peter and told him what he really thought of him. The next morning Peter told Father he was going to resign and appoint trustees to look after his wife's third stake in the business.

Alistair Kennedy, who was very close to Peter, managed to talk him out of resigning but things were never the same afterwards and the two protagonists steered as clear of each other as they could. This was in fact to have major repercussions for us all because when the company went public in 1959, Peter insisted that the family stake was put into trusts and that the next generation should share in the family wealth. We should all owe him a great debt of gratitude as Father would never have made over his money if he had full control of it.

We were also very lucky on another front in that Bob Clark, soon to be Sir Robert Clarke, was a partner of Slaughter and May, a leading firm of solicitors, and he masterminded the flotation. He was persuaded to stay on as a non executive director and as he moved from Slaughter and May to the merchant bank, Hill Samuel, which he eventually became head of, he brought city expertise to our expansion. He was also an extremely good family trustee, working throughout for the good of the whole family.

After the flotation we were in a stronger position financially but were still a regional rather than national company, strong in the North West, North Wales and North Midlands, where an agreement with Robert McAlpine's had restricted us, but unknown outside those areas. We had been allowed to build Gatwick airport, a contract Robert wasn't interested in, but otherwise had not ventured outside our territory. In football terms we were half way down the second league.

All this was to change with the award of the M6 contract to build the motorway from Warrington to Preston. This was a very large contract by any standards and much of the firepower of the company was brought to bear. The contract was divided into six sections, one of which was staffed from the Midlands area. Because of the size of the contract we had formed a consortium with Leonard Fairclough to build the bridges. They were a much smaller firm than ourselves but were destined to grow even faster than us and have now become, under the name Amec, one of Britain's top hundred companies.

The contract got off to a slow start and unfortunately we missed the good weather at the start as the large earth moving equipment Peter had ordered was late arriving. As soon as it did the weather broke and one of those summer wet periods ensued, which caused real problems. Many people do not realise how big a part weather plays in the construction industry.

The contract had Oswald Edge as director in charge. Oswald had one of the best brains I have ever come across, was energetic and his decision to go resident on site was later described by him as the best single decision he ever made.

Gradually the contract pulled around and although we were behind schedule for much of it we finished on time and importantly gained a lot of goodwill from James Drake, the county surveyor. Drake (later Sir James Drake) was a passionate believer in good roads and it was largely down to him that Lancashire now has the best county road system in the country.

We also impressed Lancashire County Council who alternated between having Labour and Conservative chairmen of their transport division. The two got on surprisingly well and made sure the same policies continued whichever party was in power.

Whilst for much of the Preston to Warrington contract we showed a loss on the books we did end up with a modest profit, largely due to the fact that both James Drake and Lancashire County Council were extremely pleased with the way we had tackled the work. What was far more important, it had given us confidence to increase our stake in the road building programme and we went for every contract Drake had with particular enthusiasm.

The whole country was desperate for new roads and the British Road Foundation, formed at about this time, coordinated the campaign for them. From 1960 to the mid seventies a great deal of road building took place. At its peak we were doing over twenty percent of the entire programme and were prepared to take a contract anywhere in England. Although we had a closely monitored agreement with Robert McAlpine to stick to our respective areas of operation, they were not interested in roads and I soon reached agreement with Malcolm McAlpine that we could go anywhere for them. I should mention that my cousin Malcolm and I had regular meetings on behalf of both companies to administer the territorial agreement.

We continued to take contracts in all other spheres of construction, factory work being particularly popular. Although we did quite a lot of general building, civil engineering was the great love of most of the senior staff, many being civil engineers themselves. Whilst this was a great advantage until the civil work dried up in the second half of the eighties, the engineers were not good at adapting to changed circumstances and part of our troubles, from the late eighties onwards, were due to the numerous engineers in the company.

We had of course the one overseas company based in Johannesburg but operating over quite a large part of Africa. In 1963, Nicky Knoop, who ran the company, was forced to flee at very short notice. He had an extremely rich wife and was anxious to try and get their assets, some of which were in South Africa, back to England. South Africa had some of the tightest financial controls in the world and getting money out was nearly impossible. They did allow postal orders of a small sum to be sent abroad and Nicky devised a scheme by which he sent thousands of them posted from Rhodesia. He believed the Rhodesian authorities may have tipped off the South African treasury but was himself warned by one of his friends in the Rhodesian government that he should not return to Johannesburg and boarded a plane from Salisbury to London instead.

This left us with no South African managing-director and Father, who was on his usual three monthly stay in Johannesburg, was forced to take the decision on who should succeed. Unable to decide between Nicky's two main subordinates, he made them joint managing-directors. Both were engineers who had showed promise under Nicky's direction but as it turned out neither were really capable of running a diverse operation. Because they both found it difficult to work together, one decided to take a large pipeline contract from Durban to Johannesburg, a 725 kilometre journey through very difficult terrain; the Durban end across the Drakensberg mountains and then through much easier terrain. It was a troublesome contract even for an experienced pipeline contractor; for one who had never built one before it was little short of madness.

We did enlist the help of a Canadian company partly owned by Robert McAlpine, who were specialists and were to supply the senior pipeline staff and welders, all Canadian or American, whilst we were responsible for the civil engineering and two staff were sent out from England to help. The contract soon turned out to be an utter disaster. The Americans and Canadians, on enormous salaries, seemed completely disinterested in the lack of progress and appeared to regard it as a pleasant interlude from the New World.

When I went out for a visit it was obvious we were in deep trouble and when I got back to Hooton and went into the dining room for lunch I was immediately asked by Alistair Kennedy how I had got on and I told him the bad news. Father then arrived and made it clear he thought I was exaggerating and I said he had better go out himself, and that if something isn't done the South African company is going bust. He did go out with Oswald Edge, Peter Bell following two weeks later. The gravity of the situation was obvious and despite being one of Father's favourites, the joint managing-director was sacked and a rescue operation organised from England. Stewart McVey, who had just been made a director of the Northern Company, was put in charge and he insisted that if he went he wanted total control of the contract. Staff poured out from England and a lot of new equipment was bought. McVey's tough attitude paid dividends with the Americans, who had been treating the contract as a paid holiday. Incredibly 650 kilometres of pipeline were laid in seven months including the very difficult section over the Drakenbergs. It was McVey's finest hour and the severe penalty clause which would have come into play the day after completion was averted. The South African company was saved.

The sixties and first half of the seventies saw massive progress, particularly on the roads front. Three road building teams were established, two from Hooton, one under Oswald Edge, the other under Stewart McVey, fresh from his triumph in South Africa. The third was from the Wolverhampton office with Owen Rich the rising star there. Most contracts made a good profit and the margins of profit rose from an average two percent to four percent, still ridiculous for the risks involved. Nor did all contracts make a profit. Alistair Kennedy had taken over the tendering department at Hooton from John Goodall, who was much better suited to the disparities involved. One disastrous contract was the spur from the M6 to Blackpool. Alistair had become frustrated by missing out on a tender a month before the Blackpool road tender was due and told me that he and Peter Bell were bitterly disappointed. I was getting very nervous about Alistair's tendering and when the Blackpool result was announced we had won it by the biggest margin in road tendering history. We had put in a completely crazy price and a crisis meeting was held in Hooton and John Goodall and myself went down to the Ministry of Transport to tell them we had made one or two major mistakes and we were throwing ourselves at their mercy! Such was the goodwill that we were able to correct the tender by over a million pounds, still well below the next offer and the contract still made a thumping loss.

Most contracts were tendered for but we did have some negotiated work which was obviously more profitable. Our best customer was BICC, who were the largest maker of cables in Britain. Their chairman, Lord MacFadyean, had been a student in Edinburgh with Alistair Kennedy and there was considerable mutual liking and respect. A great deal of work was carried out at a number of their local factories. We also made a number of sorties – against my cousin's wishes – to build them a new laboratory in London and other works in the South. Sadly this happy arrangement came to an end when BICC bought Power Securities, which included Balfour Beatty and a building company called Tersons. Although Kennedy had warned Lord MacFadyean not to go near Liverpool with Tersons they waded in and took two of the largest contracts going there, the new Royal Hospital and the IRO building at Bootle to centralise Inland Revenue activity. Tersons presumably thought the prices at Liverpool were too good to miss, well above similar ones in London. What they did not know was that the militants in Liverpool had the place sewn up and it was impossible to put up a large building without paying massive bonuses to the workforce and then you got a much lower output than elsewhere. We had soon realised it was impossible to work there and after taking a beating on two medium-sized jobs we avoided the place – although we were the largest firm in the area. Because of Kennedy's warning it did not take BICC long to realise they were going to lose a fortune in Liverpool so they decided to phase out Tersons and concentrate on integrating Balfour Beatty, which was going well. Their problem was that whilst all the Terson contracts outside Liverpool were attractive, the two large ones in Liverpool were virtually impossible to manage.

Edwin McAlpine had got wind of the problems and, seeing a great opportunity to seize a number of attractive negotiated contracts, he rang me up to say that he had spoken to Lord MacFadyean and a deal was on the table as long as we would give a price, however high, for the Liverpool contracts. I went down to a morning meeting with BICC with Alistair Kennedy due to follow at lunchtime. I had a torrid morning with enormous pressure being exerted by Edwin to get a deal before lunch. Fortunately I held out and when Alistair arrived he was brief and forthright. There is no price he said that we would undertake Tersons' Liverpool contracts. This shocked the meeting but after a pause for everybody to consider their positions the suggestions of cost plus for the Liverpool contracts instead of fixed prices was made and agreed.

We were then faced with the problem of carrying out the work and found out that every known trouble-maker in Liverpool had been taken on the two contracts. Progress was appallingly slow and BICC losses were so great on the hospital that they decided to put Tersons into voluntary liquidation, pay all the sub-contractors and suppliers and call it a day. The hospital authorities then put the remainder of the work out to tender. We did not complete the work.

I have two memorable stories of that era. The first concerns the IRO building where the electricians went on strike because a national pay rate their union leader had negotiated for the whole of Britain put them well behind what others on site were earning. I went with Oswald Edge, the director in charge, to a meeting with Frank Chapple, the charismatic union supremo. To our surprise union headquarters turned out to be in a large house in a leafy Surrey suburb of London. 'It is my birthday,' said Chapple, 'will you both have a glass of champagne with me?' and the three of us drank a glass of excellent champagne. 'Now what's your problem?' and we described the situation in detail. 'Where did you say the contract was?' 'Liverpool,' I said. 'I don't think it's in Britain, are you sure it isn't one of your African contracts, it certainly isn't in my parish.' He then gave us an excellent lunch, discussed anything but our problems and we left empty handed.

The other story concerns the Royal hospital and the endless unofficial strikes that bedevilled it. Officially the militants belonged to a construction union UCATT, which was a fairly moderate union, although the Liverpool branch was a law to themselves. Nevertheless, the union secretary was a paid official of the union and must have got fed up with his job being far more arduous and difficult than anywhere else. We sensed this and one day I rang him up and asked for a private meeting. 'I can't possibly be seen meeting you,' he said, and I suggested a quiet upmarket pub in Runcorn, which I knew was usually nearly empty mid morning. I met the union secretary in the car park which looked alarmingly full and we progressed to the main lounge where, to my horror, Mark Carlisle, the local Conservative MP, was conducting an election meeting. 'How good of you to join us Bobby, and you have brought a friend,' with which he pinned a blue rosette on the union secretary's lapel. To his eternal credit my 'friend' never turned a hair, smiled at Carlisle and said, 'You are doing a very good job.' One of the most embarrassing moments I have ever had.

The militants were to get a major setback some ten years later when UCATT called the first general strike in their history. We were in the middle of a motorway contract on the M58, much of it through Lord Derby's land at Knowsley. Our workforce did not want to strike but the militants descended and a site office was set on fire and everybody was running for their lives. The whole area closed down in twenty-four hours.

Bored with the fact that they had had nothing left to do in Merseyside they decided to go further afield and organised several coach loads of Liverpool workers to disrupt sites which were still working in rural Shropshire. There they met a very different situation from what they were used to at home. The Shropshire workforce may have earned a lot less than their Liverpool equivalents but were extremely happy with their conditions and wages and had no desire to stop working. To be fair to the organisers there was probably no intention to resort to violence but controlling coach-loads of Scouse workers, many of whom had fuelled themselves with alcohol, was never going to be easy and some ugly scenes erupted. The worst was on a McAlpine site near Telford, where a joiner had an eye severely damaged by a missive thrown at him. This got a lot of national publicity and the authorities stepped in and charged three of the organisers including Ricky Tomlinson, now a lovable character actor on television.

Whilst there was no suggestion that Tomlinson was directly responsible for the violence the court case was heard in Shrewsbury and the defendants were found guilty and prison sentences of between two and three years were handed out. These even then looked severe and they would certainly have been treated quite differently now. Tomlinson came out of jail deeply embittered, was unable to find a job on Merseyside and has made a great deal of money as a television actor and through advertisements. Only last year I saw a TV programme 'Guilty my Arse', which tried to portray Tomlinson's innocence. He had not changed at all, trotted out all the old Marxist rubbish, stated that McAlpine's treated their horses better than their workers (Father who was chairman at the time had never owned a racehorse in his life and the Liverpool construction workers were the most pampered in Britain). Even Arthur Scargill was brought on to the programme but the high spot was a confrontation between the worker who had nearly lost an eye and Tomlinson, who brought his hand forward but the handshake was refused and when he tried to make light of the man's injuries it was made clear he had met his match.

Fortunately times have changed very much for the better and when I was asked as a director of Aintree racecourse to keep an eye on the contract for their new stand, completed five years ago, I discovered that the workforce was about seventy percent Polish and a third local and everyone seemed to work happily together.

The fifteen years from 1960 to 1975 was a period of success and progress largely as a result of massive quantities of road works but also other civil work – power stations, reservoirs, etc – and some very major factory work, particularly the Vauxhall Motors factory at Ellesmere Port, one of the few automobile producing units still left in Britain.

By 1975 the euphoria for new roads had begun to wane; the opposition from those who thought the countryside was being spoilt was on the increase and the difficulties of getting over objections to new routes also led to lengthy delays as opponents found more and more ways of obstructing. In my capacity as chairman of the liaison group between the federation and the Ministry of Transport, I met a succession of ministers and I remember one meeting with Nicholas Ridley, who was keen to get on with road building. Everybody, he said, thinks the South East of England is being covered by concrete and yet we have all the statistics and only fifteen percent has construction over it. He too bemoaned the scope given to objectors and I quoted a road I knew well from Chester to Wrexham and beyond to Oswestry, where a handful of objectors, one of which we employed, held up the construction for over ten years. Our old house Glan Alyn had been compulsory purchased and was so badly vandalised it had to be pulled down. Now hundreds of vehicles use the dual carriageway every hour of the day unaware of the ten wasted years when they had to crawl along the old road.

Another concern was the desire of the ministry to save money. I had taken part in a programme with Brian Walden in the early sixties in which he showed a series of diagrams to illustrate how traffic would increase. In fact he grossly underestimated the growth and when the M5 was built we tried hard to persuade the ministry to build six carriageways not four. They were adamant four would suffice and a few years later had to widen the road at a far greater cost than the original contract for those sections.

The objectors were feeding the public two themes: that the countryside was being destroyed and that major roads could not handle the traffic they generated. Both were utter nonsense but sadly the public believed them. The widening of the M5 showed that one extra carriageway each side made all the difference. Traffic now flows freely most of the time between Birmingham and Bristol, only the link to the M6 causing difficulty.

In our company those of us who were close to the political and federation scenario realised that we needed to widen the company to become less dependent on civil engineering work. This was not easy as the civil engineers were the backbone of the company and its great success was largely due to them.

The obvious move was to take more work overseas where our competitors were making large profits, particularly in the Middle East. In 1975 our work in the Middle East really took off and we were awarded by the Kenana Sugar Company an enormous contract to build a sugar refinery on the banks of the White Nile at Kosti, some 200 kilometres south of Khartoum. The contract included a network of canals and roads and was awarded on a cost plus basis, so it was bound to be profitable. In fact by the standards of the Sudan, it went fairly smoothly and when President Nimeiri paid a visit to the contract to open the first section, all seemed to be well. The opening ceremony was one I will never forget. Lonhro, the leaders of the Kenana sugar company, were supposed to be represented by their chief executive, Tiny Rowland, who was very popular with the authorities. At the last minute Rowland sent the chairman, the ex Tory minister Duncan Sandys, who arrived wearing a panama with an old Etonian blue band round it. When it came to lunch it was announced that the president would not attend, leaving the foreign minister in charge. Duncan Sandys, who was to sit between them, refused to take his seat and went and sat the other end of the marquee next to the British ambassador. I who was the other side of the foreign minister had to make conversation to a very angry and, I discovered later, very left wing gentleman, who had taken the slight extremely badly. When we gathered that evening for a barbeque, the resident director of Lonhro, who had become quite a friend of ours, cried, 'Fifteen years of my life has been wasted thanks to that arrogant idiot!'

One of the major changes at home had been the abrupt retirement of Edmund Jones, who had collapsed at Wolverhampton station and severe angina was diagnosed. Fortunately, Owen Rich had grown in stature and was the obvious person to succeed him, although it might have benefited the area to have someone conversant with the superior systems, particularly regarding the tendering methods in place at Hooton. Oswald Edge would have done a wonderful job if he had been given the opportunity, but his one weakness was his outspokenness and his criticism of Wolverhampton methods had reached Edmund Jones's ears and caused considerable antipathy.

Whilst both main English areas were continuing to earn healthy profits, our fortunes abroad were going in a different direction. As we had a large staff in the Sudan and as the main British competition was concentrating on the Middle East, it seemed sensible to take more work there.

We had tried to establish a large overseas presence in Portugal in 1972 where we were the lead contractors in a consortium to build what effectively would have been a new motorway system for the country, going from Faro in the South to Lisbon and up to Porto in the North. We had acquired a small but solid Lisbon civil engineering company, Supico, but under Portuguese law we could not take a majority interest. This was solved by taking on a prominent banker and industrialist, Torge de Brito, who bought the remaining Supico shares and all looked set for years of profitable road work.

The Portuguese revolution put paid to that happy notion. Both John Goodall and Oswald Edge were in Portugal on the day the revolution took place and decided to take a train to Madrid, having no idea whether they would get through immigration on the border – but the train was allowed through and they got back to England safely.

A crisis meeting was held in Hooton and it was decided that I should fly to Lisbon that night and attend the consortium board meeting two days later. I chartered one of my cousin's fleet of jets based at Luton and we had an extremely pleasant flight and duly landed at Lisbon. The revolution was over in twenty-four hours without any loss of life. It could only have happened like that in Portugal. I managed to contact de Brito and arranged to have lunch with him the next day. It was a miserable meal. De Brito said it was lucky I had suggested lunch as he was about to be arrested any minute and in fact he was in jail by dinner. The consortium board meeting was a remarkable affair. The revolutionary council had sent a representative who arrived in khaki and promptly sat down in the chairman's seat and very ostentatiously laid a pistol on the table. The chairman, a genial Portuguese gentleman, whispered in his ear and he moved a place away and the meeting continued with everybody being very careful not to say anything controversial. We all had lunch afterwards and I talked to the representative at length; he was a great admirer of Castro and his great ambition was to go to Cuba. When I went to see the British Ambassador later in the afternoon he said we should arrange for him to go to Cuba as it might change his ideas if he could see how much poverty there was there.

We continued to have a presence in Portugal for some years and completed a number of contracts. Sadly the government never paid promptly – although they allowed Portuguese contractors unlimited credit – and we only survived with the advance payments we had received before the revolution.

This did not deter us from trying to get more work in the Sudan and we took on two difficult and ultimately unprofitable contracts. The first was for 150kms of road through another agricultural estate, this time for cotton not sugar. There were a number of reasons why this contract was disastrous. The conditions were grossly underestimated. Whereas Kenana on the banks of the Nile had a relatively benign climate, the region where the road was to be built was far hotter and dustier and some of the equipment which had worked well at Kenana – particularly British lorries – were simply not up to the conditions they encountered. In addition the time between when the tender was submitted and acceptance was nearly a year and too little money was added on.

I made several visits to this contract, which was very close to the Ethiopian border. There was at the time a civil war going on between the South of Ethiopia and Eritrea, which we were close to – 13km at the closest point. One of the distractions for the staff and workforce was the plight of the refugees, who would cross the border desperate for food and in the case of the women, many young and attractive, quite prepared to sell themselves to stave off starvation.

The contract was the most unprofitable in the company's history and virtually wiped out the year's profit. It was made far worse by the client not paying us in the latter stages and although we were entitled to withdraw because of non payment it was made clear to us that it would be difficult to get our valuable plant out of the country. Fortunately the strength of our balance sheet – we had large reserves of cash – came to our rescue and the share price did not suffer greatly.

We also took on a pipeline contract from Khartoum to Port Sudan in partnership with a German pipeline contractor. We were fortunate to be able to bring over a lot of our staff for the pumping stations along the route from Northern Ireland, where we had been forced by the IRA to virtually disband our operations. Unlike some of our competitors there who yielded to IRA demands, we refused to contribute and paid the penalty by having two of our senior site staff kneecapped. When I visited the various pumping stations most of the staff living in very difficult conditions said that they much preferred the Sudan to working in Northern Ireland. Again we had great difficulty in being properly paid by the client, a wealthy Kuwaiti industrialist, but we pursued him through the Kuwait courts and to our amazement eventually received a settlement which was added to the record profits we posted in 1985.

The Sudan was a far better country to work in when we went there than it became when Nimeiri was overthrown and a strict Islamic regime was installed, with attendant brutalities such as floggings, amputations and executions. Even Osama Bin Laden was made welcome for a number of years and the country now is similar to Iran, although the authorities pay a little more attention to world opinion. Although we did not work in Southern Sudan, I paid one visit there with Stewart McVey. There was tremendous poverty but the populace, which included many Christians, were far more relaxed and cheerful than they were in the North. I have just seen a B.B.C. programme on their independence and wish them all the best. So many people in England see Sudan as one country, whereas it is divided into several major tribes with fundamental Muslims in the North trying to impose their will on the rest of the country.

One thing experience in the Sudan did teach us at great cost was that, to take risky work overseas, it was essential to make sure the finance was firmly in place and, apart from one minor exception, this stood us in good stead from thereon.

We also attempted to start a company in Saudi Arabia and obtained the services of a very prominent Saudi businessman, Suliman Olayan, who was also chairman of their main airline, Saudi Air. He was obviously an immensely busy man and suggested that we should have a joint company with Prince Khalid Abdullah, who was married to a daughter of the King. I was being advised in England by Morgan Grenfell, whose two principals David Douglas-Home and Lord Carrington's son were regarded as top experts on Saudi Arabia. I have to say that neither I nor they had our finest hour over this company. They were adamant in their view that women in Saudi Arabia were relatively unimportant and that marriage to a king's daughter was very different there to one in the western world. They may have had a point but then totally failed to realise how immensely wealthy and powerful his highness was. He is of course now a famous figure worldwide but then he was completely unknown. I should have paid far more attention when he visited England, as visiting Saudi Arabia was fraught with problems. There were, in those days, virtually no hotels in Riyadh or Jeddah and you had to book months in advance and then barricade yourself in if you wanted to extend the stay. We should also have recruited a top man to head our side of the company but we simply didn't take it seriously enough. I have to say that Prince Khalid's team didn't help either. Whilst I was in Riyadh I would find I needed three days to tie down a meeting with the Prince but would spend time with his main assistant there and come to a reasonable agreement on policy. I would then go back to London to find that the London manager completely disagreed with what had been arranged in Riyadh. All the time costs were mounting and whilst we got close to obtaining contracts, none actually materialised. At the final meeting in London, at which his highness was not present, we had a complete stalemate over policy although I tried everything to reach an agreement. Afterwards Mark Thompson, who was then working for the Prince, told me he had never before been to a meeting where he had such sympathy for the 'other side'.

By this time his highness had begun to acquire his racehorse empire and his first main trainer in England, Jeremy Tree, was a regular bridge player at the Portland Club. I found him playing one evening and tapped him on the shoulder. 'Please don't interrupt me, Bobby, when I'm playing.' I waited for the hand to finish and said, 'Your big new owner, Prince Khalid and I have a company which is costing a lot of money.' A new hand was dealt and I waited patiently for it to finish. 'How much do you call a lot of money?' 'Three or four million and increasing all the time.' A fresh hand was dealt and again I waited patiently. 'May I suggest when his highness and you have lost fifteen million each, his highness might start taking an interest.'

When I started thinking the following morning I realised that Jeremy was right. The loss of half three or four million for a company making thirty a year was a nasty percentage, whereas for somebody as rich as the Prince, it was an irritant, no more. So I wrote a polite letter to his highness saying that we could not continue like this and got a letter back saying if we wanted to dissolve the company, so be it.

On reflection I handled it poorly. Inexperienced in overseas construction, other than Africa, I badly needed a competent, experienced, old hand around me and I simply hadn't got one.

Chapter 6

The Dorchester Hotel

I knew from a very early age that the Dorchester was a family hotel. It had been built for a hotel group, Gordon Hotels, but they had been unable to pay for it and the family were forced to take it over in the mid thirties. According to rumours still circulating in the family, Sir Robert, who was in his last years when the Dorchester was built, told his sons it would be a millstone around their necks, which might break the company. Nevertheless, it was left in presumably equal shares to Sir Robert's five sons, of which my grandfather was one.

My first memory of staying there was the night we got back from the long stay at Little Cumbrae in 1939. It was a great treat and I shared a room with Nanny and Billy, my mother being in an adjoining room.

Although Father must have taken us there after the war, my next real memory was the Queen's Coronation, where Father had booked seats overlooking Park Lane, and he, Rosemary, her brother Alec Gregory Hood and myself watched the procession. I remember Father and myself going to my uncle Robin's suite for a drink and Nora, Robin's wife, stroking the hair of her daughter, Carolyn, and saying how untidy she looked, which surprised me because I thought she looked anything but untidy. I had arranged to take a girl from Shropshire out to dinner with the others after the Coronation and there was an unspoken pact between us that if I took her to the Coronation she would look after me later. When late at night we asked for the key to my small single room, the man at reception said 'you only have a single room' to which my friend duly replied 'I left my handbag' and we went up without further problems.

It was a chance meeting with Robin that really started my rapport with the cousins, who Father kept his distance from, not because he didn't like them but because he didn't feel they were part of his world. The meeting was at Trawsfynydd, where we were doing a scheme, part of which included the dismantling of a dam which had been constructed before my grandfather formed a separate company. Robin was there because my cousins hoped to construct the nuclear power station being built there and Father, thinking a member of the family should be there and not wanting to go himself, sent me instead.

I got on well with Robin and an invitation to visit a nuclear site of theirs followed, plus an invitation to lunch at the Dorchester. Robin pointed out that a family discount of fifty percent was available, introduced me to the manager and asked him to look after me. This he certainly did because he asked to see me the next time I came in and suggested I used a single room for which I would only be charged a nominal rate provided I gave a week's notice before using it.

Robin also arranged for me to come to a partners lunch at the Dorchester and this led to my meeting other members of the family, Edwin and two sons Bill and Alistair and his brothers Malcolm and Kenneth. Sir Malcolm, who was head of the family, I already knew from my schooldays when I took the Green Line bus to Fairmile.

As I got to know all my cousins better I realised that there was little love lost between the two active senior members, Robin and Edwin. Both were very different in character, Robin being more austere and serious while Edwin was fun loving and much more entrepreneurial. They both held frequent lunches and dinners but Edwin always used the Terrace Room and Robin the Grill, both having tables permanently reserved for them. As I got to know Edwin better he would occasionally ask me to join him and I soon realised that a vast amount of business was being transacted in the lavish surroundings of the Terrace Room. One time I was in the foyer of the hotel and saw Edwin and a guest make for the restaurant and was about to join them when I got a warning look from Edwin – his guest was the Archbishop of Canterbury!

Gradually I was using the hotel more and more and as my progress in Sir Alfred continued I too took prospective and current clients there. Robin and Kenneth both used tables to the left of the Grill Room and I started to use a table just through the doors to the right which, provided I rang beforehand, became my table.

I always made a point of seeing as much as possible of the managers and also became very friendly with two of the staff, the head doorman, who was a Welshman whose home was not far from Llanarmon and who always asked after Father, and the head barman who had his own empire and had been there for many years. The bar had a strange selection of regulars, one of whom was an East End acquaintance of Johnny Phillipson, who Johnny always said had done some deals with his father and had promised him he would look after son Johnny if he ever got into real trouble. Known as 'the Colonel' I had found him an engaging character to have a drink with. Roy the head barman had frequently complained to me that Father and myself were the only two members of the family who ever used the bar, so one day I persuaded Robin to go in with me. To my horror, the only person sitting at the bar was 'the Colonel' who said, 'Bob, champagne for you and your friend.' I introduced Robin to Roy and beat a hasty retreat, making up some excuse for my acquaintance with 'the Colonel', which I am sure Robin didn't believe.

Edwin gave an immense Christmas lunch in the hotel ballroom for about six hundred guests. It had all started during the war as a relatively small affair but had blossomed into the major lunch on the Christmas circuit, with all Sir Robert's senior clients being invited. He also cultivated the leading politicians of the day and the first prime minister to grace the table was Edward Heath, followed by his successor Margaret Thatcher, who was to make Edwin's son, Alistair, the Conservative treasurer. The family were all put at the ends of tables and when I was first invited I duly found myself at the end of one. A different member of the family had to make the speech on behalf of the family but fortunately it never got around to me.

Whilst most of the guests drank champagne before the lunch in the adjoining room, there was a smaller room where Edwin entertained his chief guests, mainly politicians. A few of the family also joined in and although I was only asked once it was a memorable occasion. I was introduced to Dennis Thatcher, who I was having a good conversation with when Margaret Thatcher came and joined us. All went well until I saw Tim Kitson, who had originally come to the lunch when Heath was prime minister, hovering behind us. He was completely ignored by Mrs Thatcher until I got so embarrassed I asked her if she knew Tim. 'Of course I know Tim,' she said, with which she strode to the other end of the room!

The lunches got so big that the ballroom of the Dorchester couldn't hold the guests and it was moved to the Intercontinental Hotel and became an evening drinks party rather than a lunch, and it still continues in that form to this day.

Although I did not use the Dorchester for accommodation after I got my first flat in Ryder Street, there was one memorable exception when I told the manager my mother was coming over from Nassau and I would like to give her dinner. He suggested that I used the Messel Suite, the most luxurious accommodation in the hotel with a bathroom with gold taps, all designed by Oliver Messel. He did tell me that it was permanently reserved for Elizabeth Taylor and Richard Burton but that they were the other side of the world and so we could use it.

I took up his offer and Jane and I thoroughly enjoyed settling into such a fabulous suite; I had a lengthy bath, twiddling the gold taps with my toes and we had dinner with my mother, who had asked if Stirling Moss could come as a guest. My mother was a friend of Moss's Canadian in-laws and was in the middle of giving him some marital advice. After an excellent dinner we settled down for bed about midnight and about three hours later I was awoken by a furious banging on the door. It was the manager who said we have just received a message that Elizabeth Taylor and Richard Burton will be here in about two hours time and we have to get you straight out and into another suite. He was full of apologies and promised to make it up to me. I never got another bill for the next three months!

The other part of the Dorchester I used frequently was the private dining penthouse suite on the top floor. I had joined both the construction industries dining clubs, one of which had all its dinners, about three a year, always there. The other had dinners where the host wanted, and when it came to my turn to host I always used the Dorchester. My first main guest was Keith Joseph and I had ordered a particularly expensive dinner, but as he sat down he said he wasn't hungry and ate and drank very little.

When the hotel was sold the family usage came to an end. Robin the manager resigned the next day as did a number of the staff and I realised just how much they enjoyed working for a family employer rather than a hotel group. A number of us were upset at the sale and Nigel Elwes, Robin McAlpine's son-in-law, and I have often discussed it, both agreeing it was sold far too cheaply. The problem was it needed a lot of money spending on it and neither Robin nor Edwin were in favour, although it had been put into a company called Development Securities, which could presumably have used borrowings which would not have affected Sir Robert directly. Father had accepted a fairly small offer for our holding when Development Securities was formed and would never discuss the sale, nor did I ever discover where the money went.

It was all great fun while it lasted and I still occasionally go there. Peter Daresbury used to hold Aintree dinners for the BBC in the penthouse suite and I sometimes go to the downstairs night club bar to have a drink with Christopher Hanbury, who represents the owner, the Sultan of Brunei, in England. It is still a slightly weird feeling to go into a hotel I knew so well and not see a single familiar face. Such is life!

Chapter 7

Coping with Change

As the seventies faded we were faced, in the UK, with a massive downloading of civil engineering work. Not only road works were decreasing but a lot of infrastructure was in place and both government and private industry were reluctant to undertake large capital spending. This was also true of the privatised water and electricity bodies and although overseas work provided one solution there were many of our staff who did not want to leave the country.

We had diversified into a number of ancillary activities and had thriving and growing pipeline and asphalt companies. Peter Bell had been largely instrumental in the purchase of Penryn Slate, the largest slate quarry in the world, although he had asked me to go with him to the final meetings. These were all flourishing but we had not marched into the two areas which most of our rivals had turned to – building houses for sale and property development.

We had built houses for local authorities in large numbers since I had joined the company. It was very low margin, cut-throat work and I always felt we should be braver and get into private housing. The old guard were resolutely opposed and whilst Father, Alistair Kennedy and Peter Bell were actively involved there was little chance of progress, but when Alistair Kennedy retired and Peter Bell died suddenly, Father was left rather isolated as all the senior directors left had varying degrees of interest in getting involved.

In 1976 we were offered by the Bissell family a site in Stalybridge. They had sold a couple of sites which had been developed successfully by local house builders and, flush with cash, we agreed to buy it without any idea of how to develop it. At the same time Oswald Edge had been approached by a highly successful local developer, Peter Jones, to build a development for him in Portugal, our company there being still in existence. Although the revolution put paid to the Portuguese site, Oswald took the opportunity to look at Jones's local sites and was very impressed. He brought me into the picture and we offered Jones a joint stake in the Stalybridge site to start a joint development company. Although Jones was not attracted by the Stalybridge land which he immediately suggested should be called Mottram – much more up-market – he liked the idea of joining a very large company and our joint company started a succession of highly profitable developments in the Wilmslow, Alderley Edge area of outer Manchester.

Unfortunately Jones was still attracted by overseas developments and I was having a good February break in Barbados when I got a call from my finance director, Christopher Edwards, to come urgently to Florida, where he, Oswald Edge and Jones were meeting to discuss a development there. I went from the heat of Barbados to a surprisingly chilly Florida. The first thing I did was buy two pullovers and was taken to see a proposed timeshare development on Marco Island a few miles from Naples on the East Coast. Jones was full of enthusiasm but I was quite disappointed particularly with our proposed partners, a pair of brothers, one of whom was an architect. They seemed to me lightweight and certainly needed our money to get started but were still to get over fifty percent of the profit.

Against my better judgement we took on the development having been assured there would be no other timeshare operations on Marco Beach. Unfortunately two or three others started shortly afterwards and then came one of the worst property depressions to hit Florida. As far as I was concerned the obvious thing was to sit tight and weather the storm but at a crisis meeting held there our American partners said they had no money to contribute and to my amazement Peter Jones said he wasn't contributing his share either.

I was furious. Peter Jones was even then an extremely rich man and he had got us into the development. Regretfully we broke up the joint company and we took it on ourselves and successfully completed it. Peter Jones sails higher and higher up the *Sunday Times* rich list every year and I suppose it is decisions like that which has got him there. From my position it was very sad and I did not have a top-class developer by my side when I needed one at the end of my construction career.

The seventies had seen a dramatic change of fortune in the South African company. For years they had taken on a variety of work in a number of African countries and apart from Botswana had made only small profits from the efforts expended. All that changed when

Trans Natal, an African mining house, asked us to be their partner in the first coal mine in Africa – to be dug largely by opencast rather than deep mine techniques. As in Britain the mining unions in South Africa had fiercely opposed opencast mining, although it was far cheaper. At optimum the coal was so close to the surface, three feet in one place, that the authorities allowed opencast to go ahead. Our managing-director in South Africa, Sydney Ovis, was the survivor of the pair in the pipeline debacle and whilst I never rated his general ability very highly, he did get on very well with the Afrikaans and a large effort was put in from England with Father, myself, Peter Bell and his deputy John W Roberts all playing a big part in the negotiations.

Optimum was a tremendous success. By 1977 a world record was set for one dragline producing over 700,000 tons of coal in one month. In 1978 Sydney Ovis died suddenly and his place was taken by Tony Scurr, who had been sent from England when the contract started to bolster the management in South Africa. He was also very good with senior staff of Trans Natal and the association entailed a lot of hard drinking and attendance at rugby matches. The South African company was so successful that it went public on the South African Exchange. In 1985, as the political situation in South Africa had deteriorated considerably, we received a suggestion from Trans Natal that they would like to bid for us. With the company at its profitability peak and the future looking very cloudy politically I persuaded the main board at home that we should sell and flew to Johannesburg to start the negotiations. Our merchant bank in England, Hill Samuel, had a flourishing branch in Johannesburg which had always acted for us and Christopher Castleman, who ran it, was a great help to me. From the start it was recognised that our proceeds from the sale would be from Trans Natal's cash resources outside South Africa and put into a company we had formed in Switzerland to finance overseas work. My largest contribution to the initial negotiation was to insist that the price would be in sterling not rand and as the rand dropped like a stone through the negotiation this was one of my very best decisions. We did have to come down a couple of million but nothing like what would have been the rand equivalent.

The money from the South African sale came at a perfect time for investment in the USA. Since the break-up of the Jones company, I had searched for a new partner and in the early eighties found one in the shape of Frank Sanderson. I had met him through a great cricketing friend, Charles Robins, who was a director of his company, Finlas. Frank was originally a small but successful house builder in Kent. His firm was taken over by Bovis and he became chairman and chief executive. When a merger between Bovis and P & O was proposed he was to be chairman of the enlarged group, but a late rearguard action by Lord Inchcape scuppered the merger and Frank was forced out of Bovis. He started again and had built up a medium sized company, Finlas, which had three divisions, all attractive to us – house building, property development and a construction company in the London area.

Frank had both charm and charisma and I felt we could work well together, perhaps unwisely not recognising his reputation for single-mindedness. When later I was to say to one of my directors, 'I always thought Frank would be a team player because he was so keen on cricket', the reply was '... but he would want to decide his place in the batting order'.

I suggested to Frank that we should acquire Finlas and that he should join our main board but continue to run it and also spearhead the proposed entry into the USA. He accepted the offer and for a couple of years all went well. The Finlas companies all performed well, I attended the board meetings held in their offices in Suffolk Street, which became our London office. Frank seemed to have an excellent relationship with his three managing-directors and we always finished with a good lunch at the Berkeley Hotel.

We duly started prospecting in the USA and Frank found a housing company in Boston which seemed very promising and a major development at one of America's finest golf resorts, the Pinehurst Complex in North Carolina. This had fallen on hard times and was in receivership although the resort itself was continuing as before. It boasted the largest wooden hotel in the world – which worried us – but the housing potential was enormous with large houses being built and selling for millions of dollars, particularly to rich retirees who preferred the milder climate to that of Florida.

We did put in an offer which the receiver said would probably succeed but it was turned down, much to Frank's frustration. Frank suddenly resigned at the beginning of 1985 which was completely unexpected and a severe shock for me as I could see the problems he would leave behind. The general opinion was that he had discovered a housing company in the States which was too good to miss but in the event he did not buy one. Instead he concentrated on a family company run by his son, which failed spectacularly in the late eighties property crash.

He left me with the three Finlas companies. Surprisingly the one he had least faith in, the London construction company, was the one which performed well with a minimum of attention needed. The housing company had a very talented man running it, Philip Davies; unfortunately I inherited him a few years too early in his career. He was to go on after he left us to found a highly successful company, Linden Homes, and make himself a great deal of money. The real disaster was the property company which got totally out of control – more later.

Up to 1976 Wolverhampton had only had two managing-directors, Edmund Jones and Owen Rich, but when John Goodall retired in that year, Owen Rich was given the position of group managing-director, the other two senior directors, Oswald Edge and Stewart McVey, both taking a part-time role before retiring completely.

Owen did an excellent job in the eleven years he was in charge of the company. Basically cautious and careful by nature, he still recognised that the construction world was changing, although he was reluctant to spend the money needed and also to change the culture of the company. He did put in place a study of the company by a respected firm of management consultants who had originally been brought in to do a specific task. They concluded that the company had outgrown its management and that we should bring in a chief executive from outside the company. Whilst they were totally correct in their conclusion the timing was very unfortunate, Father still hanging on as chairman although by then I was doing ninety percent of the chairman's role. Had the non executives insisted on his handing over three years earlier the outcome for the company might have been dramatically different, as nobody was prepared to see a new chief executive nominally reporting to Father. I have to be honest and say that I might not have made the right decision anyway. Certainly when the non executives finally persuaded Father to stand down in 1983 when Owen Rich was still in charge, I did not have to make the decision and the next two years culminating in the 1986/86 results were the best in the company's history and included a £2.5 million settlement from the Sudan pipeline contract.

1985 was a half centenary year and we celebrated by commissioning a book called *The Road to Success* with a professional freelance writer called Tony Gray as the author. Poor Tony started off with the best of intentions and the early chapters are excellent, but he got bogged down by everybody trying to get into the act, although I had pleaded with people to let the book be readable. I had to finish off the last chapter myself and cannot say I was proud of my first attempt at a serious piece of writing. The greatest success of the book was getting Margaret Thatcher to hold it aloft on an election campaign, when she visited the Marks and Spencer financial centre we had built on the new Chester Business Park we had purchased a couple of years earlier. The picture got a lot of publicity including a caption in the *Daily Mail* the next day – 'Will it be her road to success?'

We also gave a large cocktail party at the Savoy for numerous clients, consultants and architects, followed by a small dinner party in one of the hotel's excellent private dining rooms. Three of my guests were my cousin, Alistair, in his prime as Tory treasurer, Rocco Forte and my good friend Richard Hall, on whose company I had been a non executive director for some years. I have never received such attention from a hotel. Because Rocco and his father Charles were trying to take over the Savoy there was a waiter behind every chair and the manager spent much of dinner hovering behind as well.

It was heady stuff and we left the celebrations thinking how well we were all doing after fifty years of continuous growth and progress. How little did we realise that it would be downhill from then onwards. I had written on the first page of the final chapter that Owen Rich had to face as his main two objectives the new tasks of cutting the costs of the construction company to match the workload available and helping the current chairman transform the group from a construction company to a flexible forward-looking group with four main divisions.

I still believe my strategy was a hundred per cent correct but what I failed to realise, despite the management report, was that I hadn't got the resources in the company to carry it out. When Owen retired in April 1987, I should have appointed a chief executive from outside; not to do so would prove to be the worst mistake of my business life, although it was difficult to see it at the time.

A leading tycoon of that era wrote that family companies were always resistant to change. Because they had done things for a long time very successfully in the same way they could never see that they should change to meet different circumstances. If ever a statement summed up our situation at the end of the eighties that was it! Although everybody paid lip service nobody wanted to take the radical steps that were needed mainly in the construction company, which had far too many staff, a lot of them unnecessary in an era where modern technology had cut out work previously done by hand.

On Owen Rich's retirement I had appointed Tony Scurr as joint managing-director with myself. After South Africa was sold Tony had run the quarrying division with, on reflection, rather mixed results. He had an excellent personality and was frankly the only real candidate internally – Trevor Wilson, who had done a marvellous job at Hooton, was retiring in 1989. Brian Stanley, who had been Oswald Edge's number two through the sixties and early seventies, had succeeded Owen at Wolverhampton and appeared to have been very competent, though he was not much liked by the staff. In view of Trevor's pending retirement he was the obvious candidate to take over construction as a whole and there was nothing in his previous record to make one think he should not do it very well.

In Wolverhampton, Howard Stevens took over from Brian Stanley; he was an outstanding manager on large sites and a favourite of Father and Alistair Kennedy, who thought of him as the great 'up and coming' on the construction side. He was very reluctant to accept, probably realising his limitations, but knowing he would be supervised by Brian Stanley I had no hesitation in persuading him against his wishes.

We had also bought a construction company in Scotland, Whatlings, which got over longstanding ambitions to have a presence in Scotland. We soon found that working in Scotland was difficult but the company seemed to be performing well and both Owen Rich and Brian Stanley felt it would be a useful addition. I visited several times and I remember one visit in particular: we had just been awarded and had started a ring road contract around Edinburgh. When I got to the office there were long faces and their managing-director said we are in trouble over the Edinburgh road, the chairman of the new Labour council wants to cancel it. I said, he can't without paying us a small fortune in compensation. The M.D. replied he's very left wing and determined to make a name for himself and showed me a newspaper photograph of a smiling youthful man with an enormous beard. His name was Alistair Darling and he bore little resemblance to the figure who was going to become chancellor in Gordon Brown's government. I was right on one thing: we made more money out of that cancellation than any other contract in Scotland.

The year following the record results was another good year, only fractionally less profitable and without the settlement from Kuwait, so I found the analysts and financial journalists still very much on side. It wasn't until late into 1987 that the first sign of real problems started emerging. We had issued an interim statement that disappointed the analysts because I had been gloomy about the construction outlook. Before issuing the statement I had convened a meeting at which Brian Stanley and Howard Stephens were present and asked them whether Wolverhampton would definitely meet their budget for the year. Brian replied yes while Howard looked gloomy and said nothing and it was partly his gloomy look which made me tone down the interim statement.

At this point I should explain that we had an accounting system which allowed every contract to make reserves against their profit or losses to take account of the protracted settlements which occurred on most contracts well after the physical end of the work. It had in fact enabled us to conceal large profits made in the sixties and seventies and early eighties, so that we could always have a supply of profit to insulate us against a year with some losses. This had worked very well for us, the only problem being that nobody knew exactly how accurate the reserves really were and, when Brian made his statement to me knowing the Wolverhampton reserves stood at over £30 million, I had unsurprisingly assumed he could make up any shortfall from them.

It was therefore with real shock and horror that I reacted when Brian walked into my office only six weeks later quite late in the evening, when I was having a drink with Oswald Edge who had called in to see me, and announced that Wolverhampton could not meet its target of £11 million. I said how much can you make and he replied three or four. I said you realise how serious this is Brian? and he walked out of the room without another word.

The following day I arranged a crisis meeting with Tony Scurr and an emergency board meeting the following week. I rang both the senior non executive directors, Bob Clarke and Alex Alexander, who said we must issue a statement to the press immediately following the board meeting. They also felt that somebody had to go and I said that has to be Brian Stanley; he has simply not given Howard Stephens the guidance he needed and he was in charge and agreed only a few weeks ago that profit targets would be met. I told Brian that I felt he could not continue and that he should not attend the board meeting.

He duly left the company and was extremely well compensated and got a very senior job with the Ministry of Defence. Howard Stephens, who I persuaded to stay, went back to doing what he had always done extremely well – running large civil engineering contracts.

The profit warning caused major problems with both the analysts and financial press. The analysts were mainly intelligent people who understood the industry and the risks involved. The financial press were quite different, many being young, inexperienced and extremely arrogant. At our briefing after the final results were announced a young girl arrived an hour late just as we were closing, refused to speak to Tony or myself and wrote an unpleasant and inaccurate piece the next day. I rang a friend, Chips Keswick, who said the girl is out of control, I have just reported her to her city editor and suggest you do the same. I followed his advice but suspect that she could have had something to do with the major problems I had with the financial press three years later.

The debacle over Wolverhampton affected the profits for the next three years as the losses were massive, far more than originally forecast. They had simply taken on far too much work, nearly all of it loss making. Their tendering department had made the classic mistake of tendering to the market rather than ensuring that the prices they put in would be profitable. Nor did they have sufficient competent staff to put on all the work they had taken.

I had fortunately recruited a senior construction manager from a smaller firm, where he was number two and due eventually to become chief executive. I threw him into the deep end and he did an excellent job of consolidating the two main areas and ensuring that proper controls were in place for everybody.

Unfortunately the reduction of profits from construction placed a lot of strain on the group elsewhere. The quarrying side was reliable and progress was being made in America where the money from South Africa was being invested. Our head office in North Carolina was overseeing a family construction company we had bought and they and our growing quarry side there were doing well.

But the big shortfall could only be made up from the housing division where Philip Davies was struggling to make the profits we were looking for. He had found a company headed by an entrepreneur called Eric Grove, which he felt would tie in very well with us and had substantial profits still undeclared. The problem was that Mr Grove wanted a very substantial sum and produced a letter from his solicitor, Herbert Smith, stating that he felt we did not have sufficient finance to buy the company. At this point I should probably have walked away but I was put under enormous pressure by Philip and eventually we produced a complicated deal which involved a substantial down payment, a buyout over a period and the issue of company shares to Eric, the sole owner.

The deal did produce the profits but at a considerable price. I had failed to realise as had my colleagues how much money was needed to fund housing. They had a different year end to us, October, whilst ours was April, and all the money from the year's profits would flood in at the end of October and steadily go out for the rest of the year. In addition the property division was giving me major headaches. I had been very fortunate in concluding a deal with a local developer, John Broome, to buy what is now the Chester Business Park. The deal was made to ferry spoil from the south Chester bypass which we were constructing, and made a large profit for that contract without the development being considered. We were fortunate in obtaining Marks & Spencer as our first client followed by Shell and two other smaller companies. Whilst this was going well the manager I had inherited from Frank Sanderson had a dreadful development at Wrexham and two others which were unprofitable.

We needed to bring in management and I tried to buy a small company run by an old school friend, David Parkes. His two managers were extremely keen to join us but negotiations stalled on a role for David – although we offered him the post of chairman we reserved the right to take major decisions and he did not like that.

I next turned to a company that had emerged locally, Warringtons, originally a respected but never very profitable building company, operating in Cheshire and the surrounding area. They had twice approached us to take them over but we never seriously considered buying them. They had been taken over by property developers headed by Graeme Jackson, a charismatic man who had nearly gone bankrupt in the previous property crash in the seventies but had survived and I felt he would not make that mistake again. They were extremely keen to join us and we worked out a complicated deal by which we would buy a large minority interest, over forty percent, inject our property into them but would not have their borrowings on our balance sheet.

Again it all started well; my finance director, Christopher Edwards, and I joined their board and to begin with we were impressed. I began to get nervous when they started spending substantial sums on infrastructure in the Chester Business Park, whilst we had tended to get a client, build his factory and leave the rest of the park untouched. They also seemed to have no difficulty in obtaining finance and expanded more rapidly in the South and around London. Although Christopher and I expressed reservations at board meetings our minority stake made it difficult to control them and our lack of property expertise certainly didn't help either.

It all came to a head at the beginning of 1990 when our borrowings soared alarmingly and I realised that we had to start cutting down. We held an internal meeting at Hooton and agreed we should make £10 million of savings. Had Owen Rich still been in charge there would have been no problem as he hated wastage and revelled in what he described as good housekeeping, but Tony Scurr was the opposite and liked to surround himself with a large support team. The last act I can remember him making was appointing a new and expensive head of security at Hooton without any reference to myself and in the middle of a major savings campaign.

By April I was getting desperate and was beginning to have sleepless nights and realised far too late in the day that we had to get a chief executive as fast as possible. I met the two senior non executives, Bob Clarke and Alex Alexander, and they agreed to assist and we decided on a head-hunter to be briefed by myself. Then something happened which I can only describe as one of the fateful moments which become life changing. I read in the *Daily Telegraph* that Graeme Odgers, the chief executive of British Telecom, had resigned after a major disagreement with his chairman. I had never met Graeme Odgers but I had two friends, John Betts and Michael Stoddart, who knew him well. John Betts was a shooting friend of Father's and myself who had been working in South Africa when we first met him. He came to shoot at Llanarmon for one of the main weekends and used to go on the Saturday night to stay with the Odgers in Shropshire, under an hour's drive away. Graeme was finance director of Tarmac and John described him as a red hot businessman (his actual words).

I rang John up and he said Graeme had a dreadful personal tragedy whilst working for Tarmac, his school-aged daughter having been killed with a friend in a car crash, and he felt that was probably the reason he had left Tarmac. I also rang up Michael and got a ringing endorsement of Odgers ability from him. I, perhaps stupidly, didn't ring anyone from Tarmac, although the chairman and Bill Francis, the former managing-director and the former head of construction, were all good friends of mine.

I remembered Bob Clarke knew Odgers from the days he, Odgers, was personal assistant to Arnold Weinstock and Bob who hadn't seen the report in the *Daily Telegraph* seemed to be keen also. I suggested that he should approach Odgers and see if he was interested and he agreed to do just that. We both met Graeme Odgers a few days later. He seemed pleasant enough and I felt we could work and get on together. He asked me if I would mind giving up the chief executive role and I said not only will I not mind I will be delighted to give it up. I then asked him if he could enjoy working in a family company while the family environment was still to the fore and was probably quite different from companies he had previously been with, and he replied that he would enjoy a new experience.

We agreed his remuneration which was substantially more than mine and a handshake sealed his agreeing to join us. To me it seemed to be 'Manna from Heaven'. We had got a top-class chief executive immediately and without expense and I could unload all of my problems onto the shoulders of a man I was sure could deal with them.

I had to make a phone call to Alex Alexander, who was very put out that he hadn't been brought into the negotiation and made the point that he didn't feel that Bob and I had done sufficient checking – a point he could have thrown in my face later but being a particularly nice man he didn't. I also had to tell Tony Scurr the news and ask him whether he wanted to stay on under Odgers. Whilst he knew what was coming he was obviously depressed and very sensibly decided to leave and go to South Africa where he was sure his friends in Trans Natal could find work for him.

After the announcement to the press I called a meeting at Hooton and introduced Graeme to all the senior management in the company. I also started discussing cuts and told him I was keen to close down our aviation link. The company plane had been an essential tool of management and indeed most large construction companies had one but in the last twelve months its usage had gone from 800 hours to under 300, mainly because we now charged whichever division used it for its costs, whereas previously it had been a general overhead charge.

I also arranged to introduce him to our French partners, Dumez, who had taken a minor stake in us, under fifteen percent. Their chairman, John Paul Peraire and managing-director, Andre Kemal were extremely keen on shooting and fascinated with Llanarmon and we made the visit to Paris in the company plane and everybody seemed to get on well.

Looking back I realise that if I had made more enquiries about Odgers before he was appointed, I would have realised that he was the wrong man to appoint to a company with a very strong family ambience and history. The problem was time was not on my side and I should have looked for an outside chief executive much earlier.

Later that year I went to a shoot organised by John Milne in his last days as chairman of Blue Circle. There I met a former non executive director of Tarmac, who said Graeme Odger's administrative skills are very limited but he is the best financial public relations man in the business – the analysts and the financial press loved him and Tarmac went through their best era with them whilst he was on board.

Christopher Edwards and I did indeed take Graeme around the analysts and he made an excellent impression, as he also did with the finance and media and a lot of the criticism I had encountered there began to abate.

As promised I gave Graeme a free rein with all the senior executives; he got on well with Peter Hulmes, who I had recruited to be number two in construction but who was now running it. He also got on well with Eric Grove and his managing-director but plainly preferred them to Philip Davies who was actually in charge of the housing division. I had told him that I was very worried about Warringtons and he had offered to go on the board. Wanting to protect him I said that I thought Christopher and I should continue, another mistake as it turned out.

All went well until later into 1991 when I began to get vibes that Graeme was not happy – although the only disagreement I had with him was over the previous year's results, where he had wanted to handle the analyst and financial press meetings himself but I insisted on also going.

My cousin Bill with whom I was very friendly had met Graeme at some function and they had chatted about the two companies and Bill had said how the clients loved dealing with the family and Graeme had come straight out with 'I am trying to get rid of them in ours'. Instead of reporting his remarks back to me, Bill kept quiet and it was Alex Alexander who asked me to have lunch with him and put me in the picture. Apparently Graeme had been trying to stir up feeling for months and what really upset me was that he had got Peter Hulmes, who I regarded as a friend as well as colleague, to tell Bob Clarke that the company was not happy with my chairmanship. Alex also told me that Bob Clarke was, as he put it, now wholly in the Odgers camp. 'Because Bob is a big tall man everybody thinks he is big in everything; in fact he is being very weak with Odgers.'

Odgers needed a stick to beat me with and he found it in Warringtons, where all the chickens Frank Sanderson had left me with were coming home to roost. I bitterly regretted not letting him go on the board of Warringtons as Christopher Edwards and I were unable to influence the board decisions as much as we would have liked. They did embark on an acquisition spree which came disastrously to grief with the property crash of the early nineties. Even the Chester Business Park went in a single week in 1990 from having seven major enquiries to none. Eventually Jackson resigned and it became obvious that Warringtons had to go into liquidation. Surprisingly the banks were very reluctant to see the company liquidated and pleaded with us to let Warringtons continue. Quite rightly the main board did not agree to this and the liquidation took place. I, like other shareholders, received nothing from the receivers. Odgers was able to spread the word that we had been incredibly reckless, completely ignoring that we had a thriving housing side which was later to be sold for an enormous sum of money.

If ever I needed a friend this was the moment and Alex was to prove his friendship in a very major way.

A meeting shortly after Christmas was set up between Graeme, myself and the non executives which also included Tim Kitson who I had brought onto the board when he resigned as an M.P. The meeting was held in Scott's restaurant's private room and was getting nowhere when I said to Graeme that I hoped he was not going to turn out as ruthless as some people seemed to think he was. This got him very excited and he said the last thing I am is ruthless and more or less agreed to continue as before. When the dinner broke up he was the first to leave and I said to Tim Kitson I thought that went very well. Tim agreed but Bob Clarke was not so sure and how right he was.

I went for my winter holiday to Barbados thinking everything was fine and was in the middle of a meeting in the hotel Angela and I were staying at with the solicitor who was to represent her in her action against the man whose motor boat had severely injured her the year before, when a waiter came in to say that Sir Alex Alexander was on the telephone and wanted to speak to me urgently. I went out of the room and started to say that I was in a meeting when Alex said what I have to say is more important: Graeme Odgers is determined you should retire and Bob and I are fighting to reach a deal for you. I said that I would fly straight back but he said no that wouldn't solve anything; much better to let us handle things. He then asked if my retirement date was age sixty, fifteen months off, and I said no, final retirement date is 62 and I have always said I would go then. I will have had forty-four years in the business and there are other things I want to do.

Alex said armed with that information he would come back to me and a day later he came back and said we have done everything we could. Graeme will agree a deal to take you to 62 if you give up the chairmanship at 60 but remain a non executive to 62, you will continue on full pay and benefits and will be able to take your pension at 60 so financially it is an excellent deal, and indeed it was.

I returned to England a couple of weeks later and went to a construction dining club dinner where about sixteen of us at the top of the industry met two of three times a year. I got Philip Beck, the chairman of Mowlems, to one side and said you have twice asked me if I would be interested in a merger do you still feel the same way? He replied that he did and I suggested he wrote to me.

Mowlem would have actually made a very good fit for us and Bob and Alex, who I rang up when I received Philip Beck's letter, were both enthusiastic. I suggested to Bob that as a merger would mean a major reduction in our shareholding, then just over 30%, the first thing we should do was to have an informal meeting with Philip. Both Philip and I wanted to have it in total secrecy so we arranged to meet at his flat which had a good sitting room. Unfortunately it had a communal entrance and when Bob and I plus son Euan arrived we found a good racing and Sunningdale friend of mine, Michael Buckley, collecting mail for his flat next door. He looked at us and said it's obvious what you have come here for. So much for secrecy!

I had of course to ring Graeme, who was on holiday in the Caribbean and although the news was obviously not popular with him he accepted that we should take the approach seriously and a board meeting was convened on his return. It was obvious to Alex and myself that as Dumez's attitude would be very important as their chairman was on our main board, so Alex agreed to go to Heathrow to meet his plane and explain the issues to him. When they got to the meeting Alex whispered in my ear, everything is fine, he is keen on the merger. I opened the meeting by explaining the approach and said that it is up to the board to decide whether they want to negotiate or not. After a rather inconclusive couple of comments I turned to Jean Paul and instead of enthusiasm, which Alex had forecast, he stalled completely. It transpired that he had merged with a larger company, a major French water authority, and his new boss, a powerful French industrialist, had told him not to agree to anything. Had the meeting been held a month or two earlier the outcome would have been very different.

The meeting broke up without reaching any sort of agreement and Eric Grove and I flew to Cheltenham in a helicopter chartered by Eric, a hair-raising journey through thick fog, to have lunch in his box before the races. I always stay with Barry Hills for Cheltenham and although a flat trainer Barry always enjoys going to Cheltenham to see the best of the National Hunt racing. I had just finished breakfast when I was told that there was a phone call for me. It was Bob Clarke who said, 'Bad news I am afraid. Graeme called all his executives together after yesterday's meeting except Euan and they want another board meeting to vote you out. Both Alex and I have told him that it is completely unacceptable but he is adamant.' In fact Alex, who had an acute heart condition which was to kill him eighteen months later, had told Graeme that he was making him ill and Bob had said you may win the vote but you will do major damage to the company.

I had done my sums and still thought I would win the vote although I needed Eric Grove, who I was sure would vote for me. I had after all bought his company and brought him on to the board. At his wife's funeral, she died tragically young, he had squeezed my hand on the outside of the aisle as he followed the coffin. He was, I thought a loyal friend.

My opinion changed when I had lunch with him a few days later at a Birmingham restaurant, the Plough and Harrow, then the best in the locality. Eric was nearly half an hour late and I had to listen to the head waiter moaning about half his staff being laid off and standards of service were suffering as a result of the recession. When he did arrive there was no apology and instead of talking about the proposed merger he said Graeme had rung him up and told him he was expecting his support. I said I hope you gave him a firm no and Eric said I told him I hadn't made up my mind.

As the fateful new board meeting approached Bob Clarke asked me to meet him. He was very upset at the situation and for the first time he was plainly not supportive of Graeme. He obviously thought Graeme would narrowly win the vote but at the cost of blowing the company apart. Three days before the meeting I was due to meet Bob again to discuss the trusts and I walked in expecting a very gloomy meeting. I said we can't really decide anything until the end of the week and Bob said with a broad smile, 'Forget that; Graeme has changed his mind and called off the vote to remove you.'

So things continued as originally agreed although the proposed Mowlem merger was called off. We had to find a new chairman in a year's time and it was agreed that Bob, Graeme and I should, later in the year, come up with three names each and come to a decision. During the intervening period Bob introduced to me two people, both of them answering the description as professional non executives, and I didn't really take to either of them. I had found a senior figure in the industry, Sir Frank Gibbs, who had been chairman of Taylor Woodrow and on his retirement had taken the same position with the British Nuclear Authority. I rang Chips Keswick who said he is outstanding, you couldn't have a better man, if you can get him. When it came to the meeting it was obvious to me that Frank was the best candidate but Graeme was having none of it and I should have realised that he would never agree to anyone I put forward and that my only chance to get him in was to persuade Bob to put him on his list.

In the end we were getting nowhere and after what seemed a long and aimless discussion, Graeme said, 'If you will agree to John Milne, so will I.' I had no business dealing with him other than being a client, who used a lot of the cement his company manufactured. He had taken me by helicopter to the Open Golf at Sandwich, to a number of shoots and to golf and dinner. I had put him as No.3 on my list but had thought Frank Gibbs to be such an outstanding candidate I hadn't given much thought to my other two names. Whilst John Milne was undoubtedly very popular amongst his golf and shooting friends, the only two people in Blue Circle I knew well didn't like him at all and told me he was very different in business to the social scene. I really had no alternative, he was on my list and Bob Clarke seemed happy to close the meeting with his appointment.

I also felt that we needed a change of trustee. Bob Clarke would be seventy when I finally retired and I had gone to his retirement party at Hill Samuel early in 1991. I had asked whether Graeme was going and he replied, 'No I am only having friends.' Bob in fact needed no prodding and knowing I was friendly with Chips Keswick said as long as you appoint him in my place, I will hand over. Bob had done a great deal for the family trusts and as I said at a farewell dinner we gave for him, the current beneficiaries, all twenty-eight of them, owed him a lot.

I suggested that I kept my office at Hooton for the last two years but Peter Hulmes, obviously at Graeme's behest, said we will build you one in your outbuildings at Tilstone and indeed a very nice office emerged with another room for a secretary and I still use them both to this day.

It was also made clear that my secretary, Kay Headland, would retire with me. She had been with me since I first went to Hooton and had been invaluable, although she had started to suffer from cancer, which was sadly to kill her a couple of years later. She had one invaluable asset a secretary needs – she knew instinctively what was really important to me and what had to be dealt with first.

About six months after starting my final two years in the company a very dramatic event occurred. Barry Hills rang me up early on a Sunday morning and knowing I always played golf on a Sunday asked if he could have some money on the opposition. I said, 'Why on earth?' And he replied, 'Read the *Sunday Times* and you will find out.' To my total amazement there was a front page story about a prominent industrialist and myself taking large salary increases at a time of pay restraint. I knew I hadn't taken an increase other than inflation at five per cent and it only took a minute to work out that the journalists had mixed my salary with Graeme's, mine having been the highest for the year before and his easily the largest in the last set of accounts.

I had changed solicitors as Isadore Kerman, who had been my London one for many years, had died. I switched to William Martin, a great friend of both Angela and myself at Nabaro Nathanson, where he was a partner. I rang him up to be told by a daily that Mr Martin had a very late night and under no account was he to be disturbed before eleven. I then rang Graeme who did not have a *Sunday Times* but said he would go out and buy one and we agreed I should ring again at lunchtime. Having nothing else to do I played golf and plainly nobody at Delamere Golf Club takes the *Sunday Times* because nobody mentioned it.

I cut out the usual nineteenth drinks and dashed home, where I rang William and Graeme and arranged to meet both of them in London the following morning. I took an early train and headed straight for Nabaro Nathanson, where William introduced me to an attractive, competent looking lady and said she is our libel expert. I was immediately asked to produce the evidence that my salary had only increased by five percent rather than the forty the paper had said and I gave her the last set of accounts and a current salary sheet I had brought with me. Robert Sangster had rung me on my mobile on the train to tell me there was a further piece in the *Sun* and we all read that together. It accused me of giving myself an absurd increase at a time of cut backs and had quotes from two or three people, one a Conservative M.P., who specialised on the subject. She said she could do nothing about the *Sunday Times* or *Sun* or indeed any others I hadn't seen – there were two, one being the *Liverpool Echo* – she would however immediately issue writs on the four papers and would send every other paper in the country a warning that the accusations were totally untrue and any further ones would result in an immediate writ. She assured me that would stop the pack and sure enough, although I bought every newspaper the following day, there was not a word in them.

I had gone from Nabaro Nathanson to our London office where I found Graeme sitting at my old desk in my former office talking to the *Construction News*. He handed me the phone and I found a construction journalist I knew well on the line. I explained what had happened and after expressing the necessary outrage he asked whether I was going to sue. I replied that I hadn't got round to considering that aspect. He said I should go for them, as did Graeme, who was for once being supportive.

Later in the week I did discuss what I should do with the partner of Nabrano Nathanson, who had quite a week as she was working on a big assignment for the Coal Board and had slept in the office for three nights in a row. She said that I had a seemingly cast iron case but it would take at least eighteen months to get to court and cost a great deal of money. She said she could get me immediately an apology, all my expenses paid and perhaps a small donation to charity. As I was desperate to prove to the staff the accusations were rubbish I went for the second option. In the event the apology on the front page of the business section included so many others that I was partly submerged, although I was the first named. I do regret not insisting on a front page main paper apology which is where I was libelled.

There was a sequel the following week when the *Daily Telegraph* published a small article headed 'we all make mistakes' then going on to say that libelling twenty-seven people was over the top. Also that the Business editor, who was in America, had resigned and of the two journalists left in charge, one had been sacked and the other suspended without pay. Andrew Neil, the editor, had also rushed back from abroad. I still take the *Sunday Times* and find it incredible that they could leave a business section in charge of such incompetent people. One phone call to me could have sorted it all out.

A few months later I was due to attend the monthly board meeting when Bob Clarke rang me up to say that John Milne wanted to see me and Euan and himself before the meeting. We all went in to be told that Graeme had handed in his resignation and was going to join the Monopolies and Mergers commission as their head. Milne added that he was taking a reduction in salary but that there would be a knighthood at the end and the intellectual challenge had attracted Graeme.

Bob, Euan and I went into an ante room and I opened up by saying that I thought it was the best news I had heard for years and perhaps we could now get a chief executive who would be fair to all sides. Bob agreed but said it would not be easy to get the right man.

Chips Keswick told me that I had to get on the selection committee but John Milne chose Bob Clarke and Eric Grove. Eric was a top class entrepreneur, brilliant in his field, but was never a corporate person and the rest of us were never put in the picture as to what the committee were doing. In the end they selected Oliver Whitehead who had previously had experience with Laings and had just finished a stint as chief executive of the engineering company Babcock. He seemed to have good references although Martin Laing had said that strategy wasn't his strong point. Since we were never presented with an alternative candidate the appointment seemed the best we could achieve. As soon as the announcement was made John King, Chairman of Babcock, rang me up. 'He won't suit you at all,' he said. I pointed out that I had taken virtually no part in the decision and that he had written a glowing reference. 'Of course I did, I wanted him to go,' was the reply.

So Whitehead joined us for my final year as a director and it was after I left that Dermot Smurfit told me his best director had applied to join us and he was terrified of losing him. His name had never come up and John Milne had treated Whitehead's appointment as a formality.

The last major drama in my career in the family firm came only a couple of days before my final board meeting when John Milne went to see Chips Keswick to tell him that a second rights issue was being proposed. Chips was furious, told Milne that the family had agreed to a substantial dilution of their shareholding when Odgers had masterminded a very successful rights issue shortly after arriving as chief executive, and that another so soon was quite unnecessary and that I was to put the family position at the board meeting. That I did probably far too angrily and when the new head of Hill Samuel was wheeled in I should have said that he had far too much at stake to give an opinion and at the very least they should get an impartial merchant bank to adjudicate.

At this point I should have simply left the meeting as it would have saved having to listen to Milne trying to find a couple of nice things to say and having to sit next to Eric Grove at lunch – it was mainly he and his managing-director who wanted the rights issue.

They duly went ahead with the issue and we sold our allocation the first minute dealings commenced. The share price went plummeting down not to recover until Milne's successor took over. So my forty-four years in the company ended on a particularly sour note. Happily for me life was to become much more enjoyable in the years from retirement to the present day.

The company went through a poor period regarding growth and profits until Milne retired having got himself an extra year as chairman. I met Bob Clarke at the Derby where we were both guests of the sponsors, Vodafone's chairman, Ernie Harrison. When I asked him why Milne had got an extra year he said, 'We were conned' – the same expression he had used when I asked him why they had let Euan go when the quarrying division was sold cheaply. I felt like saying surely senior non executives shouldn't be conned but he did give me the closest I will get to an apology when I saw him the following year. Milne's appointment, he said, was the worst he had ever been associated with.

Fortunately his successor Sir Terence Harrison, who had retired from Rolls Royce as chief executive, did a magnificent job and completely turned the company around. I had asked to meet him and spent an hour in his London Rolls Royce office. His opening remark was, 'If I had known how bad a state the company was in I would never have taken the job.' According to John Hignett, my one non executive friend on the board, he made Whitehead concentrate on line management and under his chairmanship the company moved to a much better level of profit growth.

I never met the final chief executive, Mr Grime, and Oliver Whitehead became chairmen, against the industry's strict advice that chief executives should not become chairmen. They were both much aided by being able to sell much of the 'family silver', particularly the housing side which went for a great deal of money and America which was also a good sale. As I have previously said the quarrying company was sold for a relatively small sum and would have fetched far more had it been kept for an extra year or two. The one piece of family silver left came back to bite them. It was Penrhyn Slate company, which was subject to a major fraud regarding sale of slate and two of the principals went to jail. It was a classic case of when you depart from the roots and leave a company isolated the management becomes much more difficult. In fact, according to one newspaper report at the time of the takeover by Carillion, it was the main reason for the takeover being accepted.

There was one final drama I was involved with during the Whitehead/Grime era, when they decided to change the company logo and colours. We had spent quite a bit of money in the early eighties on the logo and the colours, green and yellow, which were both distinctive and popular with everybody.

However, obviously there was a desperate desire at the top to get away from the old image and a change of logo and colours was announced, the new colour being a rather insipid violet. There was nothing anybody could have done about this but in my view, extremely foolishly, they also announced that the company would be called McAlpine, instead of Alfred McAlpine, despite the fact that Sir Robert McAlpine had an enormous company and had not been consulted about the change.

Unsurprisingly, Sir Robert's board were furious, particularly as they had done a couple of large joint venture contracts together and Malcolm McAlpine rang me up to say that they were going to court to fight the change and what would my position be? I replied that I could not believe my old company had been so stupid and I was totally on Sir Robert's side. He asked if I was prepared to give them a written statement, which I did and this was used in their submission without a word being altered. Sir Robert's won the case hands down and a very costly bill had to be settled by Alfred McAlpine, who apart from paying all the court case had to repaint all the plant yet again to incorporate Alfred McAlpine instead of McAlpine.

Two construction papers got onto me and asked for my comments, expecting an attack from me on the senior management. By this time I had had a deal of experience as a non-executive director, particularly on the Hall Engineering board and I said, 'This was surely a case when the non-executives should have stepped in.' By chance I was staying in the same house, a few months later, as one of the non-executives, a fellow member of the Jockey Club and former chairman of Hansons, Chris Collins and I did raise the subject with him. 'Oh, I rather like the old logo and colours,' said Chris. I gave up at that point!

Of the principals, some have fared better than others. Graeme Odgers duly got his knighthood, towards the end of his period with Monopolies and Mergers. I have not spoken to him since he left but bore him no ill will. I should have researched him better and he did provide a few much needed years of stability. Peter Hulmes soon fell out with Whitehead and left the company. I certainly did him no favours as he would have become head of Keir, who are still going as a successful medium-sized company. Eric Grove and Graeme McCullum were both arrested on tax evasion charges and spent a couple of uncomfortable nights in police cells. Graeme McCullum was quickly released and Eric never came to court but both had to resign as directors. Whereas Eric headed for a comfortable existence, Graeme McCullum went from strength to strength becoming chief executive of Wilson Bowden and then joining the main board of Taylor Wimpey.

The company itself is now part of Carillion, who took over Tarmac construction when Tarmac was split in two. The family name still goes strongly with Sir Robert McAlpine, who have recently built the Arsenal football stadium and were lead contractors for the Olympic complex. Few of the old names who provided the construction dining clubs survived the nineties intact. Mainstream construction is dominated by Balfour Beatty, Carillion, Sir Robert McAlpine and Laing O'Rourke – Laing construction having been bought by O'Rourke for the princely sum of £1. Amec is a highly successful company mainly in oil related activities. Taylor Wimpey are pure house builders. The days of fourteen to fifteen large mainstream construction companies have long gone.

The reason is simple, four governments in succession, one Conservative and three Labour, have totally neglected the country's infrastructure, preferring to spend money on work which appeals to voters, largely in health and schooling.

Chapter 8

My Shooting Field

Unlike most children from shooting families today I did not learn to shoot at a very early age. Only one boy at my preparatory school had a gun and he was allowed out with the masters and their friends on one or two organised shoots in the Welsh hills near Llanfyllin.

Surprisingly I showed no great desire to have a gun. Cricket was my main boyhood passion, and although I was given an airgun by Father at the age of twelve I never managed to kill a live bird with it. When I graduated to a twenty-bore two years later I was amazingly allowed out unsupervised and my first shot with it was in a wood near Glan Alyn where I fired at a pigeon and with the recoil I nearly fell backwards. This so put me off that for some time I took the gun out but was reluctant to fire, and it was not until I was allowed to take a back gun at one of Father's shoots and under his eagle eye had to fire a few shots that I started to use the gun properly.

It still took ages to kill my first game bird – very late in the season at a wonderful rough shoot called Stockton near Newport in Shropshire. Father hadn't really opened up Llanarmon immediately after the war and concentrated on two Shropshire shoots at Stockton and Acton Burnell, both close to Tickwood and both taken in partnership with Norman Partridge.

Stockton was a combined pheasant and partridge shoot, all wild on two farms just south of Newport. The shooting rights had been given to a local vicar who leased them yearly to Father and Norman for an undisclosed sum of cash. The keeper was semi retired and we all had many happy days there. My first bird, a hen pheasant, shouldn't have been shot because we were supposed to be shooting cocks only, but everybody was so pleased I'd finally nailed one that all was forgiven when I went home.

Acton Burnell was a different sort of shoot with several good coverts and a full-time keeper. It belonged to a well-known local family who took some days for themselves and there was always a feeling that the keeper was trying to keep the game for his employer despite the money Father and Norman put into the shoot. It all came to a head one day when having shot two drives with little result they insisted on driving a wood which the keeper said would yield nothing. It was full of pheasants and trust was non existent after that, and the lease was terminated at the end of the season.

My greatest memory of Acton Burnell was shooting a wild quail, one out of a pack which had survived through the war. I would never have fired if the keeper hadn't shouted, 'Quail, shoot them.' I wonder now how many people have ever shot a wild quail in England.

Llanarmon, our family shoot, was originally owned by a leading family in Wales, the Cornwallis Wests. Their daughter was the first wife of Bendor, the controversial and immensely rich Duke of Westminster. At some point he had bought the estate off his father-in-law and divided his shooting days between Eaton, his Cheshire home, and Llanarmon. According to one biographer most of his guests preferred Llanarmon to Eaton, a very flat low bird shoot. However the Duke intensely disliked his first wife and his mother-in-law, who he was convinced had pushed him into marriage, and decided to rid himself of all associations. My grandfather, who was on the scene at the right time, managed to secure the lease in 1923, and in 1931 he bought the whole estate with the shooting rights. The shoot consists of some of the finest terrain for shooting pheasants in Britain, and rivals any Scottish equivalent. There are three small grouse moors which in the thirties used to produce just over a hundred brace of grouse on the opening day and, although it never quite reached those heights after world war two, quite respectable bags were obtained until the nineties when almost all the grouse were wiped out by 'Louping ill', a blood disease caused by infected tick from sheep who pass it on to birds. Sheep used to be regularly dipped to prevent tick getting a hold, but in the late eighties dipping was not compulsory and with a plunge in the value of sheep the graziers who have rights on the moor had no financial incentive to dip the sheep and keep them free from tick.

Llanarmon had always been a top-class pheasant shoot and according to Father two drives, the Precipice and the Pool, featured in an article in *The Field* in the thirties as two of the best twelve stands in Britain. The war had put an end to feeding pheasants and the results were devastating to the shoot. Although shooting continued right through the war years, until 1943 tiny parties with my grandfather at the helm took place. Father only shot occasionally, perhaps after a strained relationship after his divorce. One of my grandfather's guests was Field Marshal Sir Edmund Ironside (down in 1943 as Lord Ironside), one of the generals leading the army in the very early stages of the war. Another was Lord Howard de Walden who then rented Chirk Castle. My grandfather's last recorded appearance was in early 1944 only a few months before his death. He was at the head of four guns, their bag mainly rabbits.

After my grandfather died Father headed most of the shoots, but 1944 and 1945 were the two lowest totals in the game book with 115 and 124 pheasants shot. It was not until the '47/8 season that the pheasant total was in the two hundreds.

My first recorded entry in the game book was in 1946: Master R McAlpine and Master W McAlpine; 3 rabbits. We were 14 and 12 years old. The second entry was: AJ McAlpine, Master R McAlpine, Master W McAlpine; 1 pheasant, 1 woodcock, 8 rabbits – no prizes for guessing who shot the pheasant and woodcock.

My early days at Llanarmon were outside days where six or seven of us walked in line through fields on the edge of the estate. Billy and I were on the end of the line but it was great fun; although the bags were small, it was varied and it was very good exercise.

The head keeper, Beaton, a dour Scotsman who distrusted the Welsh, was in failing health and didn't accompany us and it was Alf Matthews the second keeper who organised the rough days. Although Father and two or three friends would join in the early rough days, later on in the season I was often able to bring my friends. We were not allowed anywhere near the big stands but one day when the sport had been particularly poor, Matthews took a chance and allowed us a small wood between the Pool and the village. It was full of pheasants and to our glee we trebled the bag. Unfortunately Beaton was watching through binoculars and reported the proceedings to Father. Matthews got a tremendous roasting and we were never allowed near the centre again.

My breakthrough came when I was hurriedly pushed into the line when I was double banking behind the guns at the Pool. One of them, who had clearly overdone the party the night before, shouted 'take my place' before rushing to a hedge where he was extremely ill, poor man! I started firing away and to everybody's amazement I suddenly started killing most of them. Indeed my shooting never totally looked back from that day and as my confidence grew so did my shooting continue to improve and I became a regular at the larger days, though often put on the end of the line.

I had around me some of the finest shots in the country of which I would single out four who were just as good as the best today. Denny Thompson, whose wife owned a large estate at Sansaw near Shrewsbury, was the most stylish and elegant shot I have ever seen. Quite unlike the Percys and other great shots of today he never fired at a bird he considered out of range and as a result rarely missed. If he did it would be after lunch as he consumed very quietly prodigious quantities of gin before going on to wine and port. The other three – Jack Bissell, Neil Lamb and John Kinnerston – would also compare with the Percys, Francis Stafford and David Johnson, who make the top fifty in *The Field* today.

There was an enormous difference between the shoots of those days and today. Llanarmon had the two stands already mentioned, but little use was made of the remaining terrain and game crops were unheard of. The shoot was divided into beats with the guns walking from one stand to the other; the idea being to push birds into the next stand to be driven out again. Although very talented at cricket and golf, Father was a relatively poor shot, though he liked to kill birds. He shot off his left shoulder despite being right-handed at other sports and I always felt that if he had shot off the right shoulder he would have enjoyed it much more. A very conservative man he hated change and his continuous cry whenever I expressed an opinion was, 'Leave it to the keepers, they know much more than you do.' Whilst that may have been true when I was very young it certainly wasn't when I brought my brain to bear on improvements that could be made.

Unfortunately the keepers were equally unenterprising and conservative and as long as the bags were high they saw little point in risk taking and experimentation.

The guns too were quite different from those of today; most were either 'country gentlemen' or had sufficient money and leisure to shoot several days a week at the height of the season. Although the better shots enjoyed shooting at higher pheasants they would happily shoot at anything safely killable. They would have been amazed at a very pleasant team I had from the south of England last season who fined themselves if they shot anything which was not considered a 'good' bird.

This attitude had been passed down by their forebears who loved killing pheasants at any height. When my London neighbour Geoffrey Reeves (we had adjacent flats in Ryder Street) made his film *The Shooting Party* of an era just before the Great War, he was surprised how close together the guns stood in those days – about 15-18 yards apart, about a third of the distance you would expect today. The objective was to shoot a lot of birds. Alf Matthews frequently told a wonderful story about Llanarmon in 1919 when Bendor was in full flow. Alf was only nineteen and was employed as a keeper's helper and general factotum. He had joined the keeper's senior beaters, pickers up, etc. in a room specially provided with beer and cold food. The bag for the morning was between eight and nine hundred and everyone was in a convivial mood when Bendor's agent walked in. 'Silence,' he shouted, 'I have to tell you His Grace is disgusted with the morning's sport, or rather lack of it. I hope you're all going to do a lot better this afternoon.' The afternoon consisted of one stand, the Precipice, which was done towards the village where there was less height than the way we have always done it in my time. There were three guns provided by two loaders to every member of the line and a 'Powder Monkey' was in attendance to prevent anyone running out of cartridges. The total for the stand was over a thousand and although Alf was never told he assumed His Grace was satisfied with the afternoon's sport!

When I started shooting in the early fifties the scene was dominated by large landowners who reared a lot of pheasants. Two of Father's greatest friends, Jack Bissell and Denny Thompson, had widely contrasting shoots both owned by their wives. Enville, the Bissells' estate, was a traditional great shoot with a number of coverts where the birds flew extremely well. Jack was an ex professional national hunt jockey, intelligent, hardworking and spent a great deal of energy ensuring the shoot performed well. Denny Thompson's large estate, Sansaw, was totally flat and little effort was made to improve the quality of the birds. The two important things on shooting days were to kill a lot of pheasants at any height and have a long, extremely alcoholic lunch.

To some extent the same principle applied to Llanarmon. Father wanted the pheasants at a height he could perform adequately and although he could not alter the Pool and the Precipice, both naturally good stands, he soon discarded Ty Coch, another excellent stand, on the basis that it took too long and was difficult to get to the pegs. Although there were a number of rough days during October often combined with a grouse drive, there were only six main days pheasant shooting before Christmas: two lots of two-day shoots in November and a two-day shoot before Christmas in December.

The first of the two days was always the same, Towers Wood, probably the best though now it would be close to the worst stand on the estate, then up to Pen Y Bryn where the birds were so low that the only way to gain any enjoyment was to take them miles in front like driven grouse. The next stand Roman Camp could be mildly challenging in a gale and the fourth Greenshields Corner was supposedly named after a Captain Greenshields who had boasted to my grandmother how good a shot he was but only killed two pheasants having fired a large number of cartridges. Unless the birds flew quite differently in those days it is very difficult to imagine anybody now only shooting two birds with sixty to eighty cartridges. In the afternoon Stynog, now a stand equal of any in Britain, was shot in the opposite direction to today and large numbers of birds no higher than the top of a telegraph pole were shot. Before I was given a number in the line I used to start with the beaters and I watched one or two pheasants fly from the back of the wood across the valley at prodigious heights. I pointed this out to Father and the keepers only to be told it would never work the other way, they would only go sideways. The concept of rearing birds in one wood to feed them in another so they would fly at great heights across the valley was amazingly never considered by anybody in those days.

The second day was considerably better than the first although the opening stand at the top of the Pool is not done today because the birds simply don't fly well enough. But the Pool and Precipice are still driven in much the same way and although the Pool is better nowadays through tree felling, the Precipice has always been a wonderful stand. When Jimmy Lindley, having just won the Ascot Gold Cup on my horse of the same name, first shot at the Precipice, a bird got up from the rocks several hundred feet above him and arrived over Jimmy's head at least two gun shots out of shot. Jimmy got down on his knees and lifted his hands in prayer to the great amusement of the rest of the line.

The financing of the shoots was also very different in the fifties and sixties. Jack Bissell and Denny Thompson had very rich wives who could easily afford the upkeep of large shoots. Llanarmon was entire-

1. Parents' wedding: Just a twinkle in the eye! My paternal grandfather is between his two daughters back left, Mary on left and Jackie on right. My paternal grandmother is front left and maternal front right. Aunt Jean, mother's sister, is behind her and my maternal grandfather is on the right.

2. What a lovely little boy! Why do they have to grow up?

3. The Harrow rackets pair 1948-50 Dick Bridgeman and myself, professional Fred Crosby in the middle.

4. My mother with her second husband, Dennis Hickman, in the Bahamas.

5. My Aunt Jackie (right) after winning a hunter chase at Bangor-on-Dee. She left me all her horses including good hunter chaser Compton Lad.

6. My maternal grandmother.

7. Father with my second stepmother, Rosemary, Mother and stepfather, Dennis, all looking very relaxed at my wedding to Jane.

8. A rare sight! Me on horseback with three children. I am holding Christopher with Euan and Sara on the other pony.

9. Early photograph of Jane by Lenare, the very fashionable photographer.

10. Wedding photograph of my sister, Valerie, at her first wedding. Euan is the page and Jane Bell (later Patterson) is a bridesmaid (extreme right).

11. Bernard Argent, Father, Sara and Sally at Sally and Bernard's wedding.

12. Euan, Sara and Christopher in the garden of Lower Carden Hall. House in the background.

13. My brother Billy, looking unusually pensive.

14. Doug Francis, my near neighbour at Carden. He was a great friend and influence
in the early part of my life and was my best man at my second wedding.

15. Self and Angela looking very happy and relaxed.

16. Christening of Emma at Swettenham.

17. Angela, self, Emma and Tiggy in picture by Sony Robert. Tilstone Lodge and lake in the background.

18. Leaving Swettenham after wedding reception. As usual Bernard Argent hasn't done Angela justice!

19. Angela with Jane Armstrong – one of my favourite photographs of Angela with Jane.

20. Robert Sangster with one of hundreds of racing trophies!

21. Self in High Sheriff's uniform in the front hall of Tilstone Lodge.

22. Patricia Hodge at the front door of Tilstone Lodge during the filming of *The Cloning of Joanna May*.

23. Self in Tarporley Hunt Club regalia!

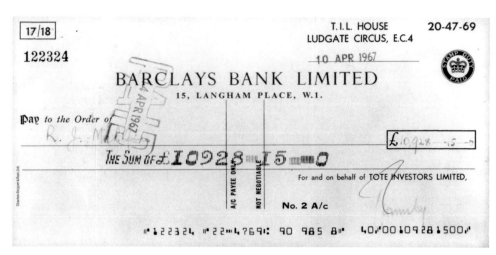

24. The cheque after the jackpot win at Doncaster in the 60s.

25. Willy Jenks riding Marieson at the Devon & Exeter in 1969.

26. Jane greeting winning jockey (Paul Cook) after a good win, Chester May week.

27. Self being presented with trophy at Haydock Park by Christine Sangster after Zip Fastener had won the Victor Ludorum hurdle. Tommy Whittle, late owner and chairman of Haydock, is on the right.

28. Two of my grandfather's racehorses on a foggy day in North Wales.

29. Precipice Wood (J Lindley) after winning Ascot Gold Cup, Royal Ascot 1970.

30. Precipice Wood by Sarah Ponsonby.

31. Cormorant Wood (Steve Cauthen) wins the Champion Stakes at Newmarket 1983 – having come from last to first!

32. Cormorant Wood after winning Champion Stakes by T.S. La Fontaine. The artist had never visited Newmarket before I asked him to go there and considerable artist's licence has been used!

33. River Ceiriog after winning the Supreme Novice at Cheltenham at 40/1. Nicky Henderson's first winner at the festival.

34. Myself with one of the early mares, La Foire II with her foal.

35. Inglis Drever winning at Sandown. He was to win three World Hurdles at the Cheltenham festival and was the most expensive yearling I ever sold.

36. Self with Steve Cauthen after winning the B&H Gold Cup (now Juddmonte) on Cormorant Wood at York, defeating Sadler's Wells, who started favourite. Doug Francis' head can just be seen between us.

37. Charles and Rose Lowther, Willy and Caroline Jenks and myself with Sadler's Wells at Coolmore.

38. A picture of Chester racecourse by Peter Smith. Richard Thomas and I are in the foreground.

39. A wonderful print of the old paddock at Ascot with all the trees and foliage on a hot summer's afternoon. How different from today's!

40. Sam Sangster's Christening.

41. A memorial race gathering of Robert Sangster's closest friends at Newmarket.

42. Myself and Victor Matthews on a hot day shooting grouse at Llanarmon.

43. My loader, Basil, who loaded for me until the early 2000s. He was a prolific drinker and smoker and a great character. He originally worked for Doug Francis and rode two winners, not for me, but he did come fourth on a horse of mine on the flat at Aintree.

44. A group at the opening shoot in the '70s. Father's fourth wife, Margaret, is holding the dog and his daughter, Sally, is next to him with Sara in front. Cousin Owen Lloyd George and his daughter, Julia, are extreme left.

45. Family Christmas shoot in Father's last days of running Llanarmon. His fifth wife, Cindy, is next to him and my two stepdaughters, Trinie and Sarah, are in front of Angela and myself. Robin Cayzer (now Rotherwick) is next to son, Christopher, extreme right. Val and Peter Shaw are with their two children, Samantha and Joanna, next right. Sister Sally is in front of Cindy and her husband Bernard is in front of Christopher.

46. McAlpine Day – from left to right: Christopher, wife Sarah, Bill, Angela, Kenneth, Emma, self, Fiona, James, Cullum, Adrian and Euan.

47. Shooting at Llanarmon in 2001 with Basil.

the Chairman

June 1989

ITE

again

R.J McAlpine

March 1988

48. The Chairman on the front of our company magazine – *On Site*.

49. A happy group at the Federation of Civil Engineers dinner. My cousin Kenneth on left, David Morrell, Sandy Shand and myself.

50. With Anthony Bamford (now Sir Anthony) at Haydock Park Plant show.

51. A large group of directors, both main board and subsidiary, at Hooton in the 70s. Peter Bell, Father, Alistair Kennedy and myself are in front row.

52. Board picture during my chairmanship. Owen Rich is next to me, Sir Riobert Clarke extreme right, Sir Alex Alexander extreme font left. They were my two senior non-executives.

53. Mrs Thatcher holds our book aloft after her last election campaign at the Marks and Spencer financial services building in the Chester Business Park.

54. A typical gathering of two sides at the end of the Marchwiel cricket week. The opposing captain, Anthony Vivian, is between Father (right) and myself. My brother-in-law, Peter Shaw, is second from the left, middle row. Former Lancashire captain, Richard Bowman, is third from the right middle row. Lifelong friend, David Marchwood, is end right of back row.

55. Not quite Tiger Woods! Teeing off in a Pro/Am at Bristol. I used a two iron in those days!

56. Myself, John Major and Alistair Goodlad at Tilstone Lodge.

57. Photograph of myself with John Lucan taken at a bridge tournament sponsored by Ladbrookes at the Ladbrooke Club. A number of Portland members were partnered with the best professionals in the world and I had one of the Dallas Aces. Although the photograph spanned two centre pages of the *Daily Mail*, the caption that thousands were being won and lost over the green baize was hardly a reflection of the evening. We were in fact playing for a trophy and the only money changing hands was on an auction before the tournament. John Lucan was the actual winner although there were far better players than either of us taking part.

ly funded by the company and Father never put a penny of his own money into the shoot. There is nothing intrinsically wrong with this; we entertained at Llanarmon some very important clients, although in my view not nearly enough and it was only at the end of his days running the shoot I was able to get more clients and prospective clients there. Many of the opposition in the construction industry also had shoots. Tarmac had in succession two excellent Shropshire shoots and I frequently shot with them. Charles Hickman, the then chairman of Tarmac and a close relation of my step-father, did not take part, but his son, Ian, who was effectively Tarmac's public relations manager, actually ran the shoot and took it extremely seriously.

Most landowners looked to friends to help with the upkeep of shoots and there were many syndicates, some of which remain to this day. The first person in North Wales to run his estate on a purely commercial basis was Harry Blackburn who had bought the Nantyr estate in the fifties. The estate which borders Llanarmon had in fact been first offered to Father for about forty thousand pounds – even in those days a ridiculously low price with a large house, cottages and several thousand acres involved. Beaton, who was still head keeper, would never have coped with the extra workload and unfortunately the opportunity was never taken up. Although Nantyr bordered Llanarmon the potential for good drives was considerably less. Nevertheless Harry used what he had to much better effect than Father. He had also worked out that the cost of shooting one pheasant equated to three or four bottles of decent wine and he provided an excellent lunch. On one memorable day in the sixties we had shot the allotted two hundred birds by twelve fifteen and an early lunch was called for. Lunch lasted for two and a half hours before we were allowed one stand in the afternoon. I had virtually not missed a bird in the morning but fired over twenty cartridges for one dead pheasant in the afternoon, and Harry having filled his party with alcohol managed to keep the bag within the ten percent allowed over the target.

The sequel was equally dramatic. Of the six vehicles that left Nantyr that evening only one reached home without incident. Black ice on the long downward hill into Glyn Ceiriog took its toll. I was the first to leave and was extremely lucky to bounce off the fence back into the road. The three behind me all went through the fence and into the field and a fourth who took another route finished upside down in a ditch. The lesson was learned, and although the breathaliser was not to come in for another few years, Harry made sure the excesses of that day were not repeated.

Llanarmon had three small grouse moors each capable of providing a day's shooting. Two of them were set out for driven grouse, the other, the Pohlo Moor, was always walked. Between the wars quite large bags were obtained though nothing on the scale of the best Scottish or North of England moors. Because like most Welsh moors, Ruabon being the exception, there was no keeper responsible solely for the grouse, the pursuit of vermin essential to keep a quantity of grouse intact tended to be done by the pheasant keepers in their spare time. The pheasants were always the priority and I had a constant battle with Father to try and get more attention paid to the grouse.

Father's first priority was the party atmosphere which surrounded the shoots and in order to have somewhere for his guests to stay he bought the Hand Hotel, one of two hotels in the small village. It had been completely run down and its bedridden female owner had just kept the bar licence. All the resources of Alfred McAlpine were brought in to completely renovate the Hand and an extension was put on and a large suite on the side built solely for Father's use. At the same time The Towers, effectively the shooting lodge, was taken down from three to one storey and a large comfortable dining room installed. Because he wanted to put as much as possible through the Hand, no kitchen was built and the food was brought up in terrines either to The Towers or the lunch huts on the moors.

Father chose the managers of the Hand himself, though in the last two he did ask for my opinion. The first manager, a Polish gentleman, with an unpronounceable name, lasted for a few years before handing over to a lady who was moderately successful before Father's last manager, the brother of George Formby, the famous, pre-war music hall star, and the brother looked very like him. Unfortunately our accounts department at Hooton, who were supposed to check the hotel accounts, completely failed to spot that Mr Formby was raiding the till and in fact he was eventually charged and received a jail sentence. Father then came to me and said that it was time I put my hand in my pocket, as he claimed to have lost £100,000. Whilst I was extremely sceptical about the £100,000, the company having paid for all the entertainment on all the shoots, I was not surprised he had lost money. In particular, he had always insisted on a lengthy menu, so he could choose any item he wanted, which led to considerable wastage. I made what I consider one of my finest replies, when I said, with a completely straight face, 'Certainly, Father.' He looked so surprised, nothing was said for several seconds, when I added, 'but there is one condition.' 'What is that?' 'That from next Monday you take no part in the management.' The hotel was put on the market the following Monday!

There are many stories over the hotel but the one I best remember was when we entertained Sir Miles Thomas, the chairman of Monsanto Chemicals, a company which we were trying to get contracts for their building work. He had brought with him a personal assistant and wife and we all tried hard to give them a good evening. I went to bed after midnight and was drifting off to sleep when the P.A. and his wife arrived next door. As the insulation between the rooms was really poor, I could hear every word and when he said what a tedious evening they had had listening to Jimmy McAlpine toadying to Miles, I became wide awake. I was still chuckling until he said, 'Mind you, he wasn't as bad as that ghastly fat son of his.' Next morning when I went down to breakfast, where Father was sitting alone, I relayed the first part of the conversation, carefully leaving out the second part. He was so rude to the P.A. that I am sure any chance of obtaining work was severely jeopardised!

My first disastrous experience on the moors was when I was shot by the next gun, the pellets missing my left eye by less than an inch, and two of them going through my lip and down my throat. Amazingly there was no major damage done but when I got back to the lunch hut I was shaking so much I couldn't get the glass of whisky I was given to my lips and somebody had to force it down my throat. Father behaved quite appallingly, being far more worried about whether the culprit was upset than how I was and desperately concerned that lunch should not be spoilt. Not for the first time I was made painfully aware of just how selfish he was. In fact the 'culprit', a genial old Etonian from a well-known Cheshire family who spent most of the season shooting, was by far the most dangerous shot I have ever encountered. A year after he had shot me I again had his gun pointing at my stomach as he followed a low dipping pheasant, 'You didn't think I'd pull the trigger?' 'Well you did last time,' was my reply. He finished his grouse career by peppering his hostess and two flankers at Dalogill. This was too much for Godfrey Bostock, the owner and one of his greatest friends, who told him very firmly he was not to fire another shot at Dalogill and if he had any sense anywhere else. Even Father was eventually persuaded to leave him out of the season's invitations, the only time I remember him dropping any regular.

Although I had heard wonderful stories about grouse in Scotland and the North of England it was not until the end of the sixties that I received my first invitation to shoot on a top Yorkshire moor. This was Gunnerside which had been recently handed over by his father to Willie Peel, a friend of the Kitsons. I remember Sally Kitson saying that the moor was the *crème de la crème* – and how right she was. We were taken to what was then known as the high moor and for the first time I was shooting with two guns. I drew the number one peg and looked out across a long shallow valley. An enormous pack of grouse set off at the beginning of the drive and appeared to be heading for the other end of the line. I said to my loader that we weren't going to see that pack, and he replied, 'Don't be so sure, they can easily change direction.' Sure enough half way across they started heading towards me and to my horror I realised the whole pack was going over my head. I put my gun up and two grouse came down with the first shot, one with the second and another with my last shot with the second gun. 'Not bad,' said my loader and when the drive finished I was surprised to be singled out for considerable praise. I had assumed all those practised grouse shots regularly shot four grouse out of a large pack – but apparently not so.

On the strength of this Tim got me an invitation to Swinton where he had helped David Swinton put together a team who shot alternate weeks, the other team having been similarly organised by Dickie Nicholson who had been a school friend of David's at Winchester. Like Willie Peel, David had been handed the moor at a very young age by his grandfather, a prominent pre-war cabinet minister who had Harold MacMillan and Alec Douglas Home to shoot regularly. Indeed it was partly Swinton which led to the grouse moor image taunts which dogged Alec Douglas Home in particular.

My first day at Swinton was not a success. I had not shot very well when at the end of the morning I had what I thought was an unusually high grouse and shot it through the beak. Feeling a little more pleased with myself I went down to retrieve the bird and found the head keeper and two others bent over the bird. 'You have just killed the only grey hen on the shoot,' the keeper said, 'and we have two alternatives: we can bury her before his Lordship gets here or you can take the consequences.' I never got the choice as at that moment I heard the thunderous sound of the twenty stone plus David Swinton actually running down the hill to see who had done the dreadful deed.

Despite this, Tim Kitson got me in his team for the following season and thus started thirty-four years of wonderful shooting on David's magnificent moors. I also managed to get myself invited to Dalogill next door to Swinton. Dalogill had been extremely cleverly bought by Godfrey Bostock who was a regular on one of the main Llanarmon days. The moor had been passed by his father to Henry Vyner as part of the Fountains Abbey Estate, one of the largest in Yorkshire. Vyner was addicted to gambling in Aspinalls and like John Derby had lost a million in one night's gambling. Unlike John Derby he did not have unlimited resources and had mortgaged the estate, which was up for sale by Eagle Star who held the guarantee. Godfrey Bostock, a Midlands industrialist, was a director of the Ionian Bank and having persuaded the bank to buy the whole estate he sold off much of it at a large profit and the bank in turn allowed him to buy one of the finest moors in Britain for a comparatively modest sum.

Godfrey and Father had a number of mutual friends, in particular Jack Bissell, Derek Boumphrey and John Midwood. He was very keen that both Father and I shot at his great new acquisition. While I was eager to do so, Father took the opposite view. Under extreme pressure Father accepted the first year's invitation but from then on made every excuse not to go.

I was by the time I started to shoot grouse in Yorkshire a competent, perhaps even better than competent pheasant shot, but grouse on the large scale was a different challenge and in the early days at Dalogill I did not shoot well. Godfrey had taken on Jim Joel's keeper Gillis who, having looked after the Joel team for a number of years, was less than enamoured to see a number of poor shots coming on a regular basis.

My first loader talked about the Harrison brothers. They hardly ever missed, he said, they would take two well in front, another two and a further two behind. This did nothing to shore up my morale though Jack Bissell was later to tell me, 'Absolute nonsense; most of the time they shot just like the rest of us, he must have seen one of them on a particularly good day.'

I well remember my first big drive at Dalogill, over a hundred cartridges for less than twenty grouse. Knowing that Gillis came around to count the cartridges I persuaded Jane, who was in the butt with me, to bury half of them. 'Not bad for fifty-two cartridges,' I said when Gillis arrived. 'And what about that pile the wife got rid of?' he replied.

However it was Gillis who paid me a major compliment in his last season there. I was the end gun and he was supposed to be flanking but he was lying down in the heather. Half way through the drive he got up and with some vigorous flag waving sent several high grouse over me, most of which I despatched. When I thanked him at the end of the drive he said, 'I wouldn't have got up for anybody else.'

What had caused the improvement was regularly shooting a lot of grouse at Swinton. Grouse fly much faster than pheasants and often jinx when they get close to the butts. Being totally wild birds they are more exciting than pheasants or partridges and the trick is to shoot well in front. Unfortunately shooting grouse is also extremely dangerous and too many poorly coordinated, inexperienced shots try their hand. Everyone has to start somewhere but I so instilled safety to my children that they frequently did not fire at birds when it was perfectly safe to do so.

The second time I was shot was at Dalogill, the culprit being an experienced shot at partridges and pheasants but not grouse. Unlike Father's Cheshire friend he behaved as well as possible under the circumstances, rushing to my butt and blubbing uncontrollably when he saw blood running down my face. In fact he had again narrowly missed my left eye and put several pellets into my loader's Barbour jacket and peppered the gun next door to me. This happened to be his host Simon Bostock – his father Godfrey having handed the moor to him some years before. A few days later a jeroboam of Lafite Rothschild '83 arrived through the post and Simon received a similar gift. We fared better than a good friend of mine, Michael Groves, who lost an eye from a direct hit on a Cumbrian grouse moor and found himself next to the same gun the following year. Or another friend, Alan Elliot, who went to hospital after being badly shot by another inexperienced shot. It was quite obvious who the culprit was but he failed to own up and as it was a two-day shoot we were all quaking at the thought of being drawn next to him the following day. My loader was quite adamant he was not prepared to be next door, but fortunately his resolve was not put to the test as we were drawn three places away.

David Swinton was my mentor at Swinton. Utterly dedicated to his moor he brought a Wykehamist's intelligence to bear on problems with it. A graph in the lunch hut of the middle moor, Ilton, gives the yearly totals going back to the 1850s. It showed a regular pattern of improving years, usually five or six and then a plateau where too many grouse were left which died off during the winter leaving little for the following year. The reason being that the Strogoli Worm present in all grouse builds up when there are too many on the ground and the females die off in the breeding season, leaving the young unable to fend for themselves. David was determined to break the pattern and with four-wheel drive vehicles available he was able to cover far more ground than his ancestors who used to go to the moor on ponies. When I started shooting there, one of the underkeepers told me that when he started working he walked six miles to get to the shoot every day there was a shoot. David was also a great believer that when there were large quantities of grouse they had to be shot hard in August as bad weather would affect the shooting for periods of September and October. Although he rarely had more than four drives a day he shot three days a week every week until the grouse were down to numbers he considered right for the following year. As he had two guns for guests in each team he received many invitations to other shoots and at his peak was shooting six days a week. When asked if he ever got bored he replied, 'I always look forward to tomorrow's shoot as much as I have enjoyed today's.' He had a quick dry wit typical of many Wykehamists. When he shot a cock pheasant three feet off the ground an astonished gun said, 'Why did you shoot that, David?' The reply was, 'I didn't want him to pass on his bad manners to his colleagues.'

Amongst many happy memories I have one when after a good day's shooting he turned to me and said, 'Don't drink too much whisky and stay when the others go home, I've got a surprise.' I duly complied and when the others had gone he brought up an old bottle of champagne covered in cobwebs. Uncorking it he said, 'Have been saving this for a great occasion. You may not have heard but Selwyn House has been sold and is closing down. Let us drink to the demise of Selwyn.' David hated his old preparatory school and would have turned in his grave when his heirs allowed a reunion of old Selwyn boys to take place in Swinton castle.

The best day's grouse shooting I've ever had took place in December 1991, days before the end of the grouse season. It was a combined Swinton Dalogill shoot with six guns from each moor and took place on the boundaries of both. There were only three drives but the total of seven hundred and eighty-four grouse bore witness to the numbers left on the boundaries and must be a record for December and probably November as well. The last drive was particularly memorable as I was at the very end of the line and high on adrenaline and not a little alcohol from lunch fired forty-nine cartridges for forty-one birds – probably my best feat on the grouse moor. The only comparison was the first drive after lunch at Colsterdale when I was on crutches after an operation on my Achilles tendon but managed to shoot thirty-six grouse by taking them way in front. David next door, who said I shouldn't be shooting, shot one less!

I have no intention of getting into the 'cruelty' argument but I will defend shooting grouse to anyone. Without shooting there would be very few grouse in Britain. At the end of the twentieth century there were large stocks of grouse across most of Scotland, Northern England as far south as Cheshire, North and South Wales, Devon and most of Ireland. There were even regular shoots in the Isle of Man. The record bag in North Wales was 1784 grouse on Ruabon moor in 1912. There were eight drives and the head keeper on a pony at a high point on the moor controlled the drives with a series of semaphore signals.

Now there are very few grouse left anywhere in Wales. There is the odd one on Dartmoor and very few in Ireland. Although Scotland still has some moors that do well there are large areas, particularly towards the west, which have gone the same way as Wales and Ireland. The great areas for grouse are the North of England – Northumberland, Cumbria, Durham and Yorkshire. Moors there are fetching astronomic prices as billionaires compete for those that come on the market. I well remember shooting at Gunnerside just after Bob Miller had bought it from Willie Peel at a then record price of around ten million pounds. A friend of his from Hong Kong asked how much Bob had paid and when I told him said, 'Is that all? A friend of mine from Hong Kong is coming next week; when he hears how little Bob paid he'll want half a dozen of them!'

David Swinton died just too early to witness the advances in medicine which are making an enormous difference. If the worm count gets too high keepers can now go out at night during the winter, trap the female grouse using clamps and forcibly dose the grouse with medicine. This eliminates the worm and although it may cause stress in the grouse the results are startlingly good. They can now also dose the grit the grouse all feed on with medicine which will also cause major improvements in worm counts. The medicine is extremely expensive but for the large moor now charging with V.A.T. nearly

£100 a bird, the improvement in grouse bags can be substantial.

Grouse now have two main enemies threatening their existence: predators and Louping Ill, a blood disease caused by infected tick on sheep or deer.

Predators vary from foxes and stoats to a variety of birds of prey, in particular the hen harrier. Whilst gamekeepers can deal with the ground predators, it is unlawful to kill birds of prey. Bodies like the Royal Society for the Protection of Birds seem oblivious to the fact that birds of prey kill vast numbers of smaller birds and are forever trying to introduce more exotic species regardless of whether their natural habitat is Britain. The goshawk, a great killing machine, is one example and sea eagles have been introduced, though they've never been here before. Hen harriers are a different situation as they fare best when grouse are prolific and as long as there are not too many hen harriers, they and grouse can happily co-exist.

A recent experiment on Langham Moor, part of the Buccleuch estate, illustrates the point perfectly. A successful grouse moor with several keepers, it was agreed that the hen harriers were to be encouraged and the breeding pairs increased from two or three to twenty. The grouse were decimated and the result was few grouse and even fewer hen harriers as they left for moors with more grouse. The keepers lost their jobs and shooting stopped. The RSPB have very successfully encouraged people to believe that hen harriers are a threatened species although there are hundreds around Britain.

Just before the grouse at Llanarmon terminally declined there was a major incident as we were walking the Pohlo moor. Halfway through a messenger arrived and whispered to David who looked extremely worried and said he had to return to the Towers. We continued and had with us the head keepers from our two neighbours, Nantyr and Vivod. In fact the RSPB, convinced that all three keepers were killing birds of prey, persuaded the police to simultaneously raid all these keepers' houses in the hope of finding evidence. The wives who were alone were treated quite roughly and the whole debacle was unpleasantly conducted. In our case it was claimed that a red kite had been poisoned and had been found on the moor.

Although at that time I had no association with the *Daily Telegraph* I received a tip that they would be interested in the story and they duly published a report giving our side of the case as well as the RSPB's. This elicited a furious letter to the *Telegraph* from Barbara Young (now baroness Young), the chief executive of the RSPB, accusing my keepers of poisoning the red kite and landowners of not looking after the habitat properly.

My solicitor then sent a letter to the RSPB asking where the red kite had been found and when an eventual reply pinpointed the very edge of the moor where keepers hardly ever went we sent another letter asking who had found the bird and for names and addresses. We received another letter saying walkers had found the bird and never got a name or address. In fact there was never the slightest evidence that my keepers ever had anything to do with the incident and no charges were ever made. The two other shoots however did have a total of twelve charges against them and the media gathered expecting convictions and severe penalties. In fact only one charge was proved – that a Larsen trap had been illegally used with a bird other than a magpie in place and a small fine was imposed.

Disgustedly the media all faded away and very little was reported. There was a sequel to it all when the Welsh director of the RSPB decided to try and mend fences and invited us down to their reserve at Lake Vernwy. We had a good lunch and saw some nice looking heather with no signs of any grouse whatsoever. The warden who saw me looking for evidence of grouse droppings drew me aside. 'Mr McAlpine,' he said, 'as long as I am not allowed to kill any vermin – foxes, stoats never mind raptors – you won't see any grouse.' Enough said.

The second and most recent enemy of grouse is Louping Ill which has increased enormously since dipping sheep has not been compulsory and the low price sheep fetch adding to the problem. Louping Ill kills ninety-five per cent of grouse and my experience at Llanarmon is typical of moors where landowners can't control the sheep. In 1987 we shot three hundred and seventy grouse. By 1994 it was down to under a hundred, and in 1996 it was wipe-out time on two of the three moors and shooting stopped from then on. The third moor, on high ground with few sheep, managed to keep a few grouse but they are now threatened with an edict from the Countryside Council for Wales, a bureaucratic quango which we pay for to manage the countryside, who have forbidden any burning without which the heather will grow out of control and become unmanageable. Their excuse is that 'Blanket Bog', which means many things to different people and roughly defined is moor on a major depth of peat, should not be burnt because burning threatens the environment. Other environmental bodies have taken a very different view but National England is currently fighting a test case over the Walshaw moors, which has profound implications for all moors with blanket bog. Meanwhile the area at Llanarmon, which has remained unburned for some years, is slowly becoming a semi-wasteland with the value of the grazing decreasing every year.

The best way to see how intense the tick is, is to take a dog on the moor. A spaniel on our last day of seriously shooting the home moor had forty-three ticks removed from his fur at lunchtime. Last year David Matthews had a ferret escape near the moor; when he found it two weeks later, it had been virtually eaten alive by ticks. I would not dream of taking my dogs on the moors at Llanarmon anymore. A very sad state of affairs

Although grouse in Wales look like suffering the same fate as Ireland and Devon, it is a happier story in Northern Britain and Scotland. There are places where large moors can make their owners substantial sums and large amounts of money have been spent getting rid of Louping Ill and getting grouse back. The best way is to have large flocks of sheep dipped extensively at least four times in the summer and the tick will gradually be killed off. One owner even built a large and very expensive deer fence to make sure that they kept off his moor and left it tick free.

Most countrymen who know about Louping Ill think it has no effect on humans but in fact it can lead to a very unpleasant illness called Lyme disease. The problem with this horrible disease caused by infected tick is that it is very difficult to diagnose and many sufferers are told they have something else. I had one victim in my four by four who told me he was in intensive care for three weeks having caught it fishing close to a Scottish moor. Another friend's wife caught it in America where tick is a big problem in one or two states. My head keeper's daughter also caught it and it took her nearly four years to be accurately diagnosed. If the tick problem continues to increase, one day Lyme disease may become a major health hazard for those roaming the countryside on land close to moorland.

As the grouse declined at Llanarmon so pheasant shooting improved. Father finally gave up shooting in 1988, much to my relief. It was not only his use of the coverts that depressed me but he'd become extremely dangerous. His arthritis caused him major problems of movement and he was finding it difficult to stand. The last time he shot Stynog the easy way I managed to park my four by four between us and it was very fortunate I did so, as a shot by him at one of many dipping pheasants rattled the four by four. When his loader/driver David tried to tell him he was shooting too low he was told in no uncertain words that after fifty years experience he knew a lot more than David. I have given the polite version!

The slaughter of low pheasants at Stynog had been so bad that year that Victor Matthews, who had succeeded his father as head keeper, came up to me after the drive and said, 'I can't stand this anymore; next year we will try it your way.' When it came to laying a game mix the following summer Victor still had his doubts but Philip Godsall, the new agent, and I paced it out for him and told him it was going to be sown, and sown it was.

The following season I waited nervously to see if birds would fly as I'd hoped and the results exceeded all expectations. I will never forget the sight of Victor running down the hill at the end of the drive to greet me with the words, 'You were right and I was wrong' – the only time any keeper has said that to me!

Poor Victor also suffered, as did his wife, with chronic arthritis particularly in his hands and he had to retire early. His son David took over, still in his twenties and extremely young to be head keeper on a large shoot with no experience elsewhere. I had my misgivings but could not have been more wrong. David has a first-class brain, incredible energy and between us we revolutionised the shoot. Three more game crops were planted further up the valley from Stynog and wonderful drives they became; further game crops were planted wherever the terrain was suitable and the result was a shoot going into the next century which bore no resemblance to the one coming out of it.

Apart from the game mixes there were other big changes, particularly over feeding patterns. Previously the pheasants were fed in the woods that they were put in after rearing. David found that by feeding them in the cover we wanted to shoot to fly back to where they were reared and roosted they would fly much better. Instead of driving the top of the Pool the birds were fed in Ty Coch, a much better cover, and Stynog birds were reared in Haffod Adams to be fed in Stynog and fly back to Haffod Adams during the drive. We are one of the few shoots left to rear all our own birds and whilst we catch up several hundred hens at the end of the season we do import about forty cock birds every year. The results have been a gradually wilder, better flying bird emerging which has added to the general enjoyment.

After Father gave up shooting I continued to get a little support from Alfred McAlpine but as my own retirement date loomed up in the early nineties this ceased, and I found myself running a large shoot entirely at my own expense. Plainly I had to let most of the days and whilst I wasn't looking for a profit I wanted to keep the losses on the low side. Fortunately my shooting friends rallied round and many of them took days, some of whom are still with me today. I continued to shoot with many of them and at the end of the nineties I was shooting between seventy and eighty days a year. This has gradually reduced to the forty-eight days I shot two years ago. The grouse days have virtually ceased as I find it increasingly difficult to see the low flying birds in time. Fortunately high pheasants are a different story and I hope to continue for a while yet. I am heartened by Godfrey Bostock who shot his last two grouse in a drive the year before his death at ninety-four and the father of a friend of mine, who thought he had shot his last grouse aged niney-six. In fact when he reached 100 it was arranged for a pack of grouse to be driven in front of him and he did shoot one. The two important things are to enjoy it and to shoot safely. The moment the safety side becomes difficult is the time to give up. Three of my four children all enjoy shooting immensely and four grandchildren all shoot extremely well – far better than their grandfather at the same age.

The improvement in younger people shooting grouse had been phenomenal. Although I only shoot now at grouse a few days a year, when I left Swinton there were already two or three who rarely missed. Indeed I could now name over a dozen guns who shoot grouse as well as any of the legendary figures of yesteryear.

Shooting is no longer the prerogative of the rich or large landowners. It is a sport enjoyed by many people from all walks of life, with increasing numbers of female participants. It has never been more popular in the countryside, and does a great deal for the rural economy. My only sadness is that fewer and fewer landowners are still running their own shoots. In my part of North Wales, Cheshire, and the Shropshire Welsh borders I can only think of four who come into that category and one of those rents a nearby estate with better terrain than his own. It is very much the age of the professional of which Gwyn Evans, who rents estates in Wales, Shropshire and Devon and rears massive numbers of partridges and pheasants for them, is the largest. I can understand my friends accepting a large rental and a couple of days for themselves. It is very tempting and although I am glad I did not go down that route I doubt if my bank manager feels the same way.

Chapter 9

Racing Ups and Downs

My first memory of taking an interest in a horse race was listening to a radio broadcast of the National in 1939. I was told I could have sixpence on any horse, made my selection and got very excited when he was called by the commentator late in the race. 'Yes, he is in front but unfortunately he has no jockey on,' said my mother. 'Surely that doesn't matter!' I replied. I also remember backing Ocean Swell in the Derby at my prep school but Harrow had very severe penalties for betting; a crime regarded as more heinous than others which might now be considered much more reprehensible.

So it wasn't until I left school and got amongst a group of friends who were keen on racing that I started to get interested again. My uncle, Sir Malcolm McAlpine (Uncle Tom to us), had won the Grand National with Shaun Spadar in 1921 and I had been fired up by his stories of the race when as a child I took a Greenline bus and visited him at his home in Cobham. So I went to the Grand National the year after I left school and have never missed the race from that year on. The only time I have not seen the race properly was when I was briefly courting a lady who lived on the Wirral and her parents took us to the Canal Turn. The horses passed in a flash and the day made worse with Jack Bissell winning the Aintree Hurdle. All I could hear was the loudspeaker announcement. The Canal Turn was definitely not for me.

However a group of Shropshire friends, Christopher Motley being the most prominent, became very keen on going racing and in my early twenties we all started going to the local meetings – Wolverhampton and Birmingham in particular as well as Bangor and the point-to-points. My first real bookmaker was Laurie Wallis who I introduced to a Cheshire friend, Christopher Robinson. Christopher was then an insatiable gambler and got into real money troubles. His father rang up Laurie Wallis and told him that he would not pay

Christopher's debts and the account was promptly closed. I was terrified that Laurie would try and charge me but he was charming and said it was very good of me to make the introduction and it was their responsibility from then on. Although I graduated to larger bookmakers – Ladbrokes, Heathorns, William Hill and Victor Chandler – I always had the odd bet with Laurie and when the business was absorbed by Sunderlands I eventually started betting again with his grandson, Simon Wallis, which I do to this day. 'What goes around comes around.'

We had some memorable days at the local meetings and two days I particularly remember were both at Birmingham. On the first we ran into David Swinton who had become Lord Masham since the prep school days when he was plain Cunliffe Lister. I had just been allowed my first sports car; a blue Jensen and David had an identical one. The girls with us had got excited by David's title and Elizabeth Thompson, one of the three beautiful Thompson sisters, offered to go with him to my Shropshire cottage to have a drink after racing. We had in fact had plenty at the racecourse and my first memory of the drive back was seeing him in my mirror ploughing through some tulips decorating a roundabout in the middle of Birmingham. We managed to get to the cottage safely where David had a couple of drinks and went on his way. I was having supper when the phone rang and a rather tired voice said I've taken your car instead of mine. The pillar of the Yorkshire establishment, commander of the Queen's bodyguard, and deputy Conservative chief whip in the House of Lords did not want to be reminded of that story too often.

The second memory of Birmingham was the day Jack Bissell had a treble, all at decent odds. Jack had a very small stable alongside Enville Hall and I imagine this would be the only treble he ever had. All were ridden by Peter Pickford whose brother Mick was Jack's head lad. To my amazement Brian Jenks who had become a great Shropshire friend asked me to become a steward at Wolverhampton. I was still in my early twenties and felt I would be quite unsuitable but Brian, who was a director and leading shareholder and head of the stewards' panel, was very persuasive and so I agreed to serve. In those days there were no aids, no cameras to guide you and stewards were dependant on their eyesight and their ability to interpret a race. Two enquiries still remain in my memory. In the first a two-year-old winner ridden by Bill Marshall's son appeared to badly hinder the second. The son, who was an apprentice, duly came before us and despite

Brian trying to get him to do the talking his father constantly took over. His final speech would have done John Gielgud proud: 'I know you knowledgeable gentlemen will do the right thing and let my son keep the race.' Unfortunately we didn't do the right thing and the Marshalls lost the race. The second enquiry concerned Johnny Haine who appeared to make little effort to win a hurdle race. Although with no cameras non triers were not the easiest for stewards to spot, Johnny had sailed close to the wind a few times and we decided we had to report him to the Jockey Club who warned him off for a period. In those days the media behaved quite differently to today and stewards' decisions were generally accepted without any of the media debate which surrounds them nowadays.

At about the same time I became a steward I obtained my first racehorse. I had been playing cricket with Ian Lomax whose wife trained horses. Women were not allowed to train horses so Ian had to hold the licence. There was a late night party after the cricket and I woke up the following morning with as bad a hangover as I have ever had and the realisation that during the alcohol-fuelled early hours I had committed myself to buy a racehorse – which nearly caused me to have a seizure. The famous comment 'Racing is a rich man's sport' was ringing in my ears and as I had no private money at that point and was dependant on my income from the family company, I hastened to repair the damage. I managed to get through to Rosemary Lomax who said, 'The horse left Ireland two hours ago, come and see him whenever you like.'

My next move was to ring my brother up and tell him that he was the proud owner of half a racehorse I had purchased on his behalf. Before Billy could reply I disconnected the call and to his eternal credit he came in for a half share. The horse Marnrack, a four-year-old gelding, had been sold by Kevin Prendergast who is still training to this day, and the one thing in our favour was the horse was ready to run. In fact the second Saturday after the purchase Billy and I drove down to Chepstow to see the horse run in a maiden hurdle. I was full of foreboding but Marnrack ran far better than I was led to expect, challenging throughout the last half mile and being beaten about half a length. Peter Pickford the stable jockey got off him and said we will definitely win next time and I was so excited I could hardly stand upright. The excitement of seeing a horse in one's own colours run so well can only be realised by those who have gone through the same experience.

I often wonder what would have happened had he been no good.

Neither Billy nor I could have afforded to keep him for very long and I, who had absolutely no pretensions to own a horse before the cricket party, might well have decided against further ownership. I would have missed out on a great deal of excitement but almost certainly would have been a much richer man.

Marnrack's next race was a fortnight later in the first race at Uttoxeter and he was odds-on in the morning papers. Billy and I drove again together and as it was quite foggy stopped at the White Hart hotel, a favourite watering hole. We in fact got no further as the fog was still there an hour before the first race and the meeting was called off, only to clear shortly afterwards and the first race would have been run in brilliant sunshine. The next selected race was midweek at Wincanton and both Billy and I, who were not supposed ever to take a day off, failed to get there to see his victory. Reading the papers the next day he did make a terrible mistake and Peter Pickford did brilliantly to stay aboard. His jumping was always a worry because he could jump brilliantly but was prone to make the odd bad mistake. Three years later he was in a £10,000 chase at Manchester, another great course, at long odds and cruising by ten lengths going into the second last he got rid of his young apprentice jockey, a last minute replacement for Peter Pickford. Ten thousand pounds was a very valuable prize in the fifties and probably worth a hundred thousand now. We continued to have great fun with him winning a number of races until he broke down irretrievably at Woore at the age of eleven and had to be put down.

His success had encouraged me to try again and Rosemary and I went to the sales in Deauville. I used to be fascinated by French resorts with elegant casinos. A group of us started going to Le Touquet soon after I left Harrow and we had some wonderful weekends there. The casino at Deauville was larger than Le Touquet but less elegant. The racecourse too was rather disappointing. The absence of bookmakers made for much less atmosphere and, though I did not then know it, the course was to be the scene of one of my greatest ever disasters a few years later.

However we were made very welcome at the sales and as my pocket only stretched to about ten percent of the yearlings on offer our choice was limited. Rosemary, a very good judge, went for a small neat filly called La Foire II which we obtained for about £1000. When we got home Ian accused us of getting so pissed that we bought a pony instead of a horse, but La Foire was to do us proud, winning nine races and starting favourite for the Cesarewitch in which she was badly interfered with. Unfortunately when she went to stud she produced nothing as good as herself.

My move to Cheshire just after Jane and I got married brought me more in contact with one of the two local courses, Bangor on Dee (Chester itself being the other). It was there that I met Doug Francis, the elder brother of Dick already a famous figure on the turf. Doug was a simply lovely man and despite the difference in age and upbringing we got on like a house on fire from the start. He had a race mare called Codine which I bought for a small sum and presented her to Jane. More importantly I got Doug interested in Carden Bank on the Leche estate, introduced him to Geoffrey Evans the agent at Llanarmon who dealt with the Leche estate, and Doug was able to buy Carden Bank and fifty acres of land for about £11,000. It is quite astonishing how cheap nice houses were in those days.

So he became a near neighbour, enlarged a couple of stables already there and moved his small string from Bangor to Carden along with his family, wife Julie and children Susan and Richard. Codine was no world-beater but very genuine and we found plenty of races for her to either win or more often get placed. By now I had two nice horses with Rosemary and had started well with Doug so launched into two more with Doug – Home Secretary and Marieson. Both used to give a lot of pleasure and Marieson in particular was constantly in the first three. He had been bought in partnership with Anthony Johnson, married to David Stern's sister-in-law Zandra. Anthony was passionate about racing but at the time we bought Marieson there was no question about him race riding the horse. Indeed as Antony didn't hunt or point-to-point, the normal route to race riding, it never entered my head that he would take it up. Nevertheless he did and to everybody's surprise came second on his first ride at Worcester. He was desperate to get aboard Marieson and this created a major problem because two top national hunt jockeys, Stan Mellor and Roy Edwards, were also vying for the ride. Doug and I both wanted him to win as many races as possible and whilst Antony was a promising beginner Stan and Roy were way ahead of him. I as usual tried to compromise but there were constant arguments, despite which Antony and I remained friends for some time to come.

Two exciting events happened around this time in the mid sixties. Codine had been ridden at Bangor in April by the champion jockey Jeff King who got off her after finishing down the field and said, 'Very moderate I'm afraid.' Ten days later Stan Mellor rode her at Cartmel on the last day of the national hunt season and had the winning ride pipping King by one ride to become Champion National Hunt Jockey. We returned to Cliff Bank where Doug had ordered crates of beer and Stan, he and I consumed umpteen beers through the night in celebration.

The second event was on Lincoln day where I had undertaken to host a table on the racecourse for a team from the electricity board who we were doing a lot of work for. They were all keen race followers and always eagerly followed my tips. Because I knew I would not have time to get to the bookmakers between races I decided to do the Jackpot which had been heavily promoted by the Tote and was causing great excitement amongst punters. I went through the card fairly quickly and picked out a few I fancied for the early races. When I came to the Lincoln I was so completely flummoxed I said to the man next door filling his Jackpot, 'What are you putting in for the Lincoln?' He replied, 'Ben Novus, I hear he's working very well.' I put Ben Novus in as a banker and the horse in the last which looked likely to be favourite as another banker.

I managed to get the first three winners and Ben Novus won the Lincoln at twenty-two to one. Suddenly I began to get really excited, which didn't impress my friends from the electricity board who were not winning anything, and after one of my two selections won the fifth I rushed down to the books to see what was happening in the last. In fact my selection and another horse were joint favourites and I decided I should lay off on the non selection. Ladbrokes told me that Dickie Gaskell, the gentleman bookmaker I knew fairly well, was in the bar and I went in to try and get him to advise me what to do. We were still arguing when the news came through that one of the joint favourites had been withdrawn and the other duly won the race. I need not have worried as three of us shared nearly thirty-three thousand pounds. This may not sound so much now but in the early sixties it was a great deal of money and I drove myself back to Cheshire full of the joys, stopping to tell Doug the good news. He totally disbelieved me until I produced a copy of the Tote slip and the following Sunday morning I organised an impromptu drinks party for as many friends as I could drum up and served Pimms mixed with champagne – the first and last time I have ever been so stupid and the hangover was horrific. The cheque when it arrived made up for it.

Whilst we rarely missed the nearby meetings, on the August bank holiday meeting we would always go to Cartmel on the Saturday. Cartmel is a unique course with beautiful surroundings near the small town of the same name. Although owned by the Cavendish family when I first started going, it was run by Colonel Pain who had a tent which used to operate after the first race and was well stocked with champagne. The course is the most inaccessible by road I have ever come across and also has the worst viewing in Britain. When I first went there were no cameras and no steward to observe what happened on the final bend before the straight and jockeys frequently took advantage of the lack of supervision. Some of the stewards' decisions were amazing and I was at the wrong end of one when George Owen and I were watching Happy Morn II, a top class hunter chaser usually ridden by my Cheshire friend John Barlow, but ridden this time by Tony Biddlecombe, Terry's amateur brother. The first two races were both the subject of objections which were overruled and Happy Morn duly won the third by fifteen lengths with my money on board. 'At least there can't be an objection this time, George,' I said as I strode happily to celebrate in the chairman's tent. I had almost reached it when the announcement 'objection – retain all betting slips' was made. I stood in disbelief outside the tent and five minutes later came another announcement 'objection sustained'. I ran back to the weighing room and found George looking very shaken, 'You won't believe this Bobby, but Tony Biddlecombe has a terrible stutter. When the senior steward said, "Did you cross the second?" he replied, "Yes I did sir." He was about to say "but I was ten lengths ahead at the time" but the words never came out.'

I was at the right end of an even more bizarre decision when Marieson ran in a hurdle there. Although Anthony Johnson was there I had prevailed upon him to let Roy Edwards ride and had for me a substantial bet. Coming into the straight he looked sure to win but was caught near to the line and appeared to be beaten by at least a neck. The judge duly called him second (there were no photo finishes) and I went disconsolately to the Pain tent to drown my sorrows. Just before reaching the tent there was an announcement that the judge had reversed the placings and Marieson was now first. I rushed back to the track to find a grinning Roy Edwards. 'As I crossed the line I said to Eric Cousins's apprentice, "I've just beaten you." The judge went up to me and said, "Do you think you won?" "Definitely," I replied. He turned to the apprentice who said, "If Mr Edwards said he won I'm sure he did."' The most outrageous race I have ever been awarded.

There was a sequel. After a very convivial afternoon drinking copious quantities of the Pain champagne I was about to go when a very young looking man came up to me and said, 'Mr Francis has asked me to ride Marieson on Monday, how should I ride him?' I was giving the usual instructions but Anthony Johnson, who couldn't come on Monday, then said, 'Just tell the judge you won a good neck.' A little man who had been sitting in the corner got up and said, 'I was the judge today, did I get it wrong?' I left so hurriedly he never got an answer.

Another amusing steward story concerned Decode, Codine's foal who was even better than her mother though much more difficult to ride. She had an extraordinary race going so wide at the far turn that she went through a patch of bluebells before rejoining the race properly, well behind the others. Last into the far turn she appeared to have no chance but coming into the straight fourth she ran on and just got up to win.

An enquiry was held not as I expected into the running of the race (I wasn't sure if she had stayed on the course) but on the improvement in form from a race over hurdles three weeks earlier. Doug and I were sat in a little ante room next to the stewards' room but the walls were so thin we could hear every word the stipendiary steward said to the local stewards.

The stipe was no other than the senior Jockey Club official Mr Christian who I later discovered had been sent up because of reports of poor stewarding at Cartmel. He gave the local stewards a series of questions to ask Doug Francis who when called expertly stonewalled most of them. Doug who was enjoying himself enormously waited nearly until the end before saying, 'Have you a flat form book? Because if you have and look up Monday's results at Haydock you will find she came a close third in a handicap on the flat there.' Collapse of enquiry.

Not all the drinking was done on the course. At one meeting we got asked to have a drink with a youngish couple and arrived at the largest country house I have ever seen. I forgot to ask the name. At another, my brother-in-law, Peter Thompson and I had ten people crammed into two large cars. We decided to have one last drink in an attractive part of Cartmel and joined a convivial group who turned out to be nine off-duty Lancashire policemen. When last orders came one of them said we will escort you off our patch and five motor cyclists went in front and four behind until we reached the Lancashire border. They peeled off in order each saluting and the last one shouted, 'Be careful, you are on your own now.' It could never happen today.

Before the Preston-Lancaster motorway was built by the family company with Leonard Fairclough as usual building the bridges, the journey to Cartmel took so long that we often stayed closer to the course, the first year choosing a large palatial hotel just outside Blackpool. We had an excellent dinner and I decided to order two bottles of vintage port. 'We don't get much demand these days,' said the head waiter; 'I'll go to the cellar and see what we have.' He returned with two cobwebby bottles and said, 'I don't know whether you can still drink these, they have been here forever so have them on the house.' They turned out to be two bottles of Taylor's 1927, probably the finest and most expensive port of the century.

The Preston to Lancaster section of the motorway was built in 1963-4 and transformed the journey. In 1964 we set off in two Bentleys, Johnny Phillipson the owner driver of the other one, driving along nearly twenty miles of uncompleted motorway. The tarmac had not been put on but the compacted stone had been made ready for it and the two cars sped at a hundred miles an hour with clouds of white dust floating behind. Jane my wife set off on the same journey on the Monday which as usual I couldn't make, only to be stopped by a member of the works management staff. 'What do you think you are doing?' 'I'm Mrs McAlpine,' she said, '... and I'm Jesus Christ' was the reply.

The winners continued to flow though sadly I was running a cricket match when I had a treble there on the Monday with Marieson, Decode and Ginger Nut, and the celebrations were left to Jane and Doug. Ginger Nut was a new edition to the host of fine horses. By a stallion called Red God, he had been bought to win mile-and-a-quarter races on the flat. His career actually finished by coming a close fifth in the Grand National. Roy Edwards who usually rode him had said he would either fall at the first or get round, but he was superbly ridden by Doug's stable jockey Jimmy Bourke. Brian Jenks had purchased a half share and said afterwards that if only Jimmy hadn't listened to Eddie Harty on Highland Wedding, who told him at the Canal Turn second time round he was going too fast, he might have won.

We gave Ginger Nut away to go hunting but he would not jump a twig. The National fences must have really scared him!

I continued to go to Cartmel through the seventies and early eighties though the winners dried up as did the champagne. Colonel Pain gave up, and though his son continued the family tradition we had to buy our own until after the last race. I do have memories of John Edwards, my next national hunt trainer there; the first not a happy one when he produced his new and extremely attractive assistant Venetia Williams to ride one of my few near certainties, five to two on in a novice hurdle. Venetia jumped the first hurdle ok but became unbalanced at the second and fell off about 30 yards after the hurdle. Nobody is a greater fan of Venetia as a trainer than myself but sometimes you do not have to be a good race rider to become a top class trainer.

The following year I had another very fancied horse and John announced he had engaged an Irish amateur and chartered a plane to fly him to the course – 'you had better have a large enough bet to cover the charter.' My fury was such that the teenage Irish amateur received a poor welcome but rode a perfect race and duly won. His name was Norman Williamson and it was to be the first of hundreds of winning rides in England for Norman who always rode for me whenever possible.

John like myself always regarded Cartmel as a great party and one year I arrived to find him red in the face and in great pain crippled with gout. He and his wife Gina had separated and he had arranged to meet three different ladies at various points on the course. 'Can you meet them and say what has happened?' he asked. Very leg weary by the end I managed to find the first two but the third was never located!

By the eighties I was going less and felt I should leave a memento so bought a large cup which was known for years as the McAlpine Cup. When Hugh Cavendish kindly asked me to lunch a few years ago I found that the motorway which had so improved the journey was now so clogged up that I was three-quarters of an hour late – much to the displeasure of my host. I was asked if I wished to present the cup which was being run on that day but felt that the race sponsor should do it. One thing that was still there was the fish tent run by some amazing fishmonger from Morecombe who supplied the best lobsters, crabs and oysters I have ever eaten. Amazingly neither Hugh nor any of his directors had ever been in it.

The sixties had been a decade of great success and enjoyment and whilst I had a number of good horses I had never had a top class one. That was to change when Rosemary Lomax bought me a yearling at one of the 1967 sales. I had asked her to buy me something fairly forward and was surprised to find myself the owner of a grey roan colt whose pedigree suggested he would need a distance. However we did run him as a two-year-old three times and he came third in the Fenwolf at Ascot only two lengths behind the winner Hotfoot. On his third run he plainly had the virus and ran badly. He had a very runny nose and now he would certainly have been scoped and diagnosed, but scoping was unheard of then and his jockey Billy Rickaby could only commiserate. Billy was a great hero of mine retained by Uncle Robin; he had ridden Zabara for him to win the 1000 Guineas and my great sadness was that he was retiring at the end of the 1968 season.

I had named the horse Precipice Wood after the famous stand at Llanarmon and he was showing enough promise at the start of his three-year-old career for us to think about the Derby and we ran him in a Derby trial at Goodwood only to be beaten half a length by an unknown filly. His new jockey was David Yates who had been a champion apprentice and was retained by Rosemary. David was a stylish, competent jockey whose nickname was 'Flapper'. Whether that came from his style of riding I don't know but Rosemary's head lad did say to her after the Goodwood race that a stronger jockey might suit him better. She did not pass this on immediately and we both assumed he was not up to Derby standard and ran him in a small race at Thirsk instead. He won this by so far that I began to wonder whether we had made the right decision and when 'the unknown filly' came up a close second in the Oaks having looked like winning until near the line, my concerns increased. I did not know that Blakeney who won the Derby the next day would finish behind Precipice Wood on the two occasions they met, but whether Epsom would have suited Precipice Wood is another matter never resolved.

His next race was the George V handicap at Royal Ascot, a three-year-old handicap over a mile and a half. For reasons I cannot remember Paul Cook rode him and had the race won coming into the straight. His winning margin of ten lengths could have doubled. One of his opponents was owned by a Cheshire worthy, Ralph Midwood, who told Evelyn Delves Broughton he was sure to beat mine because he was ahead of Precipice Wood in the race the year before when he had a virus.

Having cruised up twice running we were confident of winning the Geoffrey Freer stakes, a Group 2 race over a similar distance, one mile six furlongs, prior to the St Leger, our main target for the end of the season. I was again unable to see the race, not this time because of work but because I was captaining the Harrow Wanderers against the Eton Ramblers on Evelyn Rothschild's lovely ground at Wing, the scene of my first day's cricket after leaving Harrow. Although I could not be there I brought my portable television set and watched the race just before I was due to bat. Precipice looked to be going to win easily but got run out of it in the last fifty yards and my doubts about David Yates increased. To cap a bad day minutes after the race I was out first ball.

If I had concerns before the St. Leger, the race Yates rode at Doncaster finished the association for good. The horse got into all sorts of trouble on the final bend and after a barging match with Ernie Johnson on Blakeney we finished fourth. Blakeney was fifth. There was a stewards' enquiry and they took the view correctly I felt that the barging was fifty-fifty. In fact neither jockey covered themselves with glory and Gerry Oldham who won the race with Intermezzo told me later that if ever there was a classic he should not have won it was the 1969 St. Leger.

The 1970 season duly arrived and, although I had told Rosemary that I was insisting on a change of jockey, she started prevaricating. She was a wonderful trainer of horses and if she'd had better facilities and a more supportive husband she might have gone right to the top. She was one of the first female trainers to get a licence and I always felt that the way she had to beg for owners and spend hours with very moderate people trying to get them simply wore her out.

At any rate I got my way and Jimmy Lindley rode him in all his races as a four-year-old. His first race was the John Porter at Newbury and we were surprisingly beaten by Torpid who got first run in a slowly run race. However in the Paradise Stakes it was a different story. On another slowly run race we held on to beat High Line who turned out to be another great stayer. They finished miles clear of the third and Joe Mercer, High Line's jockey, had a large bet with me that positions would be reversed next time we met. Precipice Wood acted on fast ground but it was so hard at Newmarket, watering systems being in their infancy, that the leg trouble which was to finish his career two races later was now manifesting itself.

Rosemary had the desperate task of trying to get her star horse showing all signs of tendon strain to the Ascot Gold Cup in a summer of blazing hot weather with no suitable gallops of her own and some communal ones at Lambourn which were far from ideal either. Fortunately Derrick Candy came to the rescue and offered us the use of his gallops, easily the best in Lambourn at the time.

There was further drama in the paddock. Precipice looked magnificent and was perfectly calm until Jimmy got up when he suddenly reared up and unseated Jimmy and bolted out of the paddock towards the high street. All seemed lost but he was caught and returned to the paddock and very late they set out for the race. It transpired later that it was almost certainly a bee sting which caused the problem but it did not affect Precipice in the race. He travelled easily all the way, went to the top of the hill still going well and I was momentarily unsighted when the commentator Michael Seth-Smith who had become a good friend said, with a tremor in his voice, 'Precipice Wood has started his run and is going into the lead.' A tremendous battle developed with Blakeney and in a desperate finish on bone-hard ground we finished half a length to the good.

A tremendous cheer went up behind the winners' enclosure and with sweat pouring down my cheeks I greeted the winner and hugged Rosemary. It was a great moment for both of us. We were then told that the Queen would present us with the Gold Cup in the Royal Box and could Rosemary and I be there in ten minutes time.

In those days a group of us had a table in the Irish bar – the one place on the racecourse where the Royal Enclosure and Tattersalls members could meet, eat and drink together close to the paddock and the entrance to the Royal Enclosure. The head waiter was a good friend and seeing sweat still pouring off me he brought a damp cloth and he and Jane attempted to clean me up for the presentation.

The race itself had not been run on the traditional Thursday but on Saturday because the general election in which Edward Heath had defeated Harold Wilson had taken place on the Thursday. In addition to dealing with an incoming prime minister there had been a major late night party at Windsor on the Friday night. I have been presented to Her Majesty on four occasions since the race and have found her charming, animated, and on one, positively flowing with conversation. I have to say this presentation was different; she was obviously tired and, even with Nancy Westminster who knew me well beside her, the conversation was stilted. I felt for Rosemary who was, as the media pointed out the next day, the first lady trainer to gain a top Group 1 race.

Anyway we returned to the Irish bar where a celebration took place with friends arriving from all corners of the course. I have always felt that the closing down of the Irish bar to make way for the Ascot racing club was a major mistake. Sometimes those in charge in their lofty positions in the Royal Box really miss what makes the racecourse tick. The Irish bar was, to many of us, the most exciting bar on the course and was named because so many Irish visitors congregated there. No doubt the racecourse benefited from the large amounts they charged the elite who became members of the Ascot racing club but to shut down the only bar and restaurant where those not in the Royal Enclosure could meet their friends close to the paddock completely altered the character of that part of the course. The building of the new stand would, of course, have destroyed it anyway.

Precipice had after Ascot the choice of two races in August: the Goodwood Cup or the Prix Kergorlay at Deauville. Rosemary had no strong views and Jimmy Lindley was very anxious to go to Goodwood. 'It will be a stroll around Goodwood whereas Deauville is a greyhound track and French jockeys will do everything to block us,' he said. I was anxious to go to Deauville on the grounds that we had proved everything over a long distance and a win of a group 1 race over five furlongs shorter than the Gold Cup would help him when he went to stud. I got my way but Jimmy was proved right, except that we should still have won. It was another hot day and the course was half in the sun, half in shadow. Lester Piggott, on Reindeer trained by Vincent O'Brien, cleverly lost a couple of places on the bend to come in shadow on the stand side knowing his only chance of beating us was for him not to be seen coming. It worked brilliantly. Precipice, who pulled out everything when challenged, thought the race was won and Jimmy only realised the danger when it was too late.

Sadly it was to be his last race. The hard ground had taken its toll and we decided to retire him to stud. I kept six of the forty shares but the others were all taken up by several friends. Uncle Robin and Philip Leverhulme both took a share and we stood him at Emral near Bangor where the owners Pat and Jean Broad were close friends of Doug Francis. His stud career started well with five individual two-year-old winners, including one from a mare of Nick Robinson. He had several useful flat animals including one of mine, Preciptack, arguably the leading stayer of his year in South Africa. But his real success was as a national hunt stallion where he produced a number of really good horses including Cheltenham Gold Cup winner Forgive and Forget. I stupidly sent him for a year to Ireland where he picked up the 'bug' which eventually led to him being put down after his return to Emral. Six years after his death I collected a large silver cup at the TBA lunch for the second time for the leading British National Hunt stallion of the year.

Forgive and Forget was my worst ever disaster, in that I should have owned him. I had sent his mare, which I owned, to Precipice Wood and the first progeny, Precipienne, was trained by the Rimells, who did not think she was genuine. In addition I had sent Forgive and Forget's full brother to South Africa, where he had had a poor first season. I sold the mare for a few hundred pounds carrying Forgive and Forget and did not even get registered as the breeder, despite having arranged the mating. The full brother in South Africa, Preciptack, then became one of the best stayers in South Africa. So I asked Doug Francis to bid and get Forgive and Forget, who was coming up for sale at Doncaster. Doug got distracted and failed to be in the ring when Forgive and Forget was sold for four thousand pounds. I immediately rang Harry Beeby and offered the new buyer a substantial profit, but the horse had left for Ireland. A couple of years later the new owner had a substantial bet in a bumper, the horse duly won and was offered to me for twenty-five thousand. I told him in graphic detail what he could do with the twenty-five thousand and he then sold him for nearly forty thousand and the new owner was to win one Cheltenham Gold Cup and would almost certainly have won a second had the horse not slipped up. Not a happy story for me.

Before I leave the sixties I must refer to another flat trainer, Pat Rohan, and my growing friendship with Robert Sangster who I had met in 1965 and who was to have a major influence on my racing career.

Pat had married Mary Dutton who was Jack Bissell's niece, and Jack had horses first with Billy Dutton and then with Pat who started as assistant trainers and when Billy died inherited the yard and some good horses. Pat had a lot of ability, was very knowledgeable but to say he was highly strung would have been an understatement. He was a dedicated teetotaller and I often wondered whether a drink would have quietened him or sent him round the bend.

We had a few good horses together, in particular Stunog Wood and Oswestry Covert – two fast fillies named after Llanarmon woods. His retained jockey, Johnny Seagrave, was a competent rider if a little towards the veteran stage and he managed in Stunog Wood's first two-year-old race to get him left at the start at Aintree (starting stalls had not come in) at five to two on. Robert Sangster and I went up together for the next race at Ayr where for the first time I stayed and played golf at Turnberry. She opened at about five to four but to Robert's amazement he had two hefty bets without shortening the price. What the bookies obviously knew and we didn't was that Seagrave had flu and shouldn't have been riding. Nevertheless he steered the filly home and we collected some sizable winnings. Robert, who loved a tilt at the ring, could not believe how strong the market was at Ayr and we were to return often – not always with the same success.

Stunog Wood went on to win the Lilly Agnes at the Chester May meeting and should in my opinion have been second to Waterloo (she won by ten lengths) in the Queen Mary at Royal Ascot. Seagrave got her held in and although she was a fast finishing fourth, a more enterprising jockey might have achieved second without difficulty. It is I realise very easy to criticise jockeys, particularly those not in the top bracket. When I finally got a world class jockey, Steve Cauthen, to ride for me I was to realise the difference somebody right at the top makes.

Robert and I had gone racing together the Saturday following our first meeting when Jane and I went to dinner at Swettenham on National eve 1965. He had been introduced to racing by Nick Robinson and had two or three horses with Eric Cousins. One was called New Liskeard and Robert said he will probably win though very bad at the start. We concocted a plan on the way to Chepstow that Robert would go to where he could see the start and if the horse got away well he would lift both hands in the air and I would immediately get the money on. When I got to Chepstow I found that neither Laurie Wallis nor Ladbrokes were there and had to revert to my local bookie Sam Barnes of Crewe. Sam was a solid genuine likeable man but was not known for undue generosity over prices, and charismatic would not have been the first word to describe him. I started my dialogue two minutes before the off and had to continue for nine minutes before Robert's hands went in the air. Sam, who was getting increasingly suspicious, accepted the bet which was much larger than my norm and we started one of many celebrations on many racecourses. We also agreed to share a couple of horses together. Most of these were moderate but we did have one good one, Lord Henham bought out of Neville Callaghan's stable and sent to America.

To win the Hialeah Turf Cup had been a dream ever since I went there from Nassau where I was staying with my mother and stepfather. My mother knew Lady Barnsie Sasoon well and having discovered that Sam Armstrong, Lester and Susan Piggott and an old Harrovian friend Nick Robinson were all staying as her guests, mama got Jane and I invited to lunch. I did not have to wait long to see Lester's hatred of parting with money; although Barnsie Sasoon indulged them with every conceivable luxury, Susan asked him for $10 to go water skiing. 'Go half a mile up the beach and it's only $5,' was the answer she got! We all arranged to go to Hialeah the following Saturday and when we reached Miami Airport after the short journey from Nassau, Sam, Nick and I all took turns to buy a round of drinks. The girls decided they would like some coffee, so I whispered to Lester that this was a good opportunity for him to speak up; the look I got could be described as 'I thought you were an idiot, now I know you are one!'

Hialeah was a truly beautiful course, where the high spot was the flight of the flamingos, where midway through racing hundreds of pink flamingos took to the air. Because of Barnsie we were guests of the Chairman and I listened to talk of their biggest race, the Hialeah Turf Cup, run at the end of their season in March on turf over a mile and a half. Sixteen years later I was to be joint owner of the winner, though Lord Henham ran in Robert Sangster's colours and neither of us were there to see it.

The sixties had been successful years and whatever commentators say now, I am convinced that it was far cheaper to own horses and that competition was not as great. The Arabs have done a great deal for everybody in racing except other owners and increasingly those other owners are turning to National Hunt racing, where there is not an Arab in sight and the sport feels more like it was in yesteryear.

The seventies were disappointing for me. I did have one good horse, Coed Cochion, Precipice Wood's full brother, which I had bought very cheaply as he had a crooked leg, though that did not stop him racing for three full seasons. He was trained by Jeremy Hindley, one of two new flat trainers – Barry Hills being the other. Jeremy had been introduced to me by Robert who had a few horses with him.

Barry was a keen and I am told very competent rider to hounds and loved hunting with the top Leicestershire packs. It was there he met Penny, his second wife, equally proficient and infinitely better looking on a horse. The inevitable happened and romantically the liaison was consummated in full hunting kit at a disused railway station. I met Penny when I went to join Robert and Barry at a club called The Office. I had first been introduced to The Office by Christie Grimthorpe. It was primarily a drinking club though there were some attractive young ladies hanging around to give the club atmosphere, at least that was Christie's explanation. Not unnaturally, I had assumed that Penny was one of this group and had joined them for a drink. Nobody was more amazed than I was when I realised Barry and Penny were madly in love and she was indeed to become the most wonderful wife and mother any man could have.

Naturally the yard went through a period of disruption as Barry's first marriage ended and Penny moved in, but Barry's main owners soon warmed to Penny and their marriage became one of the strongest and most enduring on the racing circuit.

The second major event was the arrival of Steve Cauthen in 1979. Steve was only eighteen but had already been champion jockey in America and had won the Triple Crown on Affirmed. Robert Sangster had signed him up and organised for him to reside with Barry and ride his horses, and Jimmy Lindley who had retired was recruited as an adviser.

Barry had persuaded Ernie Johnson his former retained jockey to stay with the stable but the association was never going to last and from the moment Steve won on his first ride in England at Salisbury in March it was just a question of time. In fact Ernie Johnson was riding my sister Valerie's horse for Barry a month later. Before he dismounted he asked how Tap on Wood had got on in the 2000 Guineas. When he was told that Tap on Wood trained by Barry and ridden by Steve had won he went straight into the weighing room and wrote out a letter of resignation.

Tap on Wood was the start of a great era for Steve who went from strength to strength and I have no doubt that obtaining a world class jockey did Barry no end of good also, encouraging owners to send more horses and bringing new owners onboard.

Steve and I got on well from the first meeting and became really good friends. He had come from a country background around Kentucky and had reasonably well off parents who had brought him up sensibly. He mixed in straight away with Robert's group of friends like Charles Benson and myself and was soon staying with Angela and me at Swettenham. As soon as he heard about the family shoot at Llanarmon he wanted an invitation to the shoot and I will never forget his first appearance in late November at Llanarmon. It was the second major shoot of the season and we were gathered at the bar of the Hand Hotel, then owned by Father. 'Have you shot many pheasants, Steve?' asked Derek Boumphrey. 'Never shot one in my life, Sir,' he replied and I could see the old stagers round the bar thinking this is going to be a disaster. I need not have worried; put on the outside the first day he shot seven at the first stand and by the end of the second day was shooting as well as half the line.

He entered into every aspect of English life with enthusiasm and unfortunately that included the heavy partying that Robert and his friends enjoyed so much. Although Steve only really liked one drink – champagne – he did develop quite a taste for it and although he never got into trouble, there were a few worrying moments which I will come to.

More serious was the habit he'd got into, common to many American jockeys at the time, of vomiting food in order to keep weight down. In American jockeys' rooms they apparently had bowls especially for that purpose. It was in fact Angela who had been anorexic herself when younger who spotted the signs which Barry and I were oblivious to. At one dinner party at Swettenham I had promised him a gourmet dinner party with caviar, grouse and ice cream. He had two large portions of caviar, two grouse (one was extra in case one was not a young grouse) and three portions of ice cream, making visits to the downstairs loo between courses. Angela and I went to bed but Steve said he wanted to watch the late night film. We were drifting off to sleep when a great crash came from downstairs. 'That will be Steve at the fridge,' said Angela who went downstairs and found him with a bag of apples in one hand and biscuits in the other.

He was staying with us for Haydock races and I went to the office in the morning before turning up in good time to steward. I was not in the chair as it was John Derby's turn to be senior steward and sometime between the first two races there was a banging on the door of the stewards hut, elevated to watch the racing. The lady stipendiary went to the door and to my horror said, 'You can't come in here, Cauthen.' She came back and said to me, 'Cauthen insists on a word.' I went outside and hissed at Steve that he was completely out of order but he cheerfully said, 'Swinburn has a certainty at tonight's evening meeting, you should get on it.' When I got back, John Derby said, 'What was all that about, Bobby?' I replied, 'I have got some fishing for Cauthen to try this evening and he has lost my instructions as to how to get there.' 'Very good, Bobby, I like to see these jockeys taking to our country sports.' Needless to say the certainty was not in the first four that evening!

None of this seemed to affect his riding and I will always be immensely grateful that I was lucky enough to have one of the greatest jockeys the world has produced on one of my two group one winning horses.

Cormorant Wood was named not after one of the Llanarmon woods as I had run out of names for them, but some trees at Swetten-ham where a flock of cormorants (nearly eighty in all) had gathered. She was unfashionably bred by Home Guard, top class at 6 furlongs to a mile, out of Quarry Wood, who had won four races for me from a mile and a half to a mile and three-quarters. She would also have been fourth in the Chester Cup over two-and-a-quarter miles if Pat Rohan's apprentice had not dropped his hands.

The breeding was to be of great importance as Barry was convinced she would be a staying filly like her dam. She only had two races at two, winning the second over 7 furlongs at Leicester comfortably. Her three-year-old career started with a second in the Lingfield Oaks trial ridden by Steve. Although we were mildly disappointed at the time, in the light of subsequent events to finish second in the heavy going over a mile and a half in a group race was an incredible achievement.

The next race was the Oaks itself where Steve was committed to ride another of Barry's runners and the great Lester Piggott was obtained for mine. We appeared to be going as well as any until the last two furlongs and Lester finally dropped his hands a hundred yards out and we got beaten for fourth place, which was worth eight thousand pounds and some good black type for the stud book. I went out to greet the horse and Lester with my blood pressure close to the heavens. 'Couldn't you have been fourth, Lester?' 'You think I should have been fourth!' He then put his head back and bayed with laughter. Anyone who has seen Lester laughing (it can't happen very often) would enjoy the scene but I was furious and Nick Robinson made one of his more sensible remarks trying to soothe me to the effect that hav-ing an easy race might help her later on in the season. In fact far more serious was Lester telling Barry that Epsom didn't suit her instead of telling him that she didn't stay a mile-and-a-half.

As a result we ran her again over a mile-and-a-half in the Prince of Wales and again she failed to stay the trip.

The penny still hadn't dropped with either Barry or me but we decided to give her a break and have an autumn campaign.

Fortunately the first of her three races, the Virginia Stakes, a valu-able listed race at Newcastle in late August, was over a mile and a quarter. Barry and Steve came straight from America where they had a runner and continued up on a private flight picking me up on the way. I thought they both showed signs of wear and tear but the race went perfectly and we easily beat an odds-on highly rated favourite. Her next race, the Sun Chariot, was a Group 2 (now Group 1) fillies race at the Newmarket meeting before the Champion Stakes. Again with Steve on board we won comfortably and decided to go for the big one, the Champion Stakes a fortnight later.

The Champion Stakes was run on one of the windiest days I can remember. We flew down and had a terrifying landing on the Newmarket grass strip. In the race itself I can only echo *Racehorses of 1983*'s description. 'The winner Cormorant Wood produced a performance that had to be seen to be believed. With superb assistance from the in-form Cauthen she came from last to first in the final three furlongs squeezing past tightly compacted contestants, being buffeted by a gale force side wind she swept up the hill on the bridle and at the very last found enough room between Tolomeo and the only other filly Flame of Tara to lift the prize.'

Richard Baerlein wrote the next day, 'Steve Cauthen rode a miraculous race; of all his brilliant performances in the second half of the season none has equalled this stroke of genius.'

I had watched the race with Barry and Penny from the same position we watched all the races at Newmarket – on the steps at the bottom of the members stand close to the rails. We were behind the finishing post and nobody was certain we'd won. Everybody kept telling me there had been a lot of interference and a stewards' enquiry was called immediately. Steve said he had not interfered with any of the principals and it was the second, Tolomeo, who was controversially demoted.

We had a terrific celebration and Doug Francis who'd come with us drove us back from Manchester Airport to Swettenham. Doug's driving, never the greatest at the best of times, made the last miles nearly as hairy as the race itself.

We received an invitation to Washington for the Arlington Million for the great international race, knowing that the top French filly of the time All Along would also be running. I was so ecstatic that I readily acceded to Barry's suggestion that he, Penny and Steve should all go on Concorde at my expense and stay in the Washington Marriott, an excellent but expensive hotel.

Angela and I who had to dash from Sir Geoffrey Palmer's shoot in Leicestershire to catch the Concorde, a day later both had the beginnings of influenza and although the flight was wonderful we had to transfer airports in New York to go on Eastern Airlines to Washington. The airline managed to lose our luggage and it was an unhappy couple who finally made Washington quite late in the evening. We went straight to bed only to be woken at midnight to be told our luggage had arrived.

The next day we went to Arlington where all the runners were given individual stables with the national flag in the middle. Barry and I went across to the stables where Cormorant Wood looked fine and All Along to our surprise was being constantly walked around the stables.

The race itself was similar to the Oaks, we came into the straight full of running but her run petered out again in the final two furlongs and she finished sixth. A massive bill later arrived for flying the horse over and most of the Champion Stakes winnings had disappeared. A very expensive way of finding out finally that the horse didn't stay a yard further than a mile and a quarter!

At least we entered the 1984 season with that knowledge and her first run was in the Lockinge over a mile in which we dead heated with an Arab-owned horse of John Dunlop's – Wassl. Charles Benson who had a large bet on us managed to examine the photograph when it was first displayed and tried to persuade me to challenge the result, but I was happy to accept the dead heat. We again went for a mile at Royal Ascot but after looking the likely winner two out had to settle for third place. For the first time Steve said she didn't stride out on very firm ground and in her next race, the Eclipse, he was even more outspoken, 'She just won't have this ground.' Barry was also getting worried that so many races on firm ground were affecting her tendons.

I had sold a half share in her between Ascot and Sandown on the basis that there was only one English stallion – Mill Reef – I wanted to send her to and his stud fee was £100,000 even in those days. I still had her dam and two half-sisters. The deal was a complicated one in dollars with the purchaser having an option on the other half when she went to stud. After the Eclipse I was quite happy with the deal, little knowing that she would run the race of her life in the Benson and Hedges (now the Juddmonte) at the York August meeting. This was a top group one contest and Sadlers Wells who had won the Eclipse started favourite. We had walked the ground very carefully before deciding to run as we had vowed not to run her again on firm ground, but York unlike Sandown and Ascot had an efficient watering system and the ground had real cut in it. This was the first time since New-market the year before she had run on decent ground and she revelled on it. Sixth coming round the turn into the straight Steve again showed what a genius he was dropping her back two places so that he could get a clear run. At the three furlong mark she had the race won and when she burst clear two out, nothing was ever going to get near her. She beat Tolomeo by much further than in the Champion Stakes and Sadlers Wells was well behind. Her performance was also a great credit to Barry Hills who had managed to get her to the racecourse both fit and sound.

I had had what was in effect an insurance bet on her knowing that if she won the race I had sold her too cheaply and the TV recording, which I still have, shows John McCririck saying all the bookies are ecstatic except for poor Michael Simmonds who has laid a silly bet and the camera switches to Michael Simmonds of Heathorns literally tearing his hair out having accepting that it was an 'insurance' bet and laying me forty thousand to two, easily the largest amount I have ever won on a horse. The same video shows me being interviewed by Julian Wilson virtually standing on one leg as I had ruptured my Achilles tendon playing cricket – but it had not then been diagnosed.

The next day brought the sad news that the tendon had gone and she would not race again. The purchaser grabbed his option and I received a second cheque in dollars. Although I had sold her too cheaply and the purchaser sold her on to the Dubai ruling family I did get my dollars at 1.03 to the pound, probably the most favourable rate in my lifetime. She did produce one top class racehorse, Rockhopper who won seven group races though not a group one, but generally her stud career was rather disappointing.

Before leaving Cormorant Wood I should mention his unusual lad, a mature and most amusing character who worked for my company on the M4 motorway, driving a motorscraper. He adored the filly and always said how lucky he was to look after her, 'I have had three wives and not one of them was as faithful and affectionate as her.' When we won the Juddmonte, I gave him a large present, not in cash but in McAlpine shares, hoping he would save them for his retirement – but sadly he sold them soon afterwards and left Barry.

Although *Racehorses of 1984* had said her dam had produced little of any account, River Ceiriog by my stallion Broxted and out of Quarry Wood was to become a top class hurdler.

He was the next decent racehorse I had and Steve Cauthen who rode him in work at two always said he was potentially a group horse. He had quite a set-back with Barry and I took him out of training at three and eventually sent him to Nicky Henderson at the end of the year he was four.

His first two races failed to get him into the first three, though he showed some promise and I was determined he would run at Cheltenham. Nicky Henderson was less keen and felt we should go for easier pickings. In retrospect it was amazing he got into the race where all those entered ran. On the day I had a board meeting to attend at Hall Engineering, a public company run by a great friend Richard Hall. I was driven from the meeting in Stafford to Cheltenham and spent most of the journey buried in the form book and when I got to the racecourse and the Turf Club tent where I had arranged to meet up with Angela and Nicky Henderson, I suggested to the trainer that I should have a 'modest each way bet'. 'Save your money,' he said, 'and put it all on our certainty, Baby Sigh at Wolverhampton on Friday.' Earlier he had met Peter O'Sullivan who was commentating for BBC television. 'How do you pronounce this Welsh name?' said Sir Peter. 'You won't have to call him so don't worry,' was the trainer's response.

Not only did River Ceiriog win the race, the Supreme Novice Hurdle, he was one of the easiest winners I have ever had, clearly going far the best from halfway down the far side and he won as he liked. He was Nicky's first ever Cheltenham winner. The race, then sponsored by Waterford Glass, yielded me a magnificent great glass trophy plus sixty-nine separate tumblers and wine glasses. Both Nicky and I have our trophies in our dining rooms, his smaller one for the winning trainer being overshadowed by his three Champion Hurdle trophies also sponsored by Waterford.

The next race was the main novice hurdle at Aintree which both Nicky and Steve Smith Eccles, his rider, thought would be a formality. I was a little more nervous as the Aintree race was a quarter of a mile further than Cheltenham and I remembered only too well how quickly Cormorant Wood stopped once she got to the mile and a quarter mark. All my fears were borne out and although Steve partly blamed himself for being over confident, I still think stamina deficiency was to blame for our narrow defeat.

The race had one dramatic sequel. Steve, still furious after the unexpected reversal, went with his girlfriend Di Haine out to dinner and then stayed drinking while she went to bed. When he got to the hotel room he found himself locked out and went back to his car where he slept in the back until he woke up in the early hours and found himself being driven down the M6 motorway.

History does not relate who were the most shocked, the two burglars who immediately abandoned the car and fled or Steve who had to drive back to his Liverpool hotel. History does also not relate what sort of welcome he received from Di, but rather unwisely he could not resist spreading the story to some fellow jockeys and he was quickly approached by BBC television to whom he gave an interview. His only ride on the Friday was on the same Baby Sigh who had lost on the Friday of Cheltenham week at five to two on and rightly he considered that he had no chance and so would almost have a day off. However neither Nicky nor his owners who had the national favourite on the Saturday were at all pleased at the Thursday night revelry and it did not help that the national favourite fell early in the race.

It had always been expected that jockeys would drink on nights of festival meetings, their weight being the main deterrent to over indulgence, and celebration or in Steve's case drowning his sorrows was to some extent still expected. That was all to change when random breathaliser tests were introduced and jockeys had to be much more careful. In pre-war days it was apparently traditional for the Saturday night of the National meeting to be a great celebration for everyone involved, including the flat jockeys as then Aintree was a mixed meeting. I had heard the story of Tommy Weston returning to the Adelphi hotel much the worse for wear having picked up a lady on a tour of Liverpool clubs. 'How can you bring in such a doubtful lady,' said the night porter. 'Doubtful be dammed, she's the only certainty I've had in three days,' replied Weston.

It was perhaps fortunate that the breathaliser was not introduced for other professional sportsmen. The drinking bouts of Dennis Compton and Bill Edrich before and during test matches are stuff of cricket folklore, as is Colin Ingleby-Mackenzie's reply to an interviewer on television who asked him if he had firm disciplinary rules for the county team he captained, Hampshire. 'I certainly do,' said Colin with a straight face. 'I insist they have to be in bed before breakfast.'

The lifestyle of some professional footballers was notorious and I can personally attest to drinking with Robert Sangster and George Best in a Manchester nightclub frequented by the two of them. It didn't seem to affect Best's performance for Manchester United the following day and they were of course all superbly fit professional sportsmen. Nevertheless the public mood towards alcohol has changed and jockeys in particular have a duty to their colleagues.

Steve had a much happier ride on River Ceiriog in the Scottish Champion Hurdle when he led from start to finish, the first time he had been ridden that way and we all left the season full of optimism for the following one.

We chose Windsor for the opening race thinking that a valuable hurdle on an easy course would suit, but he finished a moderate third and we discovered the following day that he had a virus which was to put him out of action for most of the season. In the twenty plus years since, scoping horses before races has become routine but it wasn't in the eighties and many horses ran with the virus. This could do a lot of damage and I have always felt River Ceiriog was never quite as good afterwards. His last ever hurdle race was the Champion Hurdle in which he was Nicky's second string to See You Then who was attempting a hat trick for the stable. Nicky always said he was lucky to have River Ceiriog as he was the only horse good enough to do fast work regularly with the stable star. As Steve Smith Eccles was obviously going to ride See You Then I had to find another jockey and persuaded Nicky to engage Dermot Brown for him. Dermot had ridden my good hunter chaser Compton Lad which had been left to me by my Aunt Jackie Brutton, a great hunt enthusiast who bred hunter chasers at her Gloucestershire estate in Compton Abdale. Dermot had worked for the Dickenson family and rode as their amateur jockey, though he had turned professional by the time he rode River Ceiriog in the Champion Hurdle. He won a large number of races on Compton Lad including two four-mile hunter chases at Cheltenham at their May meeting. He did ride him when he fell in two rather more important races: the National Hunt Chase when he started favourite, and the Foxhunters where he was in the lead and travelling well when he fell three from home. I watched the race with Michael and Monica Dickenson in the weighing room where Michael seemed unduly nervous. The race following the Foxhunters was when he saddled the first five in the Gold Cup!

Although Dermot's career was to end in ignominy and disgrace as he got into the worst possible company, I have no ill feelings on the race he rode in the Champion Hurdle. He gave the horse every chance coming down the hill, led briefly at the second last and fell at the last where, had he stood up, he might have finished third and certainly fourth. I still believe he did not truly stay in the race won for the third time by See You Then and run at a furious pace, although his virus problem may have had an affect also. His tendons sadly were also causing problems and he had only one more race – in a chase where Steve rode him and made an amazing semi recovery before pulling up.

During this period I had two other good horses running in my colours although I only owned half of them. Rollahead was bought by Jeremy Hindley and I on one bright autumn morning at Newmarket. He was out of one of Bill Stirling's best bloodlines and we were very pleased with our purchase, celebrating with a late breakfast. We were joined by Micky Suffolk (Earl of) who claimed to be acting for Bill Stirling and pleaded for him to be allowed to buy a half share back. I had met Bill Stirling a few times in Africa as his construction company Stirling Astaldi was a competitor there and had found him pleasant company – so with some reluctance agreed to his request.

When Rollahead started racing Bill never once appeared although Micky was always present. Rollahead was a very fast two-year-old winning at the Chester May meeting and looking like easily winning the listed Woodcote Stakes at Epsom on Derby day. Ten lengths clear at the distance he got unbalanced down the hill and was caught on the line. We then went to Royal Ascot where despite getting loose at the start he was remounted and won the Windsor Castle comfortably. For the first time I noticed that a couple of the group surrounding Micky were taking more than a usual interest in a particular William Pigott Brown who, fresh faced after leaving Eton, I had taken around the big fences at Aintree before racing started. Rollahead's final race for me was in a Group 2 when he came second but Joe Mercer who rode him in all his races whispered in my ear, 'He should have won governor, he's getting clever.'

I told Jeremy I thought we should sell him at the end of the season and we agreed that the Royal Lodge would be his last race for us. Micky had to be told what was afoot and came back with an offer from some character in Yorkshire nobody had ever heard of. I had to go into hospital with a severe attack of my skin problem psoriasis and was lying comfortably in a Westminster hospital bed when a nurse ushered Micky in. The nurses were usually very careful as I was not supposed to have many visitors but I then looked at his cream silk shirt with coronets emblazoned on it and could see that being the Earl of Suffolk did have its advantages. He waved a cheque in front of me and continued his sob story of the character from Yorkshire having set his heart on his first racehorse, etc.

In my weakened state I was not up to arguing and accepted the cheque although Charles Benson had warned me there was trickery afoot. The character from Yorkshire turned out to be a combination of William Pigott Brown and Robert Sangster. Although both Charles and Jeremy were two of Robert's greatest friends they were both furious with him. The syndicate was to benefit little from the deception. William Pigott Brown persuaded his new partners to send him to South Africa where he accomplished little and finished up as a minor stallion in Zimbabwe. William became a friend when I started to visit Cape Town regularly and Micky's first wife Anita, a most beautiful Swedish lady, remains a good friend today. Indeed her second husband Lord Petersham (now Earl of Harrington) bought two horses off me; one a quite useful half-brother to Inglis Drever.

My last good flat horse was called Free Sweater and was owned jointly by Jeremy Hindley and myself and trained by Barry as Jeremy had recently given up training. We named the horse because we were both prolific sweaters. He showed considerable promise in three runs at two when close up in the Champagne Stakes and fourth in the Beresford Stakes in Ireland and achieved a Timeform rating of over a hundred without having been in the first three.

Our first race at three was the group three Dee Stakes which he won reasonably convincingly and we decided to go for the big one, the Italian Derby. I had managed to combine the race with a business trip to Egypt where we were looking hard for construction work. I have only made three such trips to Egypt but each time I have succumbed to the local bug accurately named Gypy Tummy. I got the Air Italia flight to Rome and stationing myself at the front of the plane I intended to lead the queue to the loo as soon as the seatbelt sign came on. To my surprise I was not only beaten to it by three passengers but both the pilot and co-pilot arrived at the front (separately) and I began to realise that half the plane was in the same predicament. Fortunately Cairo to Rome is a fairly short hop and I got to Rome safely and went to an excellent hotel Rocco Forte had sent me to. A light supper in my room and an early bed at least got me still upright the following day and Angela who'd flown over with Barry and Penny arrived and we all headed for the racecourse. It was one of the hottest days I can ever remember racing and it was fortunate I'd got the hotel to press a tropical suit I had taken to Egypt. The horse seemed fine in the paddock and just before the race started Barry said, 'You will never regret turning down that offer.' The offer being £250,000 from an Italian, desperate to have a runner. Seven minutes later I have never regretted anything more. He went into the lead probably too early and was well beaten some way from home. He ran badly in England in a couple more races but did come good at the last Ascot flat meeting, coming second in the big handicap the Festival of Britain Stakes. He was sold for a six-figure sum just over half what Jeremy and I would have got if we had accepted the Italian's offer.

As we entered the nineties nothing seemed to have changed; I still had six or seven decent mares including several relations to Cormorant Wood. We had a number of minor winners, one winning five races but nothing on the flat nearly as good as those previously mentioned. It was left to one colt, the best in looks and confirmation I have ever produced, to keep the flag flying in the twenty-first century – though sadly not in my ownership.

Inglis Drever was not named by me and I sold an unnamed colt at the Newmarket October sales on the final Saturday morning. He fetched easily the highest price of the morning, £130,000, and Richard Aston, now boarding all my mares and young stock, and I were reasonably pleased. His new owner, Piers Pottinger, sent him to Mark Prescott who aimed him at one specific race, the Tote Ebor, but unfortunately got him so well handicapped he failed to get in the race by a pound. Had I raced him myself I would have targeted him as he got older and stronger for the top staying races and I am sure he would have made his mark.

Poor Piers got a lousy deal. Intending to send him to Nicky Henderson to go hurdling he was talked out of it on veterinary advice and the horse went up for sale fetching 91,000 gns. Howard Johnson, a Northern trainer with one very rich client, bought him for the Wylies to join a large number in the same ownership.

Inglis Drever was to turn out the outstanding staying hurdler of the new century's first decade, although Big Bucks must be equally good – if not better. His three world hurdles were a record and his winnings of over £800,000 in a single season, which included a £200,000 bonus for the largest number of points for any national hunt horse that year, was another national hunt record. Although the vets predicted an early break down he had won two world hurdles before he did break down on atrocious ground at Chepstow, having been re-routed from a cancelled meeting.

The third world hurdle was a very festive occasion and I persuaded Sam Vestey, always a generous host, to open several bottles of champagne where all three of us who had owned him and a number of other well wishers toasted him. I pleaded with Howard Johnson and the Wylies to retire him but they wanted one more race at Aintree – a track far too sharp for him and a distance half a mile less than Cheltenham. He did run one memorable race there after his first world hurdle, with no pacemaker he led from start to finish only to be caught on the line.

I was to have one top-class hurdler, in the first decade of the new century. Patricia Wilkins, who had been a good friend since the early days in Cheshire, persuaded me to buy a half share in a mare called, Elaine Tully, who had won seven races on the flat and over hurdles and was by a sire, Persian Bold, I had always admired. She proved to be a great bargain as all her first seven runners won and two gained black type. We tended to sell the colts but I would buy out Trisha's share of the fillies and two of the three I raced myself turned out to be more than useful. The first sadly broke down after winning a ten thousand pound hurdle on hard ground (given as Good to Firm) at Hexham. The second, One Gulp, got better and better and won her last two races, the second a good listed hurdle at Kempton. This was the second piece of 'Black Type' she picked up and her trainer, Paul Webber, was convinced we were heading for the very top. Sadly she was to break down in the Long Walk Hurdle at Ascot, when lying second and although a mile from home her jockey, Dominic Elsworth, said she gave him the best feel she had ever done. She had never showed any leg problems at home, there was nothing wrong with the going but her tendon break was so bad there was no question of racing her again. She does now have a two-year-old by Kayf Tara, a yearling by Yates and a foal by Presenting. So there are still animals to really look forward to. Sadly though the economics of breeding horses are also changing, I was getting so little for my sales of flat horses that I gave my last two flat mares, both winners, away. The last horse we sold, out of Elaine Tully, fetched sixty-six thousand euros at the sale. When I did my sums, Patricia and I had just about broken even, so heaven help the owners of the five hundred and eighty horses sold at a lower price.

I am very proud to have bred, from a handful of mares, Cormorant Wood and Inglis Drever, both utterly different horses but both quite outstanding in their different spheres.

Chapter 10

Stewarding, Racecourse Management and the Jockey Club

I already described my early stewarding experiences but as I was a racecourse steward for over forty years, I saw some very changing times and not in my view all for the better either. The Jockey Club may have been criticised for being backward and amateurish but there was nothing either backward or amateurish in the way they reacted to changing times and constant media criticism. I have nothing but praise for the tremendous efforts put in by unpaid people motivated by their love of the sport they were supporting.

I stewarded at five different racecourses and a few times at Newmarket. In the order I joined, at Wolverhampton, Bangor, Chester, Haydock and Aintree. In all the years on those five courses I can only remember one decision I felt we got wrong and another I thought we might have got wrong, both at Haydock. There was of course also the traumatic occasion at Chester, the first time I had ever been in the chair at a big meeting.

What I will call the 'Shellshock' enquiry has haunted me all through my stewarding career. It was early on in my friendship with Robert Sangster, who had a large house party at Swettenham for the May Chester festival, and as Jane and I had gone to dinner there the night before, I knew that his filly, Shellshock, was very fancied for the Dee Stakes the next day. I was in the chair for the first time as a steward at a big meeting and was naturally nervous. My nervousness reached boiling point when, in a tight finish, Shellshock was beaten by a whisker by a horse ridden by Geoff Lewis, who veered sharply and appeared to carry Shellshock sharply right. The stewards enquiry bell went and I went across to the weighing room to see Tim Kitson and Robert Sangster close to the winners enclosure, and Tim, staring straight at me, said, 'You are certain to get the race, Robert.' We duly ran the film showing clearly that Geoff's horse had veered sharply off a straight line (he had in fact cracked a bone in his foreleg) and the filly thinking she was going to be cannoned into, took evasive action and cowered close to the stand rails. The one major problem was that the horses never actually touched and when the two jockeys were asked for their explanations Geoff Lewis made full use of this, 'Yes my horse did drift a little bit but it was fast going and we never stopped Eddery riding' (there were no Mr's in those days). Unfortunately, too, Pat Eddery was very different from the top-class jockey he was to become. Just over from South Africa, he appeared shy and nervous, and allowed Geoff Lewis to dominate the discussion. Again, in those days, enquiries were conducted quite differently to the present day or indeed most years since. There were five people in the room, the three stewards being myself, Pat Smyly, who ran the Westminster stud and Guy Lowther, the present Bangor on Dee chairman's father. The other two were the senior Jockey Club stipendiary stewards, Mr Christian and Charles Toller, the long standing Clerk of the Course. Pat Smyly was the first to speak, 'There is no doubt in my mind that the result should stand, I can see no interference.' Mr Christian then said much the same and there was some muttering about betting money and Charles Toller, who had no right to speak, waded in and fundamentally supported the other two. Only Lowther, the least experienced in the room (apart from me), said he felt the result should be changed.

I was in a nightmare situation, although I agreed with Lowther, to have three experienced and much older hands than me so adamant they were right was truly frightening. In desperation I had the film played again and pointed out that Geoff Lewis had not just drifted but had veered really sharply. The three were having none of it and I could see just how it was going to be played politically. Only three of us had a vote and mine was the decider as Lowther and Smyly cancelled each other out. If I sided with Lowther I would be accused of gross favouritism with Robert and probably of having a large bet as well (which I hadn't). In fact if I had ever thought of have a bet when stewarding, that enquiry finished it forever. In the end I gave my vote to let the result stand and felt a total coward. Politically I was vindicated. Philip Leverhulme congratulated me and the fall out was purely from the Sangster camp, not helped by Lester Piggott, who I had earlier fined £10 for a frivolous objection, telling Robert it was the worst decision he had ever seen. Charles Benson said much the same in his book but in both cases betting money did influence their views. Strangely enough viewing the same scenario, nearly fifty years later, would the stewards have reached a different conclusion? Nowadays it seems to me they bend over backwards to let the winner keep the race unless there is blatant interference, which clearly affects the result. The jury may still be out!

I still think stewarding is largely a matter of concentration and common sense and I suppose the ability to react in unexpected and difficult situations. Although I enjoyed it immensely to start with, in the end I got bored because so much was dull and routine.

The chairman of the panel has considerably more to worry about than his colleagues. One of the saddest examples came at the jockeys strike at Haydock. Charles Weatherby was probably the least experienced of the panel despite his famous name; Victor Gubbins and I had done a great deal more stewarding. The jockeys had come to Haydock determined to see racing abandoned, as they had raced on very dubious ground ten days earlier. One or two, who had come by plane, told the pilot to get ready for a quick take off again. Even though there had been an inspection, the jockeys made it clear they did not want to ride and we were all summoned outside. Charles was buttonholed by Philip Arkwright, the Clerk of the Course, and was convinced that the course was raceable. I took longer to make up my mind with both the Hills twins, who I knew well, trying to get me to say it was unsuitable. They pointed to a piece of ground. 'It seems alright to me,' I said. 'No, I meant that piece,' said one of the twins, pointing to another bit of ground. Again I said, 'I think you are exaggerating it all,' and came to the conclusion that the course was raceable. We had a discussion and all agreed to go ahead. The two stipendiaries were now under a major time constraint with the first race going off late anyway. I did say, 'Shouldn't we have the jockeys back in?' but the stipendiaries said we haven't time and dashed outside to tell the jockeys, who refused to ride and the meeting was abandoned.

The enquiry took months and unfortunately the verbal comments in the room were not recorded. The jockeys were exonerated on the technical grounds that they had not been given a chance to query the stewards' decision and the stipendiaries were rightly admonished and disciplined. Poor Charles took the brunt from our side and never chaired a panel again. He should of course have stood up to the stipendiaries and insisted on recalling the jockeys. Would Victor or I have done so had we been in his place? History will never relate.

Although I had many difficult enquiries as chairman of various panels I never had a worse one than the 'Shellshock' Chester enquiry.

A year or two later we overruled an objection by Peter Walwyn and Willie Carson and they appealed. For the appeal, the first I had to go to being at Newbury; I had no real worries, for the film was totally clear and I had read the rule book until I was blue in the face. Unfortunately when we got to Newbury things were quite different. The film, clear at Chester, had become fuzzy and Willie Carson, one of the best talkers in the business, outscored his opposite number. I feared the worst but the decision went rightly in our favour.

I was involved in three difficult cases at Haydock. In the first David Wilson was chairman of the panel and George Owen and I were the other two. George had retired from training and was the most lovely, gentle man who had been pushed into the Haydock panel in answer to media criticism that there were too few former trainers. Many trainers would make excellent stewards but George was not one of them, being far too nice and indecisive. David Wilson the chairman of the panel was also a nice enough man but took his position very seriously, far too seriously I felt. The enquiry was for interference which I felt was marginal but he persuaded George to agree with him. I had argued to let the result stand but David said we have a majority anyway, it would be much better if we were unanimous and stupidly I went with that. I knew Willy Carson, the jockey involved, would insist on an appeal and sure enough David had to represent us and come back with his tail between his legs, having lost comprehensively.

The second major enquiry was in the major sprint race of the season, when we disqualified a horse trained by Nora Macauley, a small but popular woman trainer. It was a very complicated enquiry with three horses involved and a rough finish, with the second, who was awarded the race, going for the gap on the stand rails. We were convinced that the first had definitely interfered with the second and much hinged on the evidence of the third jockey, whose testimony supported this.

The media made a real meal of it and, poor Mrs Macauley being unfairly deprived of a big winner, was the common theme. At the enquiry the Macauley team had a very experienced solicitor called Richardson and the Jockey Club's appeal panel was headed by Michael Wrigley, the father of the current Senior Steward. I had done a lot of preparation for what I knew would be a difficult situation and as a 'frustrated barrister' (I had wanted to become either a barrister or a journalist, if I had not had to join the family company) here was my opportunity to conduct a case. Things were going fairly even-ly with the jockeys on the first two completely disagreeing with each other, but when the jockey of the third started to give evidence it was obvious he was going to retract his original statement. I intervened and said to him, 'I am reading you your original statement at the racecourse, are you saying you were lying?' That completely shut him up and he didn't continue his retraction. Our decision was upheld and I was asked to stay behind and Michael Wrigley said, 'We would really like to congratulate you on the way you have handled a really difficult case.' Probably my finest hour as a steward!

The third enquiry was into Haydock's major race of the year, then the Swettenham Stakes, a group sprint race, sponsored by Robert Sangster's stud and won by his runner – although he was elsewhere. For some time I had privately decided never to get involved in a major enquiry concerning my old friend and when Lester Piggott, in a come-back season, objected to the first and second, I got up from my position in the chair and said I think I should stand down. The stipendiary put his hands on my shoulders and said, 'You stay just where you are,' and whispered in my ear the others are too inexperi-enced.

Knowing that Robert's mother, Peggy, was going to present the cup in Robert's absence to his trainer and immediately grasping the furore should the enquiry not go the winner's way, I remained in the chair with some reluctance.

We had the jockeys in and all seemed to go well. Brent Thompson was on board the horse and had been encouraged over from Aus-tralia, where he had been very successful, by Robert. Although no Steve Cauthen he was competent enough, though not the strongest in a tight finish. He stated that he had done nothing wrong and was strongly supported by Walter Swinburn, both jockeys well aware that Lester was trying to gain at least one place on them. Lester then made his usual enigmatic statement that he had been 'lent on' by both and we then played the film. This showed that Lester had not been remotely interfered with but there was no question that right on the line Brent Thompson had 'lent on' Swinburn.

Having seen the film Walter Swinburn began to change his story but before he could get more than a sentence out I stopped him and asked the stenographer to read his original statement. Using the same tactics as in the McCauley case I said, 'Are you now saying you were untruthful originally, Mr Swinburn?' 'No, Sir, but the film does raise some questions.' One that came immediately into play was where the line was. The grass had not been mown and the actual finish was far from clear and the interference was either just before or after the line.

Privately I had little doubt that Brent Thompson had 'lent on' Walter Swinburn and that it was almost certainly just before the finish and had either of the other sitting stewards felt the same I would have to agree with them. I turned to both and in order asked them for their opinion and both said they thought the result should stand. In that case gentlemen, I said, you don't need my view.

I rang Robert that night to tell him we were now even after all those years since the Shellshock enquiry, but he showed little interest. Evading the wrath of Peggy, an extremely formidable lady, was another matter altogether and I slept well that night.

The only other enquiry which sticks in my memory was one at Newmarket. For a few years I was chosen to chair a minor two-day meeting, as the Jockey Club wanted a member to be in the chair, not trusting the local stewards who seemed very competent to do it. Nothing untoward had happened but in my last year there they put on an amateur race which was contested by several well-known amateurs including Julie Cecil, Henry's then wife, and Eve Johnson Houghton. Julie Cecil and Willy Bissell, the nephew of Jack Bissell, got into a major barging match in the last two furlongs, neither keeping their horses straight, and Eve Johnson Houghton won the race narrowly.

As I went into the steward's room I remember Tommy Pilkington saying, 'I don't envy you this one,' and sure enough the film showed both amateurs totally incapable of controlling their horses, though it was difficult to say one was more to blame than the other. Julie Cecil took control when it came to the enquiry, smiling sweetly as she said, 'We didn't really do each other any damage did we, Willy?' Who just nodded.

When we conferred the stipendiary said if they were professional I would expect you to ban them both for up to fourteen days but, addressing me, if you can deliver a really major rocket, I will abide by that.

We had both jockeys back in and I started by saying that was a quite disgraceful piece of riding by both of you, when I caught sight of Julie's face and thought any moment she's coming across the table to attack me. I mumbled the rest of the rocket and they left the room, Julie turning around to glare hard at me. When I got back to Jeremy

Hindley, who I was staying with, he was convulsed with laughter and said he'd had a phone call from Julie Cecil who said if I was to go near their yard she'd put their pack of Alsatians on to me. Needless to say Julie and I had a good laugh about it sometime later.

Whilst most days stewarding followed a predictable pattern, there were some exceptions. One day at Haydock I was in the chair and arrived early to walk the course, to be told that there was a major problem with the first race, which was a charity contest between Sir Hugh Fraser and Clement Freud – part of a series of charity matches which were all being televised. Hugh Fraser had set off from Scotland in a chartered plane but the pilot had refused to land at Haydock and went to Manchester airport instead, which meant that the race took place over half an hour later, with major alterations to the television, etc. Having landed several times at Haydock myself, in chartered planes, the first thing I did was ring up and find out the cloud ceiling at Haydock, which at 900ft. should have been above the limit for any professional pilot. Sir Hugh not only lost the race but had to face a steward's inquiry and when he came in it was obvious he expected the result to be a formality, as he said that the pilot was unable to land because of poor weather. When I pointed out that the cloud ceiling was at least 300ft above anything that should cause professional pilot problems, he looked extremely surprised and, when I told him we were fining him £100, surprise turned to anger. The following day I was told that he had concluded a deal to buy Logan Airlines, which was the charter company flying him, so that he could sack the pilot concerned. There was a further sequel when years later I went to a health farm and I found myself in a sauna with Clement Freud; he started to discuss racing and told me that his televised victory over Hugh Fraser was the highlight of his racing career. I had great delight in telling him about the scene in the stewards room, which he knew nothing about despite the fact that he was writing newspaper columns at the time.

Another memorable incident came at a stewards' seminar; these were started halfway through my tenure to educate stewards and particularly to try and get some uniformity in decisions. They were in fact very worthwhile though the oldest of us tended to regard them as a bit of a nuisance. We had had an uneventful morning and were given an hour off for lunch and allowed a couple of glasses of mediocre wine. Feeling relaxed, I settled down to listen to the senior stipendiary, who announced he had two non-trier incidents for us.

The first was an easy one with a northern jockey going up and down on a horse and not doing a 'tap' but the second woke me up altogether as it was a horse owned by a friend of mine in Cheshire who I had introduced to racing and encouraged him to have horses with John Edwards, my National Hunt trainer.

My friend for some unknown reason had decided his horse, at Cheltenham, at the start of the season, should have an easy race. John Edwards was away in Spain on holiday and it was down to his assistant Venetia Williams to give the retained jockey, Tom Morgan, the riding instructions. Unfortunately Venetia had a bad fall and was taken to hospital so it was left solely to my friend to give the instructions. What was said I do not know but I am sure had Venetia been there they would have been more sensible.

The film started and about halfway through the stipendiary stopped it and said now you see Morgan has the horse nicely buried, why does he now come out – and I instinctively said the owners spent all winter wondering just that. Luckily someone behind me punched me on the back and said for God's sake shut up.

The rest of the film showed the horse full of running getting closer and a desperate Tom Morgan trying to bury it again behind two others before finishing a close second. An enquiry was inevitable but with no stable representative to interview the local stewards had to rely on Tom Morgan who apparently lapsed into 'broad Irish' and they eventually gave up and recorded his explanation. Very lucky for all concerned.

The inevitable happened and my friend had a large bet next time when the horse was comprehensively beaten.

If by the end I found stewarding unrewarding, the same could not be said about racecourse management, which I enjoyed enormously.

I first became a racecourse director at Bangor on Dee in the early sixties. For those who do not know it, Bangor is a delightful rural National Hunt course with a marvellous viewing area and no stand. Racegoers simply stand at the top of a bank and get an excellent view of the racing. Facilities were at a minimum and the lavatories were primitive.

The early board meetings were all about survival; without the Levy help that the industry has now, the course was barely profitable and badly needed capital expenditure. My co directors included Philip Leverhulme, one of the richest men in the country, Lord Kenyon and

Ryd Middleton, the owner of Chirk Castle, so I was a little surprised, to put it mildly, that such powerful local worthies could even contemplate the collapse of such a popular local venue.

I always felt that Philip Leverhulme, who did a wonderful job at Chester, never really saw Bangor as other than a minor inconvenience. He had so much on his plate elsewhere that Bangor seemed to rate well down a large list of priorities. He did try and bring in the Haydock management to improve things but they too regarded Bangor as very secondary to managing Haydock and the fee Bangor had to pay did not help the finances.

Another factor which caused tremendous problems was the attitude of the local farmer, Mr Done, who farmed both the land inside and outside the course. The course was actually owned by Sarah Rosselli, who sadly died at quite a young age, and her husband Peter became the senior trustee of the trust administrating the estate.

Peter was a good friend to all of us but he never seemed to find it easy adjudicating the differences between Done and the racecourse. Done may have had reasons for his awkwardness but he was known to us as the 'farmer from hell'. Whilst Philip Leverhulme was chairman there was an uneasy peace but when Philip gave up and Malise Nicolson became chairman, we felt the full brunt of Done's antagonism.

Malise was a competent businessman who had a very senior position in the Port of Liverpool company and was ideally suited to chair Bangor. Indeed under his chairmanship the fortunes of the racecourse improved considerably. A capital expenditure programme was started and my company was given the contract to increase the restaurant, refurbish the bars and eventually build a new weighing room. I was very concerned that the development which generated the new revenue to the racecourse was over the top but could not have been more wrong and when in my own time as chairman the saddling boxes and Nicolson building, comprising a new Owners and Trainers bar and a much nicer restaurant with views of the paddock were added, the development of the course was complete. As Venetia Williams said to me, 'I can now persuade my smartest owners to come and see their horses run knowing they will have an enjoyable day; I couldn't say that previously.'

I should say that, just before or during the first year of Malise's chairmanship, shares had been issued for the first time and locals were invited to purchase a maximum of two shares at five hundred pounds a share. This brought much needed capital to finance the reconstruction programme. Nobody expected to collect anything from the shares and the purchase was regarded as a generous philanthropic gesture from lovers of the unique racecourse.

I had joined Chester racecourse as a director the year after a fire had burned down the whole of the members stand. Regarded as a disaster at the time and almost certainly the result of arson, the fire turned out to be the best thing that had ever happened at Chester racecourse. With the insurance money we were able to build a much needed new stand, extremely well designed by a local architect, Duncan Boddington, a member of a well-known brewing family.

The stand immediately brought resurgence in attendance and with the expansion of the racing programme, the courses finances began to improve.

Philip Leverhulme told a wonderful story about the abandonment of racing in 1969 when part of the course was waterlogged from overspill from the River Dee, which is tidal along the course. The loss of revenue had almost bankrupted the course and he went with his then chairman, Lord Sefton, cap in hand to meet Lord Wigg, chairman of the Levy Board.

Lord Wigg started the meeting with a long lecture on the inability of the Chester Board to anticipate a financial catastrophe and to provide a financial cushion for the abandonment. Eventually he paused for breath and Hugh Sefton said, 'Wigg, you are talking about finance. I have been very fortunate to inherit an enormous estate and not have to worry about finance at any stage of my life and I certainly am not starting to worry now.' Philip told me, if the ground could have swallowed him up he would have welcomed it and Sefton's outburst nearly finished off the course, as there was certainly no help forthcoming from the Levy Board.

I enjoyed serving under Philip and admired him greatly. He was slightly feudal in outlook and did regard his shareholders as privileged to be there at all. At the Annual General Meeting virtually nobody dared ask any serious questions though one local worthy, Keith Rae, did two or three times suggest that a dividend be paid – only to be severely put down by Philip. He ran the course through a general manager who had risen through the ranks and thought the world of Philip.

By 1993 it was obvious that both Chester and Bangor would shortly have a new chairman. Bangor, because sadly Malise Nicolson had contracted the illness which was to end his life, and Chester because Philip, approaching seventy-five, was increasingly finding it impossible to get around with chronic arthritis.

I did not expect to get, nor particularly want, the chairmanship of Bangor but Chester was a different story, particularly as my retirement from the family company was scheduled for the following year. There were only two candidates for Bangor, myself and John Barlow, who I knew was favoured by Malise and the big question at Chester was whether Philip would leapfrog me over the heads of two older directors who had been there a lot longer. John Barlow and I had been friends since our preparatory school days together and we were able to talk over the situation without embarrassment. John offered to go and see Philip and try and get an idea of his intentions re successors at Chester and came back with a strong inclination that I was favoured to be his successor.

The Bangor succession came first and to my amazement John Barlow suddenly announced he was unable to take it on. The reason became evident later when he split up with his wife Susan and kept a low profile. So I was duly elected chairman and a little later Philip asked me to succeed him at Chester and I found myself at the head of two racecourses. I had agreed to join Peter Daresbury's board at Aintree some time earlier and was involved in Aintree's great revival. So my life had changed from construction to racecourse management.

At Bangor we continued to have to deal with our 'farmer from hell'. By far the worst effect of his actions on us was to effectively stop us from gathering any of the new summer fixtures, which were being issued as Summer National Hunt racing was being promoted. Under the terms of his agreement with the landlord we were rationed to the fixtures we already had and any further fixtures were only possible if agreed compensation was paid. Done's terms were so high that it was impossible to expand the fixtures.

He had decided to grow maize, as he was entitled to, on the inside of the track. This grew to such a height that by late summer it was impossible to see the far side of the course and only when the big screens came into existence were the public able to see racing there.

About four years after I became chairman our general manager abruptly resigned and a new one had to be appointed. I interviewed several unsatisfactory candidates when Michael Webster, who had been in that position at Sandown Park, let it be known that he was interested. His problem was that he lived in Hampshire but he agreed to take the position and promised to find a house and move his family within six months. Although he found it impossible to honour that part of the agreement and did not get a second local course as he had hoped, he did dramatically improve the fortunes of Bangor and certainly opened my eyes as to what could be done when a competent professional took charge.

At Chester I had succeeded an immensely popular and respected local legend and nobody was more aware of this than myself. My general manager Ray Wall had risen through the ranks and worshipped Philip. Although I had a satisfactory relationship it was never going to be more than that and I tried to strengthen the management by bringing in Charles Barnett, the Chief Executive of Aintree, as a consultant.

Nor did I have an easy ride with a few difficult shareholders, who, frustrated at not daring to take on Philip, now emerged from the woodwork. One particularly unpleasant one who had gone to live in the south wrote me a string of vitriolic letters which only stopped when I told him the next one from my side would be from my solicitor.

The management consultancy did not really work but it was Charles Barnett who did me a very great favour by pointing out the solution. He told me that I should approach the general manager at Haydock Park, Richard Thomas, who he said was frustrated by Jockey Club controls and would prefer a more independent situation.

Richard accepted my offer which made me very unpopular at Haydock for a while, though I am happy to say we are all the best of friends again. From the moment he arrived at Chester the performance of the race company began to improve dramatically, as it has to the present day. Richard is simply the best manager I have ever come across and would have gone to the top of whatever sphere he decided to make a living in. Indeed he has been a friend of Alec Ferguson, who knows a good man when he sees one, and I often wonder what Richard would have earned if he had taken an executive role in a major football club!

My role as chairman became much easier and was mainly to put a brake on the few wilder ideas and encourage the many very good ones. The first things to be done were to expand the bars and restaurants in the centre of the course and encourage racegoers to spend a lot more money. We also went as upmarket as we dared and were surprised at the demand for champagne, which we now sell massive amounts of. A strong marketing campaign was embarked on with a Roman day (it is amazing how many professional 'Romans' there are) and our first Sunday fixture, which attracted an enormous crowd of over fifty thousand with the car park closed an hour before the first race – the first time this had happened since the resumption of racing in 1946.

The course was not neglected either with an extensive drainage system which was so effective that when racing was nearly abandoned one Friday night, trainers started withdrawing their horses on the Saturday only to find that the ground dried so quickly and because we were able to open up a strip of fresh ground, the going was much better.

Richard's ambitions were never going to be satisfied with just expanding Chester racecourse and we examined all the local courses to see if any were suitable to approach. The problem was that Northern Racing and Arena Leisure had already taken over most of the obvious ones and we fell back on the only available local course, Bangor on Dee. Although Chester was a totally flat racing course and Bangor a jumps course there were obvious synergies, in particular the ability to have staff working on racing all the year around.

I knew that it would not be easy to bring the two courses together and that I was in a particularly difficult position, being chairman of both. Nevertheless, Richard and I finally agreed it was worth a try and I had to start the next board meeting at Bangor with the words, 'I have to tell you in my capacity as Chairman of Chester that we would very much like to see the two courses brought together.' I then went outside for half an hour while the other directors discussed the proposition before coming back and trying to conduct a normal Bangor board meeting.

I am sure Michael Webster had anticipated the approach and his own position had been weakened by telling me that he was about to take a position with a Southern racecourse who unfortunately for him did not finalise the offer.

One obstacle which was removed was the landlord being able to offer Mr Done more land elsewhere and allow Bangor racecourse to farm the land inside the course. The landlord himself had to be persuaded that the deal was a good one from every point of view but the shareholders who had never dreamt they would ever get a return on the few hundred they had invested could suddenly see a very welcome and sizeable sum coming their way, and the negotiation went better

than Richard and I had expected. I should say that the Bangor nego-
tiators (I took no part) extracted a very full price and at the end of
the day nearly everybody was happy.

Chester further widened its business interests by building and operating a package hotel under the Inter Continental franchise. This was
entirely Richard's brainchild and so far has worked extremely well,
despite increased competition from new hotels in and around the city.

A further major step forward was taken when the catering, previously a partnership between Heathcotes, a large north-west catering
company, and the racecourse came to an end and Chester took over
entirely, with all the profit on drink that went with it. Richard
Thomas had planned this move very carefully and had been able to
monitor, at close hand, the operation on the racecourse and weigh up
the difficulties that would arise if it all came under his control. He
was fortunate, perhaps, in being able to take over the senior management, so that the transfer went extremely smoothly and the large
profits that followed, particularly from the sale of alcohol, passed
into the company's hands. Not content with this, a restaurant was
opened at an entrance to Tattersalls and was called 1539, the year
that racing was first recorded on the Roodee. This is open seven days
a week and is amongst the very best in Chester. The catering company
does much outside work at the larger functions in the surrounding
area. Chester racecourse is no longer just a racecourse, it is a significant leisure company, growing all the time!

It continues to prosper and in terms of both profit and attendance
is right at the top of the country's sixty courses. Only Cheltenham,
Aintree and Ascot are more profitable; York and Goodwood who do
not publish figures are also contenders and only the same three courses have larger attendances. To reach an average attendance of over
twenty thousand a day is a remarkable achievement.

Not only does the course now draw such large numbers, but the
corporate hospitality has grown in proportion and the decision to
take over the running of it has paid large dividends. Why other courses do not follow suit is extraordinary. The Jockey Club courses are at
least in partnership so they are only giving away part of the profit but
many independent courses are still giving all of it away.

The shareholders have every reason to be thrilled with the progress
the company has made. When I became chairman the hundred and
thirty-three shares then in existence were changing hands for eight
hundred pounds. There are now three hundred and ninety-nine

shares as we gave a two for one script issue early in my tenure. If the highest price a share has changed hands is taken as a yardstick, shareholders who have kept their shares are sitting on a profit of over a hundred and seventy times higher than it would have been twenty years ago. Moreover because the shares do not currently attract inheritance tax, their dependents can receive the windfall free of tax.

My time as chairman ceased in 2008. I had promised my successor, Nigel Churton, that I would make way for him that year and although under pressure from the board to continue and never expecting to feel as well or active in the late seventies as I do, I honoured that promise. He took over one of the best run and most profitable racecourses in the country.

Racing is going through a very difficult period, similar to the construction industry in the nineties. There are far too many bad horses, too many trainers and probably too many racecourses. Prize money is at an all-time low and the industry needs to have some contraction, just as the construction industry did. Our problem is not attendance levels which actually increased in 2010. For York and Chester to be vying with each other to have the higher average attendance at over 20,000 a meeting surely proves that those courses in the right location, who put on a really attractive show for the customers will still reap the benefit.

Most leading racecourses are now very well managed. The greatest single error in my lifetime has been the building of the disastrous new stand at Ascot. Ascot was, apart from Chester, my favourite racecourse and I have been fortunate to win the Gold Cup, the Windsor Castle, the Queen Alexandra and the King George V handicap. I should have added the Ascot Stakes to those. The thrill of having a runner at the old Ascot, never mind a winner, was amazing and the walk down from the old saddling boxes to the paddock was an unforgettable experience. All the charm has gone from the new layout, which may be functional but has totally lost its original character. As for the new stand, words for once fail me. How the highly intelligent management of Ascot could have allowed architects to railroad them is beyond me. It has cost them a large sum of money, never mind the loss of crowds of people who, like me, adored the original set up. Part of the problem seemed to be the desire of the then management to make the course more democratic. I don't think they realised that a lot of people aspired to get to the Royal Enclosure, then a far more desirable place to be than it is now. At any rate they could not have a bette man in charge than my good friend Charles Barnett, who did a magnificent job at Aintree.

The two achievements I will carry to the grave are the part I played in the progress of Chester racecourse and the making of Llanarmon as a great shooting estate. In both cases the results are due to exceptional managers, Richard Thomas at Chester and David Matthews at Llanarmon. Although unlike in appearance and upbringing they both possess similar characteristics – great intelligence, the ability to think ahead and exceptional energy. If only I had had a few similar around me in my last days at Alfred McAlpine ....

Chapter 11

Aintree

My twenty years as a director of Aintree racecourse came when I was in my mid-fifties and continued until I was seventy-four, well over the Jockey Club age limit of seventy for directors – but Peter Daresbury used the reason that I was supervising on the board's behalf, the new stand, paddock, weighing room and stables to keep me on the board.

I went on the Aintree board at Peter's request, when he took over as chairman, having been on the appeal committee which raised the money to safeguard the course. Both Peter Daresbury and I have a passion for Aintree, Peter having ridden over it when he was a leading amateur jockey and I who had been inspired by Uncle Tom winning the race in 1921 with Shaun Spadam, who also came second two years later.

We were fortunate to have two outstanding chief executives – John Parrot, who tragically died whilst out hunting with the Wynnstay as Peter's guest, and Charles Barnett, a great friend of Peter's and a good friend of mine.

I soon realised that Aintree was like no other racecourse in the country. All the profit was earned at one three-day meeting, culminating in the running of the Grand National – and a large part of those profits were the television rights, with fierce competition from the BBC and ITV for them.

Peter was faced with a monumental task: the buildings were out of date and unable to handle the numbers who came to the meeting. A total reconstruction of the course was mapped out, starting with the Queen Mother stand.

The Princess Royal stand was designed to add substantial numbers to the stand and provide comfortable hospitality accommodation with a floor of private boxes and another floor for the sponsors' use. In my time there were effectively two sponsors, Seagrams, with particular emphasis on Martell a subsidiary, and John Smith, another large drinks company. Seagram's representative in England, who we dealt with, was Ivan Straker, who was head of Elmfield when I went to Harrow and captain of rugby. His father, Arthur was a friend of my parents and had taken me racing several times, particularly to Haydock Park on my first time there. We were also fortunate that Patrick Martell became a great supporter of the meeting and Peter and Charles spent a lot of time making sure the ties between us and Martell became ever closer. Golf matches were organised and on one memorable occasion we all took a trip to Herez for golf and a good weekend. I played golf on one of the two days with Patrick Martell and did not distinguish myself, but the evening was full of incident. The BBC had also been invited and I was next to Des Lynham, an interesting dinner partner. After dinner there was entertainment from Flamenco dancers who to my horror invited all of us on to the floor. The two who didn't go were Claire Balding and myself, who hid behind two pillars, but Des Lynham spotted us and we were dragged onto the floor. My Spanish dance partner could not have been nicer and told me to follow while she led!

It was a shame that the building of the Princess Royal stand led to the demolition of the two best boxes on the course, Lord Derby's box, which had been in his family for a long time and mine which was originally the Topham viewing box, which I had converted to an enclosed lunch area with excellent viewing in front. I had originally shared a box with Robert Sangster, then graduated to a large room on the outer perimeter of the stands, reachable by the only escalator on the course. I was lucky to get such a wonderful box as the Topham one and its demolition was a great pity. No doubt John Derby felt the same.

Although the room I had between boxes was not a great place to be, there were some exciting moments, two of which particularly stick in my memory. One was of Tommy Stack, who spent most of the two days prior to his winning ride on Red Rum in the room. Tommy and Liz, his wife, had originally been friends of Doug Francis but we had all done a lot of racing together. Because he did not want to drink prior to the great race I had to order pints of milk, which he consumed enthusiastically. He did go very quiet on National day itself but gave Red Rum a wonderful ride and a comfortable victory.

The other incident concerned an Arab prince, who was at that time an owner of Jeremy Hindley's and a keen racegoer, who was to become our agent in Oman. To my amazement several policemen burst into the room and told us that a death threat to his highness was being taken very seriously by the Home Office and they had been ordered to stand guard over him. Two more police with very powerful looking guns arrived on the scene and the room became very crowded with a very nervous looking Prince surrounded by police. A number of hangers on, who I assumed to be policemen off duty, became bored, found the ample drink supply at the bar and helped themselves liberally. The Prince, one of the most enthusiastic drinkers I have ever known, did the same and by the end of the afternoon it was difficult to tell who was the most inebriated, the uninvited guests or the Prince.

Although my company had put in a tender, the cheapest price went to Birse, a medium-size firm. I was extremely nervous about employing them but my fears reduced when they declared their management team and the man in charge was a former employee of ours, who I knew to be very capable. In fact all went well until four months from the end of the contract, when he told me he was taking a new appointment but would continue to keep an eye on our stand.

The last four months and particularly the last week before the National meeting were a nightmare. Six days before the Thursday we had not got a certificate to use the stand, and this was only obtained in the last twenty-four hours. Corners were cut all over the place and money was needed to put right shoddy work done at the last moment.

Both Peter and Charles Barnett had done a tremendous job on two main fronts: getting more from the television rights and persuading the sponsor to increase his contribution. Two major crises occurred which could have had a major impact on Aintree. The first was the false start, which caused the race to be abandoned. The starter was employed by the Jockey Club and was their senior starter and like many of their employees had a military background. We would have much preferred Gerry Scott, who was a retired national hunt jockey and was very capable. 'Captain Cock Up' as the Senior Starter was called by the press, had had disputes with the jockeys and fussily insisted on a line of horses going almost up to the tape, which was stretched across the course. It was almost an impossibility, in the nervous moments before the race, to get such a line and photographs taken showed an inexperienced lady rider so close that the tape could not rise properly. Instead of firmly disciplining her, the starter tried to start the race and one false start took place but the riders were properly recalled and a second attempt was made. I was watching from my usual place on the roof, on the second floor of the Princess Royal stand, and I turned to the man next to me and said, 'The starter has lost all control of the race; he will never get them off.' My words were unduly prophetic as the starter, having made a second attempt to start the race, screamed out false start but did not give the proper flag signal and the recall man, who had not heard the false start shout, assumed the race was on and left his position. The leading jockeys, fired on adrenalin, continued for two circuits, though it should have been obvious that the race was not taking place. Nobody covered themselves with glory but the media, rightly in my view, put most of the blame on the starter.

I was immediately confronted with a personal problem in that both Peter and Charles had arranged to go on holiday and as the sole representative of the Aintree board, I was due to attend a Jockey Club meeting on the following Monday. A message arrived asking me to see the Senior Steward, Stoker Hartington (now Devonshire), who was about to announce the formation of a new body which became the British Horseracing Authority. He obviously felt he could do with the Aintree situation like a hole in the head, and having asked and heard my views, was not at all happy I was going to blame the starter. Nevertheless, he agreed to let me reply to any questions but in the event, despite all the drama in the press, there were none.

The enquiry dragged on for months and was taken particularly seriously by Rod Fabricius, who was the acting Clerk of the Course. Eventually common sense prevailed and led to instructions which are in force today – that the starter should be on his rostrum well before the tape is released and that two or three qualified people should help on the ground to bring the field into a good line.

The bomb scare of 1997, which caused the switching of the Grand National from the Saturday to the following Monday, was a disaster which was always likely to happen, as the race was an obvious target for an IRA hoax. Unfortunately a device was found by a motorway bridge which led to closures of motorways just before the hoax at Aintree. The directors had been issued with radios and instructed to proceed to Charles Barnett's office if there was a problem. Angela and I were giving the connections of the Aintree Hurdle winner a drink in our entertainment room when the summons to Charles's office took place. I have never seen Charles look more miserable as he knew, as we all did, that racing was over for the day. The police have given us no option, he said, the hoax code is the same as on the motorway incident and although we have to formally agree to give the instructions to evacuate we must do it. The order to evacuate the stands went out but we stayed talking about the alternatives facing us when the phone rang and Charlie said we will leave immediately. Standing up he said the bomb could go off any minute and we sprinted for the exit and made off down the course towards the finishing line. Peter and Charles prided themselves on their fitness and were soon well ahead but I was really struggling. Fortunately the lady representing Seagrams stumbled, and I stopped to get her to her feet to the cheers of the crowd the other side of the course – and we were able to proceed more sedately.

We all finished up in a temporary building on the side of the course, past the start, which was used by the police. Peter and Charles soon negotiated themselves to a more central post but Richard Fildes and I were left there, as was Peter O'Sullivan and a number of the BBC team. After an hour, the heating broke down and the building got extremely cold. None of us were enjoying it but Peter O'Sullivan began to look particularly grey. I found a senior policeman and said I really think you need to take Sir Peter back to the centre of Liverpool or you might get some really adverse publicity – and sensibly he did just that.

That left Richard and myself with a dwindling band and for a long time the mobile phones would not work. There must have been thousands of people trying to use them. Eventually I got through to Nicky Henderson's secretary. Nicky always stays with me for the National. 'They are all at a local hostelry opposite the course,' she told me and seem to be having a good time. Richard and I were eventually taken to the same pub, close to ten o'clock, but our wives and guests had long gone. We both had a very large drink and hired a taxi to take us home. My memory of that drive is the Liverpool taxi driver's astonishment at the rabbits either side of my front drive. 'What on earth are they?' he said. Plainly there are no rabbits in central Liverpool.

Charles did an amazing job over the weekend to ensure there was no bomb and sealed off the buildings so that the race could take place the following Monday. Despite receiving further hoax calls the searches of attendees was so rigorous that they were ignored and a highly successful race took place. As I have written in the chapter on politicians, I was asked to look after Sir John and Norma Major, who were in the last days of a disastrous election campaign for the Conservative party.

Over the years one of the greatest problems we had was with the antis, who targeted Aintree fiercely. There are sadly deaths of horses at every national hunt racecourse and whilst a couple of horses put down at Sedgefield will attract no attention, the same at Cheltenham or Aintree will. Horses get put down all the time at all sports from eventing to hunting and those of us involved with the management of Aintree have looked at every way to make the course safer. Peter and I went to look at the heavily modified Beecher's Brook, where a pathetic trickle of water stood in place of the brook where Captain Beecher sheltered underneath the fence. 'I hope the captain doesn't come out of his grave and clobber us for what we have done!' said Peter.

Sadly the two fatalities in 2011 and 2012 caused more media pressure and in the former the fact that the race was run in the warmest temperatures ever and in the latter that one of the fatalities had won the Cheltenham Gold Cup, certainly didn't help. What the public doesn't seem to understand is that the easier the fences are made the faster the horses go and it is speed which is the main problem. The course management does a great job with an excellent watering system to make sure the going is always on the soft side and the days of Nicholas Silver winning on fast ground have gone forever. Whilst the ground can be made as safe as possible, I side with the famous trainers who believe that to tamper with the fences any further would destroy the race. Dick Francis, who was always my guest for lunch on the Friday of the meeting, was adamant that the race was being ruined well before we got to the modifications of 2011. Jamie Osbourne once said to me, 'Thank you so much for giving us those lovely little National fences, they are so much easier to jump than the Mildmay ones.' It is surely time that those of us who love the race said enough is enough!

Racing is going through easily the most difficult time in my lifetime. By far the largest single problem is prize money, which has sunk to a level which now is ludicrous. The famous saying 'racing is a rich man's sport' has always been true but now the word 'very' should go in front of 'rich'.

Because racecourses, which have been unprofitable in the past have been rescued by either the Jockey Club or bought by Northern Racing or Arena Leisure, there seems to be a view that it would be terrible to close a racecourse down. This cannot be right, unprofitable courses take the fixtures from those who can offer better prize money and racing would be better off without them. Top flat jockeys are already leading the way by refusing to ride at the small meetings where low prize money does not make it worthwhile to take the risks of costly suspensions.

Sadly there are also too many trainers. At present you can pay anywhere between £30 and £80 a day for a horse with a licensed trainer. Whilst there are many making, deservedly, a very good living, there must be others on the breadline, who would be better off earning a living elsewhere. The same applies to all the attendant populace who make up the racing industry from vets and farriers down to stable staff.

Racing needs to come back as a leaner, healthier industry than it is now and it also needs a strong management body, which, in my view, it does not currently have and it can do without distractions like Racing for Change, which costs over a million pounds a year, which could add a thousand in prize money to a couple of hundred underfunded minor races!

Chapter 12

Robert Sangster, Charles Benson and other friends

Though I have bracketed Robert and Charles together in the same chapter and though they were both very dependent on each other they were very different people. Robert had much the softer character of the two and was always a loyal genuine and close friend. Charles whose great passion in life was gambling and I had some stormy times and I was always mindful of Colin Ingleby-Mackenzie's early comment: Charles is great fun to be with, just don't get too close. Both had first class brains but whereas Robert could have made a fortune in business, Charles was always going to lead the life of a bon viveur, addicted to and passionately fond of gambling. Probably neither would have any great regrets about the lives they led. Instead of making his mark in the business world, Robert was, with the help of John Magnier, going to change the racing industry in a major way and Charles could look back on a life which had contained more pleasurable moments than most people experience.

I met Charles on the racecourse in the late fifties and knew him well enough to ask him and his wife, Carol, to our National party at Carden after Nicholas Silver's win in 1961. Our paths crossed more when I went racing with Johnny Phillipson, although Carol never approved of Johnny – on one occasion describing him as a bookmaker's runner. Johnny's first racehorse was all set for a coup over hurdles at Haydock against a fancied one of Charles's trained by Tom Jones. They were having a tremendous battle going into the last when both got beaten by an outsider of Fred Rimell's.

Robert came into my life on National eve 1965 when Jane and I received an invitation for dinner, although neither of us had met him or his wife Christine; in fact the invitation was inspired by Nick Robinson who was staying with him and had told him it was time we both met. Robert and Christine had bought Swettenham Hall, a most attractive Georgian house near Macclesfield, some distance from Carden.

It may sound trite to say that the dinner sparked an instant friendship but we had a lot in common. We spent most of the next afternoon in his box at Aintree, on National day and the following Saturday went to Chepstow, where the coup on New Liscard took place. I also got to know quickly their close friends, in particular Tim and Sally Kitson, who were staying also for the National and were regular visitors to Swettenham.

In the early days of our friendship, Robert and I would lead very normal lives as both were working full time but racing whenever we could. Robert had not yet got the bug for the big time on the flat and enjoyed national hunt just as much. His horses were all with Eric Cousins, who trained at Tarporley and was extremely successful under both rules and we had great fun following our horses at the local meetings. We would go together to Cheltenham with a group of similar-minded friends and join Robert at his box at Aintree. Weekend parties at Swettenham and Carden were frequent and Robert's party trick was to take us outside after lunch and stand at the back of the house, where the ground sloped sharply downhill with the rive Dane at the bottom. He would bring out the golf clubs and say with what club do you think you can get across the river? We will have a sweep and the one who does it with the highest club takes the money. In fact the shot looked very intimidating but was deceptive and instead of taking a wood, as I did the first time, it was achievable with a well hit eight iron. I only fell for it once!

We would race at all the local racecourses and particularly Chester and Haydock. Neither of us aspired to a box and we would get a wonderful waitress, called Ginger, to reserve a table in the main dining rooms and drink prodigious quantities of champagne. In those pre-breathalyser days, after racing we would often find a pub to have a drink in which suited us both as our houses were quite far apart.

Robert had introduced me to his friends and in turn I did the same with mine and Brian Jenks in particular struck a chord with Robert and joined the 'inner circle'. All went well until Brian changed wives and although I was determined not to lose a great friend, Jane, who was very close to Belinda, disliked his new wife, Rose, intensely and the feeling was mutual. Brian who had always come to stay for Aintree and the Chester May meeting, ceased coming and although Jane was delighted, I was saddened. Good friends were important to me.

Robert was never going to stay indefinitely being a minor player in the racing world and when he moved to Vincent O'Brien and Barry Hills, he ceased to be Eric Cousins's biggest owner although he always had some horses with him. Sadly Eric was the big loser; he adored Robert and though he continued training for several years, he could not bear to see others reap the main benefits from Robert's wealth and ambition. His daughter, Wendy, was to work for Robert at Manton until his death, as his racing secretary.

I thought at the time that Robert and Chris had an idyllic life. Both were attractive people who seemed extremely happy with each other. Robert was working hard in the family business, Vernon's Pools, and Christine was bringing up small children whom she adored. They had a lovely house in magnificent surroundings, a wide circle of friends and for a few years after our first meeting all went extremely well. Robert had most of the family business under his control as Vernon, his father, had made it over to avoid the dreaded death duty scenario. In many ways Robert got his wealth too early and I am sure he would have been a happier man if he had had to work harder for it. But the great mistake was the decision to abandon Britain to become a tax exile in 1974. I thought at the time that to tear up his roots, give up a regular job and go to a country, France, where he couldn't speak the language, was the height of folly and I was proved absolutely right. Christine followed him loyally with the children giving up her beloved Swettenham which was let to friends, and although she made the very best of life abroad she was never really happy there. To a degree I blame Vernon, who was still very involved with the business and saw an opportunity to get back in the saddle whilst the family wealth was preserved abroad.

Charles Benson and Robert had known each other for a few years on the racecourse before they started a close friendship in 1973, which lasted until Charles's death in 2002. In his book, *No Regard for Money*, Charles wrote that a mutual sense of humour brought them together but in fact it was a mutual dependence. Charles was attracted by Robert's wealth and lifestyle and Robert, a surprisingly shy man, needed Charles's extrovert behaviour to provide the life he was looking for. In 1974 Charles stayed at Swettenham for the Chester May meeting, the scene of the traumatic Shellshock enquiry, the worst half hour of my stewarding career. In his book Benson wrote that the decision to let the result stand was the worst he had ever seen. Although a gross exaggeration after a substantial loss to his pocket, I have some sympathy with him. As I have said before it was not my finest hour.

Robert's friendship with Charles started about a year before Charles got involved with one of the great mysteries of the later part of the twentieth century, the disappearance of Lord Lucan. Lucan had for a period been, arguably, Charles's closest friend; they had lunch or dinner together virtually every day and played golf at Sunningdale on Friday mornings. They were in fact having lunch on a Tuesday when Benson, whose car was being repaired, told Lucan that he had to be at London Airport for four thirty to catch Robert Sangster's private plane, which was to take him and other guests to the Isle of Man, where Robert had arranged for them to speak in favour of a legalised change in the Betting Act there. Lucan offered Benson the use of his car and suggested that Lady Charlotte Curzon, Benson's then girlfriend, who was at the lunch, could drive him to the airport and then drive the car back. What happened on the drive back is somewhat of a mystery as Lucan, without a car, borrowed one off Michael Stoop, which was the car he used in his final drive.

Benson arrived back from the Isle of Man on the Thursday of the Lucan nanny's murder and was alerted to the problems on the Friday morning when a friend rang him and told him that police had been swarming around Lucan's house all night. Benson rang up Gerald Road Police Station, explained he was a close friend and was told to ring Inspector Gerring; he was then told he would be interviewed the following week. He then alerted John Aspinall and between them a lunch was arranged at Aspinall's house for six of Lucan's closest friends. Benson describes the lunch as one with cold food from the fridge and moderate white wine. He said that nobody had the slightest idea where Lucan was and the idea that a plot was being hatched to spirit him abroad was ludicrous. In fact at the meeting Aspinall, convinced Lucan was a murderer, declared that he must fall on his sword, the only course left open to him.

Benson was extremely critical of the police investigation and never wavered from his conviction that Lucan killed himself the following day, when he realised the enormity of the error he had made. As Benson said in his book, and in several conversations with me, 'We will never know exactly how he hid his body but I believe he did to himself what he intended to do to the body of his victim.' Michael Stoop, who I had a couple of in-depth conversations with, had exactly the same view. In fact those closest to Lucan had little doubt about the final outcome.

Benson was frequently called upon by the media as the saga dragged on and made several television appearances. He told me that he had confronted a senior policeman and told him that Lucan was definitely dead. His reply was, 'I know that as well as you but it's more profitable to keep him alive!'

Although there is not one shred of credible evidence that Lucan ever went abroad or is still alive, the media is still fascinated by the mystery. I remain utterly convinced the Benson view is the right one.

The following year both Robert and Charles stayed at Carden for the Chester May Festival races, a pattern which continued until my own marriage failed. However it was Robert's which collapsed first over one of the most traumatic weekends I ever remember. Tim Kitson and I had arranged to give a joint dinner party for friends at the Portland Club, the bridge club where we were both members. We were to fly the next day with Sally to Malaga to stay with Robert and Chris at a palatial house they had rented in Marbella and both Tim and I were greatly looking forward to a relaxing time. At Malaga airport we were met by two of the Sangsters' then closest friends, Billy and Annie Hart, who were returning to England on the same plane after a few days stay with Robert and Chris. To say the Harts were emotional would be to put it mildly. They were both in tears and tried to tell us the Sangster marriage was on the rocks. Neither Tim or I believed them, both of us being convinced that far too much alcohol was the cause of the problem.

When we got to the villa it was obvious that things were tense but Robert had arranged golf with Sean Connery and Tim Vigors and he and I spent the afternoon on the golf course. At dinner in the villa I sat next to Christine and started telling her that marriages went through rough patches and she must stick it out, when I suddenly found Robert, who had moved from the other side of the table, breathing in my ear, saying don't give her that line of bullshit. That certainly shut me up for the rest of the dinner.

The next day, the Saturday, consisted of drinks, lunch and more golf and there were sufficient friends around to ease the tension and we went back for a quiet dinner, after which Robert insisted on going to a nightclub in Marbella. I remember we all set off in a large black Range Rover but Chris would not go into the club where Robert had arranged for Tim Vigors and his German wife Heidi to join us. I remember having the longest dance of my life with Heidi; she must have been an excellent dance partner because long dances are not my normal style but sufficient alcohol and a competent partner can achieve wonders.

Eventually we got back to the villa and Robert said he had to look at things in the study while Tim and I decided to play a couple of games of backgammon on a lovely, ornate set in the middle of the drawing room. We were halfway through our game when Robert came out of the study holding a letter in his hand and made towards the stairs leading to the first floor bedrooms. At the same time Chris came in a dressing gown to the top of the stairs and said to Robert, 'Please come to bed, darling, it's very late.' Although I was concentrating on trying to win the backgammon, Robert must have dropped the letter which Chris picked up and took to the bedroom. Tim and I finished, said good night and I made my way to the little bedroom I was in on the ground floor. I do remember looking at my watch and it was four-thirty.

I went straight to sleep and was woken up just after seven by what I initially thought was a pounding in my head but it turned out to be Tim banging on the door. 'How can you sleep through all this dreadful drama?' said Tim. I looked totally bemused and he said Chris read the letter from Robert's girlfriend and that has finished everything. Sally and I have spent the last two-and-a-half hours trying to talk them out of it but they are adamant they should break up and you are to go with Robert on the morning plane to London and Sally and I will accompany Chris and Kate – who was still a baby and the only child there in the afternoon.

I quickly dressed and joined Robert in the main room where we had played backgammon. Although he had been through a traumatic ordeal he looked a better colour than Tim, who had begun to resemble Banquo's ghost on a bad day.

I don't remember much about the journey back. Robert was extremely calm and described Susan in glowing terms; he was obviously extremely smitten and said he was heading for Australia to meet her as soon as possible.

In fact that meeting turned out to be extremely expensive for me. Robert and I had a few horses together and one of them, Lord Henham, was being trained in America and the amazing news came through that he had won by a nose the Hialeah Turf Cup, the richest race in Florida, at 66/1. The agent who was managing the horse said it's wonderful news and I have an offer of a quarter of a million dollars provided the sale takes place before the next race at Woodbine, Canada on Sunday. I said I will take entire responsibility, Robert I know will take your shoulder off to get the sale. The agent then said I can only take instructions from Robert and I can't get hold of him, he's booked out of his hotel in Melbourne. Don't worry I said, he rings his secretary every morning; I will get her tomorrow and come straight back to you.

The following morning I rang Miss Markey, his secretary, at nine in the morning and a conversation ensued. 'Miss Markey, I need you to ring Mr Sangster immediately and tell him we have a wonderful offer for Lord Henham and he must contact the agent to clinch it.' A pause and then Miss Markey said, 'For the first time ever Mr Sangster has not rung me yesterday nor yet today.' I then say, 'But you know where he is?' 'Oh yes, Mr Bobby, but I am not to tell anybody.' I then say, 'I'm not just anybody, I am his great friend and racehorse partner.' 'I have my orders, Mr Bobby.' Kay, my wonderful secretary, had always thought Miss Markey was not the brightest pebble on the beach and I suddenly realised her instincts had not deserted her.

Thinking quickly, I said, 'Let's play a little game, Miss Markey, is it San Francisco he's gone to?' 'I can't disclose, Mr Bobby.' 'No,' I said, 'it must be Hawaii.' A sharp intake of breath told me I had got that right and I closed down the conversation.

In fact we had just bought a travel agency off an old racing friend, John Slesinger, and I said to Kay, 'Ring Mr Slesinger up and tell him it's vital I know where the smartest, most fun hotel is in Hawaii, where two rich love birds would go to.' In fairness to John he gave me the phone number of the hotel which I duly rang up and was told there was definitely no Mr Sangster staying there.

Andrew Peacock, the cuckolded husband of Susan and leader of the opposition in the Australian parliament, was far cleverer. He rang up the same day but realising Robert would be under an assumed name described him and Susan in detail, said he had mislaid Robert's name and got put straight through to their room. Robert answered the phone and said, 'Sangster here.' 'It's Andrew Peacock this end' – Game, set and match! Needless to say Lord Henham failed to oblige at Woodbine and finished up as a stallion in Port Elizabeth earning us nothing. Years later I was staying at the Nunnery, Robert and Susan's home in the Isle of Man, and I said, 'Robert it's my turn to have that Hialeah Cup.' 'Fine,' he said. I walked into the drawing room, took the cup and was going out when Susan appeared. Her look of horror told me she was certain I was taking the family silver but it now resides in my dining room, a poignant reminder of what could have been.

Robert soon brought Susan to England and she found herself the girlfriend of the most 'up and coming' racehorse owner in the country. Robert had started a partnership with John Magnier, who had married Susan O'Brien, daughter of legendary Irish trainer Vincent O'Brien.

For once I was ahead of Robert having met both of them on a trip to Ireland to stay with Susan Francis, who was managing a stud there. Susan had told me that Vincent had installed a landing strip with a windsock, etc. and she had squared the groundsman and made sure Vincent would be away. I hired a company plane and set off for Tipperary, where with some difficulty we located the landing strip and duly landed and taxied to where Susan and a car were waiting. I had just given her a peck on the cheek when out of the bushes stepped Vincent. 'How nice to see you, Bobby, fancy you calling in like this.' To say I was embarrassed would not do the scene justice but Vincent went on with, 'You must bring Susan to dinner. We'll see you both about eight.' When we approached the gates of Ballydoyle, a car came down the drive at great speed and narrowly missed us. 'Who on earth was that?' I asked. 'Until a few days ago that was my boyfriend, John Magnier; now he has met Sue O'Brien I don't think I will see him for dust.' After we had a most enjoyable dinner the couple returned and we all had drinks after dinner.

The racing and breeding empire headed by Sangster, Magnier and O'Brien did include others, who mostly couldn't stand the financial pace and dropped away. The plan was to buy and race the very best yearlings bought in England, Ireland and America and then syndicate the top group winners for breeding purposes. Although the racing side would lose money they hoped the breeding would show a large profit. Previously the big owners like the Aga Khan, Lord Derby and a host of other immensely wealthy owners had raced for fun never expecting their sport to show a profit. The Sangster, Magnier partnership was to change all that.

The first horse to do so was The Minstrel, the top two-year-old of the previous year but who could only manage to come third in the 2000 Guineas. The favourite for the Derby was Blushing Groom, owned by the Aga Khan, who had also become a close friend of

Charles Benson, whose social skills were seen at their very best on the day. The Minstrel was second favourite but when I joined Robert and Susan's party for lunch, Robert was not confident, having been told by Benson how good Blushing Groom was. In fact The Minstrel won in a tremendous finish with Hotgrove, owned by Philip Leverhulme, my chairman at Chester, with Blushing Groom third.

I had watched the race with Nick Robinson, still one of Robert's best friends, and we both decided we would have a quiet drink at the Iron Stand bar. To our horror we found Christine with Annie Hart there both sobbing their eyes out and although we tried to pour the most expensive champagne for them Christine was desolate. In a few months her life had changed completely and the prospect of not being able to celebrate with Robert obviously overwhelmed her. Had she known that Susan would insist on going with Robert to meet the Queen her grief would have been even greater.

When I returned to Robert's table a great celebration was in progress and Benson having managed to cheer up the Aga Khan was all set on arranging the evening's party at Annabels. The story which did the rounds was that he simply changed the floral arrangements from the 'Aga's' colours to Robert's – but he always fiercely denied it. It was a tremendous party with Lester Piggott, the Sangster O'Brien jockey, eating more than he would normally have permitted himself.

From then onward Robert could do no wrong on the racecourse, winning the Irish Derby and the King George VI with The Minstrel and then the Arc de Triomphe with Alleged who won the same race the following year.

My one major fallout with Charles occurred in the year before Jane and I separated. Charles was often desperate for money to fund his gambling and was helping Jeffrey Barnard write a spicy racing column entitled 'Colonel Mad' for *Private Eye*. He was also supplying Nigel Dempster with information for his gossip column in the *Daily Mail* and I was a natural target amongst several others for both outlets.

One evening Jane and I were having dinner when the telephone rang and a voice I hardly recognised started ranting at me. It took me a minute or two to realise it was Charles and eventually I got him sufficiently coherent to get the gist of what it was all about. It transpired he had been stupid enough to write in *Private Eye* about Victor Matthews, who owned the *Daily Express* and that Victor had told the sports editor to warn Benson to expect the sack from his full-time job as one of the paper's two racing correspondents, Peter O'Sullivan being the other. Benson had been told that Victor was in possession of two anonymous letters and he had leapt to the conclusion I had written them.

I pointed out that I knew Victor extremely well, that we regularly met in the construction dining groups and that anything I wanted him to hear would be said to his face. Moreover I said I would arrange a meeting with Victor the following day to clarify the situation and keep Charles informed. I duly rang up Victor's secretary early the next day and had no trouble getting a meeting fixed for the late morning. When I got to Victor's Penthouse office at the top of the *Express*'s extremely impressive headquarters, I found Douglas Bader also waiting to see Victor. When the secretary came and told me to come through I whispered, 'Surely the guest waiting here should go first.' 'No,' she said, 'I think you are more important than him.'

I duly went in to the largest boardroom I had ever been in with Victor at one end and was beckoned to sit down at the other end of the table. Advancing towards me Victor said how would you like it if these idiots wrote about your wife like this? He then put in front of me several excerpts from Colonel Mad, the only one I can remember saying Lady Mathews accompanied her husband to some smart racing dinner and in case she could not hold her knife and fork properly Sally Hindley was put close by to give her instruction.

As I had received similar treatment, though on rather different themes, I knew exactly how Victor felt and had the dilemma of wanting to extricate Charles from the sack without being too sympathetic to him. I suggested that Victor must meet Charles to clear it all up, knowing that there was nobody better than Charles at getting out of a tight corner. I also asked to see the letters which Victor duly produced. Both started with a sentence to the effect that how could a talented businessman employ somebody like Charles Benson, who was so utterly disloyal to him. My strong gut feeling was that they had been written by a woman and suspected that there were several who might have wanted to write them.

Victor and Charles duly met a day or two later and Charles using all his legendary charm totally extricated himself, though he was extremely careful not to let Barnard write anything further about Lord or Lady Mathews. The whole episode did to some extent clear the air between us although I was even more wary of Colin Ingleby-

Mackenzie's words: have fun with Charles but don't get too close!

1977 saw the second marriages of Charles Benson and Nick Robinson and Robert's was to follow in March 1978, when he and Susan were married in his private chapel at the Nunnery on the Isle of Man. The celebrations started with an eve of wedding party and went on for three days. A large number including much of the leading Irish racing fraternity flew in the afternoon before and the cloud base was very low. I was playing golf against Robert who was continuously looking at the sky wondering whether planes would be able to land. Not surprisingly I gained one of my largest wins on the golf course as a result.

My own marriage was very much on the rocks and I stayed alone with Dudley Cunliffe-Owen and his wife. Charles Benson made two major speeches to welcome everybody, the first at a party in the Palace Hotel, which our company had recently built. Susan had invited a number of single Australian ladies and Charles singled out in his speech two about to be eligible bachelors, Bobby McAlpine and the Earl of Suffolk.

In fact the one Australian lady staying at the Cunliffe-Owen home was Nicky Spice, who had already had two husbands and was working in Di's interior decorating business in Cobham. Although the weekend passed innocently enough, we were thrown together and the seeds were sown for the most intense and traumatic relationship that followed.

It was with Nicky by my side that we went to the Derby as Robert's guests to see his colt, Hawaiian Sound, narrowly beaten by Shirley Heights. Robert had brought over the brilliant, tiny American jockey, Willie Shoemaker, to ride and Barry Hills, who had one narrow miss with Rheingold, was destined yet again to just miss out. Robert arranged a celebration party two days later which I had always promised Zandra Johnson I would take her to if Robert had a Derby party, and despite the combined pressure of Nicky and Susan Sangster I stuck to my word. At the party I sat next to Bill Shoemaker's lovely wife, Cindy, who at close to six feet tall towered over Bill. After an excellent dinner and full of wine I asked Cindy if it was difficult for her with someone as small as Bill: 'Bobby,' she said, 'when two people want to do things together it is amazing that nothing seems to stand in their way.'

The day after both Zandra and I and Robert went separately to Harrow where our sons were taken out on 'Speech day' and where it was traditional for the parents and boys to all have picnics on the 'colts' ground, the other side of the road to the sixth form ground, where the 1st XI was playing a club I belonged to. I had started playing in the game a year or two earlier and went straight there to be told I was opening the batting. At the party the night before Robert had said it's ridiculous you playing cricket tomorrow, I bet you £50 you don't score twenty runs. I took the bet and was moving slowly but surely to a decent score when, on nineteen, I was suddenly aware of a commotion on the sight screen; completely distracted I missed the ball and was given out LBW. I then discovered that Robert in desperation at his bet going down had sent his two sons to the sight screen to jump up and down. It worked well and when I went to join the picnic, instead of lunching with the team in the pavilion, Robert was so amused you would have thought he had won another Derby.

We moved on to Ascot. For some years I had stayed with the Hanburys, as had Robert, and it was there that my relationship with Nicky really took off, as although she was supposed to return to her house at Windsor nearby, she ended up having breakfast at Queen's Lodge, the Hanburys' house.

It was after Ascot that I virtually moved in with Nicky, although I had the company London flat to fall back on. We made several visits to the Isle of Man to stay with Robert and Susan and on one of them I was persuaded by Susan to go with them to Australia for the Melbourne Cup. Robert had no Melbourne house and his considerable entourage stayed at the Hilton hotel, where he and Susan had an enormous suite, where everybody met at noon for drinks before moving to one of the city's restaurants for lunch. Charles Benson was very involved with Robert's itinerary, which involved a number of major racing lunches and dinners and where he really came into his own, either writing down things for Robert to say or speaking on Robert's behalf. Robert had already built up a sizeable racing empire there and his name was a household word. He was certainly the most sought after English guest to visit Melbourne that year. Although he enjoyed the racing lunches and dinners, some of which were for men only, Susan got quickly bored of seeing Robert at the centre of attention. I was never a good 'air traveller' and although we travelled first class in one of Singapore Airlines' most spacious jets, the three-hour delay in Singapore and change of plane led to a much less comfortable second leg. When we arrived at Melbourne after the longest single journey I had been on since the piston-engine flights to South Africa, I was frankly out on my feet.

We were met by Nicky's parents, who were delightful, and taken to the hotel where we were given a pleasant suite and discovered Susan had booked us in as Sir Robert and Lady McAlpine. Although Nicky's parents gave no outward sign she said afterwards they were horrified at the subterfuge and the fact we were in a room together. I was far from pleased myself, particularly as Susan insisted we continued the deceit and a few days into the stay a dramatic incident made me really wonder about her outlook on life. She rang me up and said, 'Bobby, you are not going to the boring racing lunch tomorrow, nor are you having the usual drink in our suite, you are meeting me outside the front entrance at exactly 12.15 and Nicky is going to see her parents.'

At twelve fifteen on the dot I went to the front entrance to see Susan waiting for me. 'Jump into the back, Bobby; by the way this is Andrew Peacock, who is giving us a lift to Rupert Clarke's lunch party.' Andrew did the driving and Susan managed to get out of him some exciting details of his recent affair with Shirley McLaine before we reached the Clarkes' enormous house and an attendant dashed up to park the car. The one thing I was not going to do was to walk in with the leader of the opposition parliamentary party and his former wife, a few years after one of the most sensational divorces Australia had seen. I latched on to Derek Nimmo and his lovely wife and we walked a few yards behind Andrew and Susan. There must have been three hundred people in the marquee all talking at the top of their voices. Five seconds after Andrew and Susan walked through the door you could have heard a pin drop. When I managed to buttonhole Susan, I asked you have told Robert exactly what is happening? No, she replied, he is so wrapped up in his racing he doesn't worry what I do. I then marched her to a phone and made her ring up Robert, who had fortunately not left for his lunch.

I have to say our lunch was great fun. Sir Rupert Clarke, the host, was Australia's leading banker and his bank took over the Clydesdale bank, which our family and I have always banked with. There were a number of eminent politicians there and I was seated next to Lady McMahon, the wife of a former prime minister. The high spot of the lunch was Lady Clarke introducing Derek Nimmo, who was next to her. She finished the introduction with a great sweep of her arm which unfortunately knocked the beaker of pimms Derek was drinking into his lap also soaking his Garrick Club tie he always wore. A seasoned trooper, he swiftly recovered.

The main point of the Melbourne week was of course the racing and on one of the days, just before the 'Cup', I went with Nicky and her parents. Her father insisted on showing me the 'Men Only' club stand, which he was very proud to have joined and we spent two races there. I have often asked Australians racing in England if this stand still exists and was recently told, no, it was one of the great bastions of male supremacy but like everything else it eventually had to go.

The Melbourne Cup day itself was amazing. We all started racing early and my first glass of Australian champagne (in reality sparkling white wine) was consumed just after ten in the morning. We continued to drink it until eight in the evening when we left for a major dinner party. It says much for the quality that I didn't have a major headache the next day.

I watched the race away from Robert and Charles, who stuck to him like glue, and found some English friends nearby. When I looked at Robert's horse, which was the favourite, it was obviously lame in front and when I shouted this out to my friends I nearly got lynched by the Australians nearby who told me I was talking nonsense (that is the polite version). I was proved right because the horse was pulled up after three furlongs.

Those were good days for Robert and Susan but they were not to last, as her flamboyant behaviour and love of publicity increasingly got to Robert. A year or two later we all went to the Guineas meeting at Newmarket and Robert bought us all tickets for a charity lunch. To my surprise I found myself sitting between Jerry Hall and her friend David Bailey's wife. I frankly wasn't finding either of them easy going and when I got up to get some cheese, Jeremy Hindley said you seem to be struggling, change places with me and see if I can do better. I had the great pleasure in seeing a real put down when after his first remark Jerry Hall said, 'Will you not interrupt me when I am talking to my friend' – and continued to ignore him and talk to Mrs Bailey.

When a few months later Robert with Charles in attendance went to meet up with Jerry Hall in Los Angeles, the media were on to a major story as her estrangement with Mick Jagger was front page news. Jeremy was one of the first to ring me up. Are we really going to have that woman come into our lives? was his opening remark.

Robert and Charles had started their journey in Australia where they had stopped off to consult Kerry Packer, who advised them how to avoid the media. In England we all held our breath to see if the budding romance between Robert and Jerry would take off. Di Hanbury headed straight for the Isle of Man where she gave Susan the excellent advice to sit tight and let her talk to the media. Whenever the phone rang Di answered it and she managed to prevent the publicity loving Susan from saying a single word to the press in the four days her husband and Charles were staying with Jerry Hall in Los Angeles.

The romance fizzled out and Robert came home with his tail between his legs and a cheque book in his hand. Some expensive jewellery was bought and Di Hanbury got her reward as her interior design business was given a major refurbishment of the Nunnery.

I often asked Charles what really happened in those four days but for once he was extremely reticent and all I got was that there was a lot of time spent in bed and he got much the best of it by making friends with Jerry Hall's sister.

Robert's racing empire continued to increase but so did his overdraft and, as I was privy at that time to his finances, I got increasingly concerned at the level of expenditure. His parties were legendary and the one he gave for Susan in 1982 at the Nunnery must have cost a seven figure sum. But the real expense was the racing both in Ireland and England. In Ireland the production of stallions had worked well for a number of years. The Minstrel, Alleged, Storm Bird, Detroit, Golden Fleece, Lomond, El Gran Senor and, most profitable of all, Saddlers Wells, which was to provide Robert with serious income in his latter years.

A racing journalist commenting on the difference between Vincent and Aidan O'Brien (no relation) pointed out that while Aidan has four immensely rich owners Vincent only had Robert, although he did have a few horses from wealthy Americans.

Robert with his heavy involvement in the largest and most successful stud in Ireland was always going to be a potential target for the I.R.A. and sure enough at the end of the seventies he received a demand for a substantial amount of money or he would be eliminated. He was naturally extremely worried and felt particularly vulnerable in the Isle of Man. The Nunnery was easily accessed from a number of points and the Manx police took the threats very seriously. He was not helped by receiving conflicting advice from a number of friends and business associates, some of whom thought he should make a payment.

The problem reached a peak when Angela and I were his guests at Phoenix Park racecourse in the early eighties. We had lunch in the central restaurant and then made our way over to a large box to watch the racing. The journey across was a remarkable one with Robert, myself, Angela and Vincent O'Brien escorted by several policemen with rifles at the ready. During the short walk Robert was keen to talk to me, and I, aware that he was the likely target, tried to put a few yards between us. When we got to the box there were armed police outside and although we were free to move around, Robert never left the box for the rest of the day.

In the end, it was Ken Paul, his accountant and adviser, who determined the outcome. Ken had been with Robert since his days in Vernon's Pools and was a close friend, as well as a major financial adviser. He told Robert that he simply couldn't pay clandestine organisations and would be extremely unpopular in England if he did so, and it was this advice which prevailed. Gradually the threat receded and Robert was able to lead a normal life again, but it was probably the most unpleasant experience of his life.

The purchase of Manton put further considerable strain on the finances. Manton is a wonderful place tucked away off the main roads just west of Marlborough and when Robert installed Michael Dickenson as his main trainer in England, there were a few jealous ones wishing they had been given the opportunity. Both Angela and I had had horses with Michael, my best one being a good hunter chaser called Compton Lad, who would probably have won the Foxhunters if he hadn't come down three out. The next race was the famous Cheltenham Gold Cup, where Michael saddled the first five, a feat which will probably never be repeated.

Having been right at the top of the National Hunt tree, Michael was desperate to prove he could do the same on the flat. He had enjoyed tremendous support from his parents and was used to an environment surrounded by friends and relatives. To be moved from Yorkshire to the South of England without any of the help he had in Yorkshire would be daunting to anybody. Moreover as he was told to spend what he wanted he embarked on a major reconstruction spree. When I caught up with what was going on I was so impressed with the marketing man from a relatively small local company, who had talked Michael in to spending a double digit number of millions, that I took him on myself and he did well with us.

Robert was the opposite of hands on and rarely visited Manton until Michael started to have runners. Unfortunately he was not given older proven horses and his first runners were all two-year-olds. His first season was a disaster and the second started equally badly before Robert lost patience and asked Barry Hills to take Michael's place. I have a few memories of Manton in Michael's day – and one sticks in my mind when I was asked by Robert to take Keith Miller around the stables. It was all very impressive and we reached what Michael called his laboratory. Pulling out a jar he said, these are the finest Canadian oats in the world; we sieve them to get out any impurities and just to make sure we sieve them a second time. 'Don't seem to make them run any faster,' said Keith in a loud aside. 'Keith,' I said, 'we won't get lunch if you make another remark like that.'

Keith also took part in a cricket match staged at Manton after Barry Hills had taken over. The players were racing people and celebrities and I managed to talk myself into getting a bowl just after Keith, then approaching seventy, had come to the wicket. My gentle leg spin needed assistance from the pitch and my first ball for once a decent length spun quite viciously. Keith got a thick edge and was caught by the keeper and with a wide grin he walked back. The umpire shouted, 'Come back Mr Miller you are not out.' 'Of course I'm out,' said Keith. 'We want to see you bat not McAlpine bowl,' said the umpire. 'Too bad,' said Keith heading for the pavilion, and a drink when he reached it.

Barry had always wanted to train at Manton. At least twice on the way back from a western race meeting he had taken me off the M4 to have a look at the complex, which he declared was the finest place to train racehorses in Britain. When Robert sacked Michael Dickenson and offered him the opportunity to take over, he never hesitated, leaving his eldest son John to train in his old Lambourn yard. Unfortunately he never bothered to obtain a proper contract of security of tenure which was to catch up with him when Robert put the estate on the market at the end of the eighties.

1984 was a notable year in Robert's life story; it was to be his last year as Britain's leading racehorse owner. He had earned this accolade five times – first in 1977 – but the bursting of the Arab billionaires onto the British racing scene was to change the balance of power on this front. Robert initially welcomed the arrival of the Arab princes, correctly seeing that the market which he had dominated would be given a major boost and that his bloodstock would increase in value as a result.

In Patrick and Nick Robinson's book on Robert they tell a story of Keenland sales in the mid eighties when Vincent O'Brien and Robert were outbid at 13 million dollars by Sheik Mohammed and Vincent puts an arm around Robert's shoulder and says we've met our match, Robert, let's go and have a drink. Robert's story to me was very different. Vincent, he said, was told not to go a dollar over ten million and when he went first to eleven and then to twelve he and John Magnier nearly had a seizure and it was only by forcibly propelling Vincent from the sales ring to the bar that they stopped him bidding futher.

But the real drama of 1984 for Robert was the meeting of his third wife, the second Susan and the ending of his marriage. Angela and I had just got married ourselves and were introduced to Susan and another lady at Chester races, where Robert was still a steward. 'This is a friend of ours from the Isle of Man and she has a friend in Cheshire so I was asked to bring them over and we will all have a drink after racing,' said Robert.

I saw through this at once and a day or two later a gossip column dropped heavy hints that all was not well with Robert's marriage. In Charles Benson's book he states that the actual breakup took place before Melbourne Cup week and that he agreed with Robert that instead of staying with Robert in their Sydney house the week before racing, Robert would move out and stay in a hotel leaving Charles to console Susan as best he could. When they all moved on to Melbourne to stay at the Hilton hotel Susan was anxious that all should appear normal and that the Australian press should not get the story. It must have been a very uncomfortable week, quite different from the one Nicky and I had spent in the same hotel a few years earlier.

Susan hung on for a while in the Isle of Man with her daughters, no doubt hoping Robert would relent and come back, but that was never going to happen and he started a third marriage with the new Susan, who everybody called Sue. She had already married two millionaires and had a daughter, Melissa, from her second husband. Strikingly attractive, she was far more streetwise than Susan and quickly realised that Robert's lifestyle needed to be reined in if his finances were not to get completely out of control. The first to go was Vernair, the company flying Robert all over Europe. Whilst still supportive of his racing empire she encouraged Robert to examine carefully where money could be saved and he was no longer the soft touch when bloodstock agents and trainers came with numerous 'bargains' to sell him. Certainly in the early days of the marriage she was less than popular with many of these gentlemen who had benefited from the high spending lifestyle.

The one instance where no expense was spared was the 1986 party at the Nunnery for his fiftieth birthday. Guests came from all over the world and the cabaret was headed by Paul Anka, who flew from America with a backing group of over twenty musicians. There were two bands and a major firework display which he put on close to midnight caused a major uproar, with the local radio station inundated with complaints from residents who could not sleep. One local MP even appeared at the gates in his pyjamas and questions were asked in the Manx parliament.

I had decided to stay not with the Cunliffe-Owens but in a specially large bedroom at the Palace Hotel as I thought Angela might enjoy seeing the hotel and casino we had such fun building years earlier. What I had forgotten was that when the money ran out the size of all the bedrooms had been drastically cut and the especially large double room was the equivalent of a modest single in a normal hotel. Luckily we went to bed so late that we managed a few hours though neither of us are good sleepers, particularly in a small bed.

The following day Robert and Sue gave everybody lunch in a marquee on the racecourse where the Manx Derby was run and the birthday boy duly won it. Worth ten thousand pounds to the winner it was the Isle of Man's richest race of the year but Robert who didn't watch the race was so enjoying himself that it was with the greatest of difficulty that Charles and I got him to his feet and persuaded him to go to the presentation.

Although Sue had persuaded Robert to cut down his previously unbridled spending on racing she was supportive and accompanied him to the major meetings – however they rarely came to either of the great National Hunt meetings, Cheltenham and Aintree. Robert had lost his enthusiasm for National Hunt but Charles was as keen as ever and never missed a day of either meeting. For Cheltenham he stayed with the Chairman, Sam Vestey, and spent most of the meeting in his box where, because his host had to look after the major races and the royal family – particularly the Queen Mother, he considered himself partially in charge. Sam used to find this very amusing, and greeted visitors with the statement, 'Oh, you've had an invitation to Benson's box have you?'

The first meeting the three of us would get together was the New-market Heath meeting where we would usually stay with Jeremy Hindley. On one occasion the house was so crowded that I was asked to share a room with Charles. He went straight to sleep and began to snore in an outrageously loud way. I tried pummelling him, shouting at him, but nothing would wake him up and eventually I went down-stairs and tried unsuccessfully to sleep on the sofa. How Caroline, his wife, ever stood it I do not know. Although Charles and Caroline always stayed with us for Aintree, the first meeting we all got togeth-er was the Chester May festival which Robert and Charles loved and where a number of trainers, particularly Jeremy Hindley and Barry Hills, would stay as well.

We did have one year at Swettenham when Robert got so disorien-tated that, looking for the bathroom, he wandered into our bedroom (which used to be his) stark naked and I had to lead him to the bath-room he had been allotted. Angela was quite shaken at the time. For Royal Ascot Robert and I both stayed with the Hanburys at their house, Queen's Lodge, where the hosts always gave a large party on the Thursday night. Robert and Sue had one of the four new boxes opposite the paddock with generous balconies to see the horses in the paddock and Robert, who usually had several runners but who rarely saw them saddled, could time his entry to the paddock to arrive at the same time as the jockeys. Angela and I always went to lunch on the Tuesday and I would often go for a drink after one or more of the late races on the other days. More and more celebrities used to come to the box – Joan Collins, Anthony Andrews, Nigel Havers and Ronnie Wood being regulars.

It was during the last days of the box just before the new stand was built that I had my most dramatic moment in it. I had driven down from Cheshire and arrived early, stopping for a couple of cups of cof-fee en route. It was swelteringly hot and I had on a particularly heavy morning coat and waistcoat. Angela was trying to keep my weight down and I had virtually no breakfast. I remember having my first glass of champagne when Tim Kitson arrived and started talking about the Lords and Commons bridge tour of Europe. The next thing I knew was I was lying on my back with Bill Gredley pouring water over my face and John Gosden saying he'd summoned the course doctor, who arrived a couple of minutes later. He took my blood pres-sure, which he said was unreasonably low, and then told me I would have proper tests in the ambulance room. A couple of paramedics arrived with a stretcher, which they insisted I got on and I was carried ignominiously though an inquisitive crowd to the ambulance room. There I discovered that Ascot had some of the most modern equipment of any racecourse in Britain but despite every effort to find either a heart condition or stroke they could find nothing, and I was eventually allowed back to the box. There I was greeted with total incredulity because nobody had expected to see me back. Robert admitted later he thought I was a 'goner'. Tim Kitson was trying to ring the family (Angela was not with me) to say that if they wanted to see me again they had better hasten over and Nigel Dempster, at whose feet I had fainted, was looking very pensive. I did have the presence of mind to ask Sally Hindley to make sure Dempster didn't print anything and she said she had already asked him to keep quiet. The afternoon ended on a hilarious note with Nigel Havers pretending to take my blood pressure and giving me a lot of advice to drink plenty of water and keep out of the heat. 'But you're not a doctor,' I said. 'I know,' he countered, 'but I've played so many I know more than most of them.'

I went back to William Barlow, who I was staying with – the Hanburys having sadly split up the previous year – and the following morning the papers arrived. I knew from William's face as soon as he opened the *Daily Mail* I was in trouble, and sure enough I was Dempster's lead story with for once a good photograph in a morning coat at a happier Ascot and some nonsense about my proving tougher than the reinforced concrete I was used to.

In fact, when a few days later I went to my doctor for a full check up with extensive blood tests, he was to tell me that I had a simple faint which always looks terrifying to other people. He also gave me some excellent advice: never go without breakfast, it is the most important meal of the day, and if you must drink a lot of coffee, drink plenty of water as well. I didn't tell him Nigel Havers had already given me that information. My tests were fine and my cholesterol was excellent, two points less than the doctor's, which as he rather sourly said I didn't deserve with the lifestyle he supposed I was leading.

The Derby was a meeting I always went to with Robert, as did Charles. The old Epsom stand had no spare boxes and my cousins had the largest box on the course, having built the stand. There was a private room with a few large tables and Robert had one of these with Lord Howard de Walden on one side and Prince Khalid Abdullah the other. The room had its own stand to watch the racing and I was next to Robert when Khalid Abdullah had the hot favourite, Dancing Brave, who should have won the race but was given too much to do by Greville Starkey – an excellent jockey normally but not on this occasion. Robert put his hand on the prince's shoulder, 'Bad luck, Khalid, that's racing for you.' The glare he got from His Highness silenced even Robert.

On another occasion Charles was not with us as he was in hospital recovering from a heart attack. As we set out Robert said, 'He's supposed to have no excitement but has insisted on hourly bulletins. I don't know what will be worse for him, ringing him up or getting him agitated if I don't ring.' Robert and I had both changed in London but Sue insisted on putting on her dress near the course. We found an upmarket, smart new housing estate with trees and hedges and Sue disappeared behind one of them. A man came out of the nearest house and said, 'You all look as though you want a party. I do have a bottle of champagne in the house and a spare bedroom for your wife to change in.' Robert politely declined his kind offer.

I had been asked to be a Godparent at the christening of Robert's elder of two sons with Sue and still have a picture at home of Sue looking absolutely stunning holding Sam. As the two younger children grew up and went to prep school, the school sports day seemed to coincide with the Derby and Robert, who did not want to take a box in the new stand, would go to the prep school and my longstanding invitation came to an end. I did go for some years with Ernie Harrison when Vodafone sponsored and then to the Jockey Club lunch for its members, but when Ernie died and the Jockey Club wanted to save money and scrapped the lunch, I gave up and missed the race.

Whilst Charles's health steadily worsened in the nineties, Robert's seemed excellent – but one thing they had in common was the breaking up of their marriages. Charles was the first and it was extremely amicable, Charles admitting that his lifestyle would tax the patience of any wife. Caroline, known by her friends as Chubby, was a delightful, attractive lady who had loved the racing and social side of Charles's life. What she probably did not realise at the start of the marriage was just how strong Charles's addiction to gambling, mainly on horses, was. Although he received some wonderful information from some of the leading trainers in the land, he could not resist betting on almost every race at a meeting. His girlfriend between marriages, Sue Elwyn, who later married and lived happily with my good friend John Hall, described his addiction as almost a disease. When he ran out of money he became a completely different person, she told me; he would grovel to people he wouldn't normally talk to if he thought they could supply him with betting money.

He was an excellent and sought-after public speaker, who got away with some outrageous comments, particularly on friends he knew well. (See my note on the Derby Club on page 258.)

I have already spoken of Charles's speech at Robert's fiftieth birthday. When he started the speech at Robert's sixtieth, which was held in Paris, to another large audience, he referred to Robert's children's inheritance being frittered away. He was just about to get into the Jerry Hall saga when Robert suddenly waking up to what was about to happen, staggered to his feet and removed the microphone from Charles. This was the one occasion I ever saw Robert make a major speech himself.

Charles was well known for the holidays he took which were lavish and often paid for by someone else. The late Jeffrey Barnard once listed in a newspaper column a free overseas holiday for every month of the previous year – and this at a time he was working full time for the *Daily Express*. The three holidays he would never miss were a lengthy stay in Barbados with Robert Sangster, a period on the Aga Khan's yacht in mid-summer, which lasted until he eventually fell out with the Aga, who was separating from his second wife, Sally, a long-standing ex-girlfriend of Charles, and his trip to Australia in November with Robert.

Robert's finances worsened at the end of the eighties and, faced with a major property recession, he put Manton up for sale. This was a tragedy for his great friend and trainer Barry Hills, who had no contract and frantically looked for a buyer. Surprisingly none of the Arab entrants into British racing showed interest, although the magnificent complex should have been ideal for them. Faced with not knowing if he would have a yard to train in the following year, Barry Hills was forced to give his son John notice and made plans to return to his yard. He handled this extremely cleverly, buying a house much closer to his gallops and by threatening to give up training completely, which would have meant the loss of many jobs in Lambourn, he persuaded the local council to give him permission to turn part of his old yard into a housing complex – and the profits were invested in a magnificent new yard close to his new house and gallops.

Robert, unable to get a meaningful offer for Manton, installed his son-in-law, Peter Chapple Hyam, who trained there for some years, initially very successfully. One year he had two outstanding horses in his yard, Rodrigo de Triano and Doctor Devious. Robert, who now needed to make sales, sold Doctor Devious although Chapple Hyam begged him not to. When he won the Dewhurst, Robert had to congratulate the new Italian owners and got a good press the next day for being so sporting. In fact he asked me to go with him to a little back bar later in the day where we consumed a lot of champagne and he could drown his sorrows in relative peace. Robert then said to me, 'I have to pretend to be the greatest sportsman around but you know me so well and can listen to what I really think.' Rodrigo de Triano did win the Guineas for Robert but Doctor Devious won the Derby with Rodrigo de Triano down the field. Not the most festive Derby we went to together.

I'm afraid Robert continued to sell his best prospects, particularly to Sheik Mohammed, much to the annoyance of his trainers Barry Hills, John Gosden and later Brian Meehan.

His worst financial moment was nothing to do with horses but his failure to join the John Magnier, McManus, Tabor, Lewis syndicate, who under the guidance of Joe Lewis, a genius in his field, made a fortune by investing on overseas currency exchanges. Their success transferred them from being rich to immensely rich and Robert, who had been invited to join but had decided to play safe and leave his still substantial trusts in the hands of English investors, was left far behind.

Nowhere was this more obvious than Barbados, where Robert was to spend increasingly more time and become a full resident there after leaving the Isle of Man. The high spot of the post Christmas holiday was a pro-am golf tournament, initially mainly sponsored by Robert and partially organised by Charles with assistance from Sally Hindley. Benson also did the auction and in the early years many of the top English professionals took part. The format was that the tournament was teams of three amateurs with a professional and the auction took place on the eve of the final day, with a draw for partners also organised by Charles. On one memorable occasion Charles had decided that Robert needed a good amateur and without his knowledge organised Albert Finney, who was doing the draw by putting a piece of paper with the right name in the corner of his mouth to be produced at the appropriate time. Finney partially swallowed the piece of paper and attempted to regurgitate it causing hysterical laughter from those of us who realised what was going on.

As the Irish contingent grew richer their grip on the tournament increased and, although it continued to be co-sponsored by Robert and John Magnier, the balance was shifting from the first to the second.

Barry Hills and I decided we had had enough of Barbados and with Dick Bonnycastle moved to Cape Town, where we rented a house in Constantia and had nine excellent consecutive winter holidays there. The three of us did go back to Barbados for one last visit a few years ago, when Sandy Lane, which had been bought by J P McManus and associates, was closed for reconstruction. J P, a most generous man, had tried hard to persuade Robert to sell him Jane's Harbour, making an offer of at least double the market price, knowing that Robert would hate the noise and dust with hundreds of workmen rebuilding the hotel. Robert stubbornly refused to take the offer and it was not until after his death when Jane's Harbour was put up for sale that J P stepped in and bought it from his children.

So Barry, Dick and I stayed in a hotel recommended by one of Barry's owners. It was incredibly expensive and the restaurants even more so. The influx of the multi-millionaires had definitely had a major impact on pricing and Barbados bore little resemblance to the island I first visited a very long time back.

As the nineties progressed I often wondered whether Robert's move to Barbados led to the breakup of his third marriage, although, like Charles and Carolyn, he and Sue stayed on good terms apart from the odd row over alimony.

When I moved to Tilstone and we jointly sold the Swettenham estate, he had the vast acreage of Manton to move what mares he wanted to put there.

Charles's health was in a slow but steady decline, diabetes being followed by a heart attack only to be then followed by the cancer which was to finish him off. He bore it all with courage and good humour and was admirably looked after in his last weeks by three ladies, one of whom was Carolyn.

I still think my obituary of Charles for the *Daily Telegraph* was one of the best three I wrote for that paper and the only paragraph they left out was Sue Hall's description of being attached to a gambling addict. I got a lift with Nigel Dempster from the church to the wake, held in Sue Sangster's sumptuous London flat. Nigel, who was in his last weeks of working for the *Daily Mail* and was beginning to show signs of the illness which was to kill him, had obtained a car and driver from his newspaper and hadn't lost his powers of observation. As we entered the flat he said, 'God, I didn't realise she got that good a pay-off.' Robert took a group of us to lunch, which he insisted on paying for and a major chapter had drawn to a close.

Whereas everybody knew that Charles was dying nobody ever dreamt that a couple of years later Robert would do the same. He came to Chester in May the next year as usual, alone and in good form, and asked me to go to his Spanish house in September for a week. I arrived at the house and walked straight in. As there was nobody about I found the fridge and helped myself to a cold beer and waited for Robert to arrive, which he did half an hour later with Mick O'Toole and Fonsie O'Brien, two friends from the early Irish racing days. We played golf every day in the middle of the day and the heat there, though not as intense as July or August, was still considerable. He seemed fitter and healthier than he had been for some time and we had long talks about life in general. He had introduced me to his young Australian girlfriend at his daughter Kate's wedding, where she was hidden away from the main reception. She appeared both nice and very attractive. He confessed to me that although she wanted to commit he did not and hoped very much to have a reconciliation and go back to Sue.

How or if this progressed I do not know because I was never to have a proper conversation with him again. He should never have played in the Barbados mid-January tournament but showing all his great courage he did and was put straight on a plane for London, where he was taken in a complete state of collapse by ambulance to a hospital where he was operated on for pancreatic cancer. He did rally and when I rang him up he was his old jolly self. 'I went up to the pearly gates but St Peter took one look and sent me back again. I'll be with you for Chester as usual.' Ten days later when I went to visit him I was met by a grim faced Ben. 'You can go and see Father if you wish but he is completely out of it and you might want to remember him as he was.' He died the next day.

The funeral drew hundreds of friends and I was terrified I might be asked to do an address. Fortunately the family had the good sense to choose the most accomplished public speaker around, Colin Ingleby-Mackenzie, who was at his very best. The wake was equally memorable, held in part of a large hotel with Robert's pictures and trophies on display.

He would have been proud of his family who managed later to put a large part of his bloodstock for sale at the absolute top of the market. Robert, like myself, felt that timing was part luck and part good judgement.

Jane's Harbour and the Spanish house have both gone but Manton remains in the family and winners are still flowing from the present incumbent, Brian Meehan. Although his colours are no longer on display, his family have very close likenesses and he would be amused that Sam, in his early twenties, has taken his mother, Sue's, silks and had a winner the year before last at Royal Ascot.

Chapter 13

Cricket

Cricket was a big part of my life, yet when I look back at other sporting aspects, particularly shooting, squash and rackets, where I realised my full potential, I have to be mildly dissatisfied with my achievements on the cricket field. I did become a rather stodgy but effective opening batsman and I did make a lot of runs, but nevertheless I always felt I could have done better. The day when Gubby Allen took me into the net at Marchwiel and made me turn my right hand around the bat was the major turning point and but for that I might never have achieved anything worthwhile.

Marchwiel, the family cricket ground, was one of the finest private grounds in the country, on a par with Arundel and Hoveringham, two other lovely grounds I have played on. It was in existence when my grandfather bought the house and surrounding land in 1912 and then enlarged it after World War One and built a pavilion. It had a perfect country setting with the house and gardens on one side and woods on the other. Father was a good club cricketer, bowling what would now be described as a brisk medium pace and batting between six and eight in the order. He was probably at his best in the thirties and during the war years and by 1950 when I started to watch him play regularly he was forty-two and his pace was slowing.

At some point in the early fifties he stopped playing for Wolverhampton and took over the Marchwiel village side. Although they were called a village team, because of the excellence of the ground and because the family were financing it, talented cricketers locally wanted to join and we had a well above average team. We played the local sides, Brymbo, Monsanto, Wrexham, Oswestry and further afield, Ruthin and Colwyn Bay. Ruthin had, I remember, a terrible wicket. Father had broken his thumb and I was lucky to avoid the same fate on a couple of occasions. Colwyn Bay were by far the best side we played regularly, as a couple of masters from the local public school, Rydal College, were outstanding cricketers and I never remember Marchwiel winning against them.

The great blow for Father came when he failed to inherit March-wiel, my grandmother having made a will just after my grandfather's death in 1943, which she never altered. The house and cricket ground went to his younger sister, Mary Bell, who Father had little time for, though, because of the ground, he tried to come to terms with her.

Father had run two other private sides in two two-day games against Market Drayton, a good Shropshire club, and at Aigburth, the Liverpool county ground, where we played a good touring club, the Northern Nomads. He had also built up a week of 'Country House' cricket culminating in a two-day game against the Free Foresters.

The cricket in these games was always of a high standard and the entertainment was lavish. When I briefly invested in a lobster business, in my late twenties, we always had lobsters as a starter and finished with several bottles of good vintage port. Father's great cricketing friend was Ken Cranston, who had played for England and captained Lancashire. Ken was an outstanding bat, who should have played for many more years in the England team than he did. He was also an exceptionally nice man who really enjoyed life but he did have a very controversial first wife – Mary. The two stories I remember best were when the men were playing snooker at Tickwood and a rather bored Mary came up to the table, laid her ample bosom on it and said, 'Now putt these!' At the flat I had in Parkgate, after a local match, I invited Ken and Mary plus two cricketing friends to have a final drink and Mary asked if she could see the rest of the flat. When we got to the bedroom she immediately started undressing with the words, 'We must be quick,' and was amazed when I fled back to the sitting room. She certainly didn't do Ken's cricket career any good but we benefited by having him at most of the country house games, which raised standards and he always captained the side against us at Aigburth. Father also had several other friends who were good cricketers. Tony Ledgard, who was to become the famous secretary of Delamere Golf Club, was one and Geoff Cornu, one of Father's closest friends, another. Two very good old Etonians, Ken Boles and Ian Lomax, played for many years but when Father's friends started dropping out I was able to recruit more of my own.

Charles Robbins, who was an outstanding schoolboy cricketer at Eton and who later played a season for Middlesex, was extremely helpful at recruiting good club cricketers and on occasions ex-England or county performers. Colin Ingleby-Mackenzie was a regular and other famous names who played were Ted Dexter and Phil Edmonds. Two others, less famous but just as good, were Michael Sturt, who did play a season for Middlesex as an amateur, and Michael Groves, an Oxford blue. Anthony Vivian, who was a soldier in charge of the Royal Welch, recruited a good side against us and produced Frank Worrell, the captain of the West Indies. Frank was out first ball from Ian Lomax, caught in the slips. He so enjoyed the game he came with us to Market Drayton and Aigburth. He made plenty of runs but the Market Drayton side hit his bowling all over the ground. The following year he brought Garfield Sobers, then totally unknown in England. I had been told he bowled slow chinamen and opened the batting against him. His run up seemed very long for a slow bowler and the first ball hit me in the middle of the stomach, to the hilarity of the pavilion. The Marchwiel wicket was always a little lively mid-morning and I made twenty-eight of the worst runs ever against him. He was doing far too much with the ball! His innings finished with two magnificent sixes, off Ian Lomax, the second hitting the pine trees in the wood behind the bowler, still on the way up!

In 1969 we all decided to get together to take a side to Rhodesia and then to South Africa. The side on paper looked very strong. We had one ex-England cricketer, Alan Moss, and seven or eight who had played county cricket. I produced a brochure which led the opposition to think we were much better than we were. I was unable to shake off a severe bout of tonsillitis and had gone to my GP in Malpas and then in desperation to Father's in Wrexham. Both had given me antibiotics, which did me no good and it was not until we got to Durban that I found a doctor who took a throat swab and told me he was amazed I was still standing. He also said that the National Health Service in Britain only had two antibiotics, whereas in South Africa they had the choice of sixteen. He gave me some pills which completely cured me in five days, but by then the tour was over.

We had started with two games in Rhodesia, which was then under Ian Smith, who had declared U.D.I (unilateral declaration of independence). As a result, the governor, Sir Humphrey Gibbs, watched the first match and Ian Smith the second. The first match started at 9am and broke for breakfast. On paper, I had three excellent opening bowlers but Ian Lomax lost his action half-way through his first over and Alan Moss was not really fit. It was left to Derek Wing, an excellent minor counties opening bowler, to keep things under control – but once the shine went off the ball, the opposition ran riot. They were, in fact, the full Rhodesian side and an enormous crowd, who had been totally starved of sport because of U.D.I., cheered them on. Somehow we managed to draw the first game and did much better in the second, which was also a draw.

The hospitality everywhere was fantastic and most of the side both enjoyed themselves and tried their hardest. The exception was Ian Lomax, who, out of form, sulked and was thoroughly difficult throughout. I stayed on to do some work whilst everybody else went home, the exception being Ian, who went back to Rhodesia with another member of the side. They had obviously got designs on girls they had met there. I travelled back from Johannesburg, with the first stop Salisbury, and watched the embarking passengers. The first two were Ian and Jim, both extremely drunk and having tried to throw something at the engine (they probably wouldn't have been allowed to board nowadays) they staggered on to the plane. I left them to it until the next morning when I went down and chatted but managed to get off the plane early, collect my luggage and the first two people I saw through customs were Rosemary and Jim's wife. I stationed myself behind them and when Ian and Jim came through both wives threw themselves into their arms. As I had both arms high in the air and was blowing kisses, I have to say both husbands had the grace to look highly embarrassed.

My grandmother's will did have some benefits: I was not going to inherit the cricket ground there was less pressure to play for the local side and I could run more games for the many touring club sides I played for. For two years I managed the Harrow Wanderers side against the Eton Ramblers, on the Evelyn Rothschild ground at Wing, the scene of my first game after leaving Harrow. There I found that having got a very good side together, I was to lose five of them because of the Cricketers Cup (the old boys competition) being played on the Sunday. I even managed to get Aidan Crawley out of retirement. Besides running the Marchwiel week, I ran games for the M.C.C., two local touring clubs and started a series of matches against Christopher Morley's XI at Shrewsbury school. We both got very good sides in what was one of the best school wickets I played on. Christopher lived in a lovely Shropshire house, Wenlock Abbey and the party was always held there, apart from one occasion, when

Christopher Thompson allowed us to use Aldenham Hall, another great country house. One of the other side got very friendly with a niece of the host, locked himself in a drawing room and assumed all was well. He got the shock of his life when his host came through a secret panel, which slid open to give him access!

The highlight of my later career was to play at Lord's for the M.C.C against the Argentine. Having missed out at Lord's as a schoolboy, opening the batting was a great thrill. My illustrious partner was Peter Richardson, and we did make thirty-nine runs together, before I was out LBW. My main problem until then was not to be run out by Peter but I got into double figures and enjoyed every moment. The Argentine side also played at Marchwiel; they were mainly descendants of Caribbeans, who had settled there, and they would have been the equivalent of a good minor counties side.

All went well on the cricket front until my marriage collapsed and I no longer had a base to have people to stay. Johnny Bell and I had to this point got on well together. He could have been an extremely good cricketer, bowling leg breaks at quite a fast pace. Like myself he never learnt to bowl a googly, an essential part of a top leg spinner's armoury. He was also a good middle order batsman.

I had my problems with him in the company as he never settled down. Although his father did an excellent job and was highly respected, he was not particularly popular as he lacked the warmth that Father could produce to the outside world. Johnny had the warmth but could be both stupid and arrogant. I did try and give him decent posts in the company, which anybody of ability could have taken advantage of, in particular putting him on the board of the overseas company in charge of plant. Instead of trying to do well, he upset everybody, the climax being a trip to the Sudan on which he spent an additional week coming back via Bangkok, which was not exactly on the route but which held a peculiar fascination for him.

During the second year after the split he announced without consulting me that he was taking over the cricket week and for the first time I missed the week entirely. I did partially make it up with Johnny and played against him for two of the sides in the week. Sadly, Johnny's cricket deteriorated as his weight ballooned and he became so heavy that he was eventually unable to play at all.

Although originally the richest of all of us, as his parents had passed to him a large shareholding, he lost a lot of his money in the property crash at the end of the eighties and his finances went downhill at an alarming rate from then on. Unable to finance the cricket ground, the Marchwiel club amalgamated with the Wrexham and cricket is still played to this day, though the future of both the house and grounds is still in the balance. The house owned by John's children has been on the market for nearly four years and several sales have fallen through.

Johnny himself moved to Bangkok with his former brother-in-law, William Gibbs, and as I write they both share an apartment there. It is a very sad time for a great house and cricket ground – once one of the grandest in North Wales.

My last cricket game was played for the Free Foresters on Miles Clarke's private ground, near Malpas. An excellent little ground, entirely conceived by Miles, a real enthusiast if not a great player! I bowled seven overs of leg breaks and got four wickets. The following day I could hardly get out of bed and crawled to the bath where I put half a bottle of Badedas into the hot water, it still barely got me upright. At the age of sixty-one I finally called it a day and if my cricket career was not the greatest I had a great deal of fun playing with extremely nice people.

Chapter 14

Politicians I have known

Although politics never became a serious part of my life I did at one time strongly consider trying to become a member of parliament. It was at a time when to some degree M.P.s could still decide how much time they would devote to their constituents, and I was influenced by my first Cheshire M.P., Mr Grant Ferris, who neither lived in the constituency nor spent much time in it. What finally knocked any idea of becoming an M.P. on the head was my experience on the selection for the Nantwich constituency, which was then considered one of the safest Conservative seats in Cheshire. The chairman of the committee I was drafted onto was Jack Grubb, a very influential local who was also chairman of the Magistrate's bench at Broxton. He was an excellent chairman, had a very nice large house in Malpas with an extensive garden, and we spent several weekends there or in the Conservative office in Nantwich interviewing candidates. When we got to the last chosen, wives would be invited to accompany the candidates. This would prove to be a major factor in the final selection process.

Because the constituency was so attractive an enormous number of people applied and we selected about eighty for interview. I took a particular interest in two. Bill Grosvenor was a close friend of both Raymond Mould and my brother-in-law, Peter Shaw, and they thought he would be an excellent M.P. A distant relative of the Duke of Westminster, I had expected some help from that quarter, though in the event none materialised. The other was selected by head office and I had asked Tim Kitson to find somebody who would perform well. He told me the candidate, whose name escapes me, was very bright and Ted Heath himself wanted him as an M.P. Unfortunately what he did not tell me was that he was a Jew and, though one would like to think a nice rural constituency would have no prejudice on that score, you would be entirely wrong and the moment a member of the panel prized out of him that he was a practising Jew he had no chance of progressing.

Bill Grosvenor did far worse. Suffering from either a heavy cold or flu he sweated profusely through the interview, could not answer the simplest questions on local matters, and did my standing on the committee no good at all.

As my two candidates had fallen by the wayside I had to settle on somebody else and Archie Edmondstone seemed to me an ideal choice. His only problem was that his wife was very reluctant to make her home in Cheshire and when we got to the last four, wives were made to stand up and answer questions. It was obvious her heart was not in it and her honesty ditched Archie's chances.

The hot favourite was the Duke of Wellington's eldest son and the only mistake he made was to make the running too early. Highly intelligent, he had researched local affairs to a degree that he knew more about them than most of the committee. He also did not have a wife which was to count against him at the final selection meeting.

This was thrown open to all the constituency members of the party and, whereas all the committee had in depth knowledge of the two final candidates, most of those attending would be influenced by the final speeches and the performance of the candidates on the day. The Duke of Wellington's eldest son, the Marques of Douro and Nicholas Bonsor, heir to a baronetcy, were the final candidates. Both old Etonians and both articulate and personable.

By the time of the final selection both candidates had their supporters. The Bonsor camp had gently spread a rumour that the Duke of Wellington was not in good health and was not long for this world so that the Marquess would not be able to hold the seat for long. In the event, the Duke is still alive today at the age of ninety-five, whilst Nicholas Bonsor's father died a few years after he was elected and Nicholas had to sell up his Cheshire home and live in Buckinghamshire. But what really won the day for Nicholas was his attractive and intelligent wife, Nadine. She had broken her leg and sat on the podium with her leg in plaster. When she was asked a question, she gallantly got to her feet and you could see the audience warming to this brave lady. You could also see the female activists thinking how great she would be on their coffee mornings, etc.

So, against the odds, Nicholas Bonsor won the day. He is a very nice man who I have had several drinks with since. Although he did become a junior minister he was not the best candidate and seven or eight of our discards, including Archie Edmondstone, made future cabinet ministers.

The whole business left me feeling very cynical and disillusioned and I realised that the Grant Ferris style of handling a constituency was no longer acceptable and that it would be very difficult to combine being a member of parliament and running a large complex construction company. Although I decided to concentrate on the latter it brought me into contact with a number of leading politicians including four prime ministers. Indeed when my cousin Alistair became Mrs Thatcher's party treasurer he brought all the leading Conservative ministers into our orbit. I therefore give a pen picture of my brief acquaintance or, in the case of one or two, slightly better knowledge of them:

Harold Wilson I only met him once when the chief guest at a reception given by the Mayor of Ellesmere Port, who made a point of introducing him to me. He gave me a long hard look and obviously decided I was not a supporter because after one question about local construction he moved hastily away.

Edward Heath As one of my closest friends, Tim Kitson, was his private secretary I went to two major receptions in Downing Street and met Edward Heath a number of times. He was always cheerful and courteous and started off the conversation with the words 'how nice to see you again', although I felt Tim had probably prompted him on this point. I also attended a Conservative election dinner held in the Duke of Westminster's private dining room. Heath was between Robert Sangster's mother, Peggy, and a leading Conservative lady activist. Tim had warned me that Heath was exhausted from the campaign and his head kept falling in the soup as he tried to stay awake. As both ladies had far too much to drink, he had little chance of achieving his obvious desire of falling asleep but the whole performance made me realise how exhausting an election is for Prime Ministers – I was to see the same thing with Margaret Thatcher a few years later.

Edward Heath also came into my life through Tim Kitson at the crucial election he lost at the end of his premiership. Tim and I were constantly on the phone and I pleaded with him to try and persuade

Edward Heath to go to the country quickly and not let the 'Winter of Discontent' get worse. For once an onlooker like me read the situation better than the principal and as Philip Ziegler wrote in his excellent biography, Heath uncharacteristically dithered far too long.

When the final showdown between Heath and Margaret Thatcher for the party leadership took place, Tim Kitson rang me up and asked if I wanted to back an absolute certainty. I replied that had always been a great ambition and he told me put on a bet for him and the former Prime Minister and mentioned a not inconsiderable amount of money. The odds were five to two on and I thought I would help myself and had the same amount for myself as for Kitson and Heath. Tim had done the count and of course had failed to realise how many M.P.s professing loyalty to their leader were going to vote differently. The same was to happen to Peter Morrison and Mrs Thatcher some years later.

I met Heath a few times later at lunches or dinners organised by Tim who remained close to his old boss and mentor right to the end.

Margaret Thatcher I first met Margaret Thatcher at a lunch organised by Clive Beck, who was chairman of a large scaffolding company. I had lunch with Tom King a few days before and told him I was about to meet his new leader. He was seething about the way she was tackling the fireman's strike, then a leading political issue. 'She is trying to cash in on the public belief that firemen are heroic figures whereas most of them have other part time jobs and make a lot of money. I have more of them in my constituency of Bridgewater than anybody, so I should know.' He then suggested I ask her a question and I replied that if I was going to do it, which would be difficult, he should not only write out the question but give me plenty of backup as she had a week earlier demolished my construction colleague Bill Francis at a similar event. The lunch went well and Mrs Thatcher dealt extremely competently with a number of questions on housing statistics, building industry prospects, etc. After about forty minutes of questions I lent over and asked Clive Beck, who I was next to if I could ask a political question. 'Please do,' he said, 'it's getting very boring.' I then stood up and repeated Tom King's question, which I knew by heart. The effect was electrifying, Mrs T was furious! Thinking for one moment she was coming over the table to attack me, I shrank back. 'Are you a frightened man, Mr McAlpine?' 'I am absolutely terrified, Mrs Thatcher,' was my reply, which had the table rocking with laughter but infuriated the leader of the opposition. She fired some statistics at me to which I gave some of Tom King's answers back. Clive hastily intervened and that was the end of a most interesting lunch. My main surprise was how violently Mrs Thatcher reacted, which I had not expected.

The next time we met was at Edwin McAlpine's private room in the Dorchester hotel and the meeting is described in my chapter on the hotel. I met her a few times when Alistair was treasurer and she did address our construction dining club in Alistair's London house. The meeting started at 11am and precisely on the hour at 12 she looked at her watch and said, 'Gentlemen, I always have a scotch at noon; Alistair will you provide some and I suggest you all do the same.' Needless to say most of us followed her excellent advice and the morning was a great success.

Another dramatic occasion was a visit to the Marks and Spencer's financial services office block on the Chester Business Park, where I was to show her around as a last part of the election campaign, which would turn out to be her last. Our book, *The Road to Success*, was hot off the presses and I waited for a chance to present it to her. What I had not bargained for was the 'Iron Lady' to be as exhausted as she was, just as Edward Heath had been. She was totally at the end of her tether and David Wolfson, who was on the campaign bus, told me later he had never seen her like that before. Twice I had to put my hand on her shoulder to prevent her keeling over and in front of two fiercesome looking armed protection officers, one a lady, whose hands were never far from their guns. I did eventually give her the book and she held it up. It made an excellent photograph for the press the next day.

I was moved up from the back of St Paul's Cathedral by my cousin Bill to sit next to her at Uncle Edwin's funeral, but apart from a smile and a few whispered words we had no real conversation.

Sir Dennis Thatcher I have also described my meeting and conversation with Dennis Thatcher at Edwin McAlpine's Christmas lunch but a much more exciting meeting with him occurred at a reception at No.10. Alistair had asked Angela and I to dinner after the reception and I had accepted although my wife would have preferred a quiet dinner. The reception was lively enough as I was introduced to Esther Rantzen, who was about to host a T.V. programme specialising in deriding companies who had fallen foul of the media. In our case we were trying to keep open a quarrying company in South Wales which had existed for over a century and provided much local employment. One of our senior staff had planned to quarry some land but it turned out that the landowner objected to the plan, even though we had the Council's permission to quarry it. We were totally unprepared for the media backlash that was unleashed.

Late in the reception Alistair came up to me and said Margaret has gone to the television station for an interview by Thames television. Dennis has asked us for drinks in the main drawing room, so join us as soon as you can. I found Angela and we headed for the drawing room where an amazing sight awaited us. Rolling around on the sofa were Dennis Thatcher and Alistair's then wife Romilly, who was trying hard to evade her 'captors' grasp. Sir Dennis came up for air and seeing a group of Alistair, Ian Gow, Sir Reginald Bracewell-Smith, Angela and myself looking on, shouted at a uniformed flunkey, 'For God's sake get them all a drink.' And then proceeded to continue wrestling with Romilly on the sofa. Eventually she extricated herself and although a little dishevelled, took it all with good humour. The next day I was rung up by Anthony Bamford, who had been to *Anyone for Dennis?* a big theatrical hit. 'Rather boring,' he said. 'You should have been at the real thing,' I replied, 'it was anything but boring.'

John Major John Major was a good friend of my next door neighbour and local M.P., Alistair Goodlad, who indeed joined his cabinet. Probably because of this Angela and I found ourselves hosting a well-attended local Conservative gathering with John and Norma Major as the chief guests. Large as Tilstone Lodge is we have no room to sit down a hundred people, so lunch was divided into two and I sat next to Norma Major in the dining room while Angela sat next to the Prime Minister in the drawing room. Drinks were served before lunch in the hall and John Major and Alistair both made speeches from the main staircase. A very pleasant occasion and, as the *Chester Chronicle* said, would provide photographs for the drawing room and indeed they are there as I write this.

I then attended no less than five receptions at No.10, two of which I sat next to John Major at dinner afterwards. He was easy to talk to and perhaps I stupidly began to think he was more than a casual acquaintance.

When the last days of his premiership dawned just before the 1995 General Election, a snap decision was taken to direct him to Aintree Racecourse, where the Grand National was being run on the Monday following an IRA bomb threat, which had the course evacuated just before the start of the race on the Saturday. As I was the senior non-executive director, Peter Daresbury, the chairman, offered me the alternative of looking after the Princess Royal or John Major – and having met him several time I settled for the latter.

The Prime Minister's car arrived with a large police escort and we had to fight our way from the car through a large crowd to the private box with a balcony where Major and his party could watch the race. I stood one side of him with Norma on the other and said that I would commentate for him and would he like a commentary at every fence or just the main ones. He seemed completely disinterested and was obviously 'going through the motions'. The race was won by Tony Dobbin for Stan Clarke, who I knew well and I would normally have joined in the celebrations in the Winners Enclosure. As it was I had to accompany the Majors, who could not wait to get away, to their car through a very hostile crowd who shouted insults and booed loudly.

The following summer I went to Lord's for a test match as a guest in a private box with some good friends I played cricket with. I noticed that John Major was in the box next door and when I went to use the toilets behind the boxes I found him talking to his son Euan. 'Hello sir,' I said, expecting to be recognised. When he didn't reply I gave him chapter and verse but he glared at me and I could only conclude that his disinterest stemmed from the fact I was no longer of any use to him. Edwina Currie, who got a lot closer to him than I ever did, described him as the coldest man she ever met. I would like to second that!

Willie Whitelaw Apart from Tim Kitson, Willie was probably the politician I got to know best, entirely because he had a gun in the Swinton grouse shoot – as I did for thirty-four years. Stories about him on the shoot were legendary but I was not there when the most famous incident took place. A large pack of grouse came through and Willie, who was a poor shot, fired a number of times but the only casualty was a wounded cock grouse who began to waddle slowly back; one of Willie's two, tall bodyguards said, 'May I sir?' drew his pistol and shot the grouse through the head. There were two incidents on the shoot I was involved with, both when Willie was Home Secretary. The first was when he arrived with a Yorkshire police Range rover with a large bubble on the roof boasting all the latest gadgetry. Willie went at lunchtime to ring the home office but came back and said to me, 'Bobby, can I borrow the phone in your Range rover; none of the police gadgetry is working.' The next day he came with the same request but a policeman insisted he went to the village several miles away where security could be assured. Not surprising as the loaders and keepers had listened the day before to the stentorial voice bellowing instructions to his office.

The second was during a long break for fog which had stopped shooting. We had all run out of conversation and I asked David whether I could ask Willie a question on the HIV scare which had gripped the country. I had just been to America and during a lengthy airport wait I had read an amazing article in the *New York Times*. This was several pages long, written in a scholarly way and completely demolished all the concepts which were currently prevalent in Britain – that AIDS was about to decimate the population in just the same way that it was doing so in many parts of the African continent. The *New York Times* had examined nearly three thousand cases in New York State and discovered that only four or five related to heterosexual intercourse between whites. All the others related to Black or Hispanic victims or homosexual activity. The paper had concluded that there must be a gene in non-whites which made them more susceptible to infection and that homosexuals were at great risk.

Willie chaired the committee Margaret Thatcher had put together on aids and Sue Masham was also on the committee. Two of the most worthy and honourable people I know but hardly best equipped to deal with this particular subject. Anyway I waded in and attempted to argue the *New York Times* case with Willie. He looked thunderstruck and after a lengthy pause bellowed, 'Are you seriously asking me to discriminate against non-whites and against the homosexuals?' David Swinton, convulsed with laughter, said jokingly, 'Why not Willie?' I have never tried to get on to another subject faster than I did that day.

He was a very amiable conversationalist and we talked a lot about Northern Ireland, where I frequently went on business. We were the largest British contractor there at the time. He gave me one excellent piece of advice: 'Stay at the Cullodon hotel, where I stay. The security there is far better there than any other hotel near Belfast.' I took his advice and never had a moment's worry.

Michael Heseltine I first met him when John Taylor, a well-known London architect, had him and his wife as guests of honour at the opening of the Saatchi and Saatchi building in Berkeley Square. I sat next to his wife and Angela sat next to Michael. I found his wife charming but Angela said she struggled for conversation. The next time was a foundation ceremony on the last section of the M4, when Paul Channon performed the ceremony on his last day as Minister of Transport. Paul was a member of the Portland and I played bridge with him a few days before the ceremony. We had joked about it and I was expecting a fairly relaxed day. I got to the site early and it was a blazing hot day and as there had been no rain for some time the ground was very hard. My main duty was to present Paul with a spade with the handle engraved in silver with an appropriate caption. I realised that he was not going to be easily able to cut the ceremonial sod, so I asked the works manager to dig up the ground so that the spade would go in without difficulty. He found a large piece of string which he pushed into the ground so that I would see where it had been disturbed. When Paul arrived I knew as soon as he got out of the car that something had happened. In fact Mrs Thatcher had sacked him the day before and the announcement was made the day after the ceremony. He looked furious, hardly greeted me and we went together to where the ceremony was to take place. To my horror there was no sign of the string and in desperation I handed Paul the spade. He tried to dig but the spade bounced back and furious, he handed it to me saying, 'You do it.' I had no more success than Paul and a voice behind said, 'You two idiots have obviously never been in a garden, give it to me' – and Michael Heseltine stepped forward and dug a piece of turf perfectly, to loud applause, leaving Channon and myself both feeling the description Michael had given us. It transpired that security for the Ministers had gone over the ground, seen the string and, thinking it might be attached to explosives, had removed it.

When he became Secretary of State for the Environment in John Major's government he was the obvious person to ask as the Construction Dining Club's next guest. Brian Hill, chairman of Higgs and Hill, was the host by rotation but Cliff Chetwode, chairman of Wimpey, insisted on addressing Heseltine before asking him to speak. He had carefully prepared his statement but went on too long and I said to Brian Hill, who I was next to, 'I think the Secretary of State is asleep.' At that moment Chetwode paused for breath and Heseltine opened one eye and said, 'Have you finished because if you have I would like to say something – and that is that your industry has had a good few years raking it in at the country's expense and I intend to make sure you don't continue.' Chetwode tried to intervene and said, 'But you are our sponsoring minister' – to which Heseltine replied, 'You are the last people I intend to sponsor.' At this point Brian Hill whispered to me, 'Have you ever seen Gooch's middle stump sailing through the air?'

Heseltine then made an aggressive speech and invited questions. I tried to question him on the 'Green Belt' pointing out that there were now exceptions that could be made. 'As long as I am Secretary of State there will be no exceptions' was his uncompromising reply. When it came to dealing with a piece of land opposite Chester Business Park, which had been cut off by the South Cheshire bypass and which was crying out for housing, he overruled his own inspectorate's recommendations plus those of both Chester and Cheshire Council.

I was to meet him in more relaxed circumstances when he had given up politics and twice we shot at Dumbleton, the Hambros shoot in Gloucestershire, where he had a gun. The first time I was between him and one of the best shots in the country. Inevitably all the birds seemed to come from the side where the great shot next to me felled most of them. At lunch, which is in an old cricket pavilion, I attempted to talk to him. He obviously thoroughly disliked my cousin Alistair (the feeling was extremely mutual) although he admitted Romily, his wife, had nearly saved his life when he had a heart attack in Venice. He was frankly not easy to talk to but it was a very different story when one evening I was sitting alone on the club table at Whites and he asked if he could join me. I doubt whether he had recognised me but he couldn't have been nicer and we had an animated conversation on several subjects, including Iraq – 'Blair was told by Bush, you are either with me or against me, there is no middle way.'

We also talked about shooting which Heseltine, like many Tory M.P.s, was very fond of. He said, 'When I started I was shooting one in twelve, now it is one in six. How do I know? Because, I also carefully count my cartridges at every stand.' I found this both endearing and honest; one in six is probably being still the worst average of any regular Dumbleton gun. The important thing I have always felt is that people should enjoy shooting however good or bad they are at it, safety always the first priority.

Cecil Parkinson Several times a guest at construction dinners and from the start we had something in common in that early in life he had been a partner of Billy Hart in a construction company near Stockport. When I said I just couldn't imagine him and Billy in partnership, he roared with laughter and said they didn't see each other often – he did the work but I was good at getting the contracts. I found him particularly easy to talk to and have no doubt that but for getting his girlfriend pregnant he might well have become prime minister. He might have made a good one.

Chris Patten A friend of both Tim Kitson and Alistair Goodlad, he used to stay with Alistair who one hot day brought him and his wife to our swimming pool where Angela, her daughter Trini and I were all sunbathing. I got them chairs and asked them if they would like anything to drink and Mrs Patten said she would love a cup of tea. Angela made no attempt to move but Trini saved the day by saying, 'I will get one.' When he went to Hong Kong as governor a little later I followed his career with interest though he was not popular with the Portland Club, nor Hong Kong regulars from the Keswicks downwards.

Tim Kitson went to see him when he was No. 2 at the Home Office and asked what planning permission we needed. I gave him the main two we were after, the Co-Operative land at Weston near Crewe and the land opposite the Chester Business Park. Tim later announced excitedly that Patten had told him the Weston permission was coming through – whereas what we desperately needed was the Chester site.

Lord Tonypandy As George Thomas, Secretary of State at the Welsh Office, he opened the St Asaph section of the A55 coast road from

Chester to Anglesey. I represented the company and presented him at lunch with a silver stag – at the time I was collecting silverware for the table. I sat next to him at lunch and we got on exceptionally well. When lunch was finished he said, 'Have you thought of becoming an M.P.?' and I replied that I was thinking about it. 'You would make a lovely young Tory M.P., Bob, and they really need people like you.'

He later became a very good friend of Edwin McAlpine and was one of two to give addresses at his funeral. He was of course a quite outstanding Speaker of the House of Commons.

Tom King A very engaging politician who I got on well with from the start. I have already described the question I put on his behalf to Margaret Thatcher but I was to meet him regularly shooting as Michael Stoddart used to bring him when he took days at Llanarmon. He was involved in two incidents there, the first of which he may have been unaware of. We were about to shoot the wood on Peter Greenwell's land which was always difficult for parking. Panton Corbett was trying out an exotic four wheel drive vehicle when he lost control and skidded and went into the side of my range rover, causing considerable damage. A few seconds earlier Tom King had been leaning against it and would undoubtedly have been seriously injured or even killed if he had not moved. The second incident was at the same wood where Tom was unfortunate to be put near the house bought by somebody who had just retired from his job in Birmingham. As soon as shooting started the owner came out of the house and a tirade of invective was directed at Tom. It had never happened before nor did the owner cause a problem again.

Tom King was a most likeable man who, with the right breaks, would probably have done even better.

James Prior Another friend of Tim Kitson, very much in the Heath camp, who I met several times. He took an interest in our industry when I told him early on that I thought the Treasury were difficult with us, and he confirmed that later when he told me that the Treasury were really our enemy. I shot next to him at the Reith moor when we were both Tim's guests. It was in torrential rain and very cold. Lord Cowdray with his one arm was my other side; both shot remarkably well and neither complained about the conditions.

When Heath lost the leadership to Mrs Thatcher, he stayed in the Cabinet but was never to achieve the very high office he might have attained if Heath had stayed in power. Obviously very able, I found him one of the easiest of politicians to talk to and had many in depth conversations with him as a result.

Kenneth Baker Was joint PPS to Heath with Tim Kitson and as a result they shared an office in the Commons. He was usually there and on one occasion we all played bridge until well into the night, Donald Marr, a Portland friend, being the fourth. He was always friendly and unlike Tim his career continued in politics at a high level. As Home Secretary he was one of the entourage behind the Queen at the opening of G Mex in Manchester and looked as surprised as anybody when she talked animatedly about racing to me for nearly fifteen minutes.

Norman Tebbit Came several times to the Construction dinners and was my guest on one occasion. I always looked forward to seeing him because I admired his politics, but if I was honest I would have to say I found his contributions to our discussions a little disappointing. He seemed to lack the stature of some of the others, but perhaps I am being unfair.

Nicholas Ridley He let me down badly when at a young age (early thirties) I was in my year as chairman of the Midland section of the Federation of Civil Engineers. He was a junior minister and was to be my chief guest and speaker at the annual dinner in Sutton Coldfield, the high spot of the section's year. He cried off two days before, offering one of his officials in his place. I managed to get Bill Dugdale in his place who had been at Eton with him and said his crying off was typical of the man.

I met him in much happier circumstances when he was Minister of Transport, at the annual meeting the chairman of Ministry of Transport's liaison committee (myself) had with the Minister. He was very forthcoming and we talked animatedly about the road system which he was keen on enlarging and improving. He smoked non-stop through our conversation.

Alistair Goodlad My M.P. for the first years of living at Tilstone Lodge and as he lived so close we became good friends. His land was three fields from me and we shared a water pipe which was always causing problems as it had frequent leaks, which took a lot of finding. On one occasion I rang up the secretary to the chairman of United Utilities and said that there was a bad break and could Sir Desmond Pitcher do something. 'I couldn't possibly bother the chairman with something so trivial,' she told me. I then said, 'Could you tell Sir Desmond I share the pipe with Mr Goodlad, who is in the cabinet.' Next morning when I got to the scene there were five United Utilities vans there!

He was an excellent constituency M.P. and had the safest seat in the North West; much of the rural area of what used to be Crewe and Nantwich had gone to his constituency, Eddisbury. The only time I have ever seen him rattled was in the 1995 election when his majority went from five figures to a few thousand. He retired from the Commons soon after and was talked about as the European Commissioner before being given the job of High Commissioner in Australia. He asked us several times to stay with them but sadly we never made it.

Stephen O'Brien My current M.P. and also an excellent constituency M.P. who is extremely popular locally. He has all the assets I believe an M.P. needs: a good former career in industry (he was a main board director of a large quarrying company), an attractive and energetic wife and an excellent personality himself. He was probably unlucky not to make the Shadow Cabinet but currently he has a ministerial post on Overseas Development and has made several trips abroad on fact finding missions.

Sir Timothy Kitson A great friend since the mid-seventies and many of my meetings with politicians in this chapter are due to him. Promoted from Whips office to be parliamentary secretary to Edward Heath he became a close friend as well as a colleague of Heath. Although destined for high office had Heath won the February 1974 election, his career in politics came to an end when Margaret Thatcher won the leadership of the Conservative Party. She was never going to have as a minister anybody as close to Heath as Tim was.

An excellent and popular M.P. he was proud that his constituency, Richmond, was one of the largest in terms of square miles in the country and he once drove me the entire width (over sixty miles) to prove how wide it was. He soldiered on in Parliament for some years before making a second career in business. He was for some years chairman of the Provident Financial Company and a main board member of the Leeds Building Society, as well as picking up a number of non-executive directorships, including an early one in our company.

It was of course on the shooting field that we really became close. It was entirely due to him that I became so involved in shooting grouse. When I joined his team at Swinton I really got into the top echelon of grouse moors, as Swinton under David Swinton was for many years one of the very best run moors in England. When he had to have a pacemaker, the surgeon put it in on the left side, not realising that Tim shot off that shoulder rather than the usual right-hand side. He offered to do it again but Tim was I think happy to retire and never shoot again.

Peter Morrison The M.P. for Chester was part of a powerful Conservative family and his elder brother, Charles, was a close friend of Tim Kitson. He had not been a particularly popular M.P., mainly because of a lack of a wife and rumours about his sexuality. He did tell me that he had a national Sunday newspaper on his tail and made sure he was escorted everywhere by a series of attractive ladies, one of whom was Chubby Benson. Although he did achieve a higher ministerial rank than his brother he will be chiefly remembered for being part of Margaret Thatcher's campaign team and, although not the top man, got the blame for her just failing to get sufficient votes when seeking re-election against Michael Heseltine.

By an extraordinary coincidence I had asked him to shoot at Llanarmon the day after the count, and he left Margaret Thatcher's side to fly back from Germany and arrived at Llanarmon about midnight. Two of us waited up for him, myself and Tim Kitson, who had performed a similar role for Edward Heath and also got the count wrong. Peter did not seem to realise how disastrous the situation was and, still pumped with adrenalin, had two large whiskys before heading for bed.

I had visited him in his office when he was a minister and he showed me his collection of cuddly toy animals, a very surprising sight in a senior politician's office. He died at a comparatively young age and received a slanted obituary in the *Daily Telegraph*.

Chapter 15

Clubs – a big part of my life

My life seems to have consisted of belonging to a host of clubs from an early age. Many were of the sporting variety – cricket, squash, tennis and golf – but I have also been a member of two of London's most famous clubs, Whites and the Turf; also construction dining clubs to say nothing of a premier bridge club, The Portland. I list them all below as they have played a very big part in my life.

The Wolverhampton Tennis and Squash Club The first club I ever joined, aged sixteen, mainly in the first instance to have tennis lessons from the professional, though I became a member of the squash side and played first string until Jimmy Tildersley came along. We played very good clubs locally as far as Leicester, though Birmingham Priory was always a difficult match. Gallons of beer was consumed afterwards and fortunately there was no breathalyser in those days. It had a thriving drink and dinner section and was a great place for a young bachelor to meet girls. Both my first girlfriends belonged to the club.

Queen's Club I was a member for a few years after leaving school in order to play rackets but although they had a cheap subscription for the young, it soon became too expensive for someone who didn't live in London.

The Liverpool Racket Club A marvellous club to belong to in the fifties and sixties. Sadly the rackets court had gone but there were three squash courts, an indoor tennis court and a fives court. It had an excellent dining room and comfortable bedrooms. Unfortunately, having started in an up-market area of Liverpool, by the time I joined the area was anything but and the club was burnt down in the riots which engulfed Liverpool in the seventies. It was rebuilt in a safer area of Liverpool but I have never been to see it.

Manchester Racket Club I found this when I left the Liverpool equivalent. It did and still does have a rackets court and is quite famous for its real tennis court. Also a thriving lunch and evening drinks side, but no bedrooms and in quite a dingy area of Salford.

Jesters Club The premier social squash club and I ran a match against Oxford University for two years. A particularly nice tie and sweater!

Escorts Club A good but slightly lesser standard club than the Jesters and I played many matches for them. The subscription was so small I never cancelled it and am now an honorary member.

In fact I went to their annual dinner last year and asked Simon Wallis, who is now one of their best players to look after me. The dinner was at Queen's Club and as I walked through the car park, a voice said, 'Is it Bobby McAlpine?' The speaker was Andrew Myrtle, who I had not seen at Queen's since the public school rackets final of 1950, although we had played cricket together a few times since. There were a few other veterans at the dinner but none nearly as old as me!

Bowden Tennis Club A leading tennis club in the Manchester area and, for a couple of years, Mark Pattinson and I played as first pair in their Sunday matches. I was unable to play on Saturdays because of my cricket commitments.

M.C.C. Father virtually put me down at birth for this premier cricket club and I became a member without having to qualify on the field, though I did play in one or two games a year for them and for a number of years I ran a fixture against Wolverhampton Cricket Club. I used to go to Lord's with Father and two or three of his friends to watch the test matches. As it was impossible to get seats in the pavilion for the Ashes series, Geoff Cornu, who lived in London, volunteered to get up early and spread a number of cushions out to keep seats for us. In those days we would always go out for a long lunch and often missed some of the main action in the first part of the afternoon.

My most exciting moment in M.C.C. colours came when I opened the batting for the club against the Argentine. To go out in the main square at Lord' s is very exciting, particularly as I had failed to make it to the Eton and Harrow match there. Although I only just got into double figures, ex England cricketer, Peter Richardson and I put on a respectable thirty-nine runs. A very memorable forty minutes at the crease.

I Zingari A distinguished touring club and, although the standard of matches is no better than the Free Foresters, it is a more prestigious club to belong to. It has a particularly attractive tie, which I often wear, a mixture of gold, black and red. Sam Vestey and I always wear the tie on Gold Cup day at Cheltenham.

I was wearing it when I won the Juddmonte Group 1 race at York and was interviewed on television by Julian Wilson. The president of I.Z., who was watching television, wrote to me and said the last person to wear club colours when winning an important race was Lord Rosebery.

Free Foresters A high standard touring club, which always, until recently, had a fixture at the family cricket ground at Marchwiel. I played one of two qualifiers against the Leicestershire gentlemen at the Oakham school ground and was dropped in the first over by the Dawson twin who ran Sunningdale preparatory school. I went on to make a hundred. History does not relate whether I would have sailed in.

Gentlemen of Leicester I was recruited whilst still at school by Joe Brankin Frisby, who was a great friend of Father's. Not only did I run a fixture for them at Repton School but I also took a side there for a two-day match in their festival fortnight and finished the weekend with a game against Oakham Town, a particularly enjoyable fixture. We all stayed at the Crown hotel, Oakham, where the landlady kept some very good vintage port for us. She said the only people allowed to sample the port were my cricket side and a favoured local shoot.

Cheshire Gentlemen and Staffordshire Gentlemen Two similar clubs to the Leicestershire equivalent and mainly for locals who wanted some weekday cricket, though neither club had a festival week or fortnight. I played selected matches for both clubs.

Northern Nomads A touring club whose members came mainly from Cheshire and Lancashire clubs; they had a fixture at Marchwiel and first Father, and then myself ran a two-day side against them on the Liverpool county ground at Aigbarth. We introduced some top-class Test and County cricketers into the game, including Frank Worrell, Ted Dexter and Phil Edmonds. Kenneth Cranston, England and Lancashire, captained the Northern Nomads for a long period and we had two ex-Middlesex players, Charles Robins and Michael Sturt as regulars.

The Butterflies A club confined to the old boys of six or seven public schools. It had a fixture against Harrow, which was easier to apply for than the Free Foresters and I played in it several times. A very attractive set of club colours.

Delamere Golf Club My main golf club from the days I started playing in the early sixties. The secretary was an ex cricketer called Tony Ledgard, who had played cricket at a high level and was a regular in Father's sides. He did a great deal for the club and behaved in a mildly autocratic manner, similar to a couple of famous secretaries at Muirfield. As a result most members held him in high regard but there was a significant minority who did not. The suggestion book has some wonderful exchanges between Tony and a few members who wished to restrict the activities of dogs on the course. My most memorable moment with him was when I was trying out a new driver from the club house and aimed it at the wood, which nobody was near; to my horror the ball went like a boomerang to the right and ended up missing, by inches, a member coming down the eighteenth fairway. I rushed to the assistant professional, who had let me borrow the club, who said you are in terrible trouble, you have just missed the most difficult member of the club. Sure enough, the member arrived breathing fire and thunder and rushed into the clubhouse to report me to Tony. A couple of minutes later, a bellow from Tony summoned me to the steps of the club. 'I hear you let go of a wild shot and nearly killed a member!' 'I am afraid so, Tony.' 'How could you get so close and then miss him? You would have done the club the greatest service if you had been more accurate.' All said with a straight face!

We have had a Sunday school for years, who tee off at nine o'clock and everybody throws balls in the air to divide up into three and four balls. When I spent my year at Windsor, although I had Sunningdale to go to, the one thing I really missed was Sunday at Delamere.

Sunningdale Golf Club I was a member for forty-two years and only resigned at the end of 2009, when I felt the course had become too difficult to continue. I originally joined to play a lot of golf with the Hanburys and Hollands but there were many friends who were members including Colin Ingleby-Mackenzie. Sam Torrence became an honorary member and Robert Sangster and I used to play nine holes with him and Michael King as partners. Sam was wonderful to play with, giving tips the whole time to improve my game. My two memorable occasions with him were, first, partnering him at a pro-am at Wentworth; he was excited because a minor actress, who was the girlfriend of Dennis Waterman was playing in front of us. Sam said it was too distracting to tee off and when she reached the first green she holed a good putt and wiggled her bottom in delight. 'How are we going to follow this?' said Sam, who couldn't wait at the end of the round to introduce himself. A year later they were married! The second occasion was in Barbados, where he was playing in the annual tournament organised by Robert Sangster and John Magnier. The day after it finished he suggested nine holes and he gave me seven shots. I played the game of my life and won three and two and collected two hundred U.S. dollars. That night there was a beach party at the house Barry Hills and I were sharing and Christy O'Connor junior had everybody in stitches by asking how Sam could have lost to any golfer who had so bad a swing, which he demonstrated. I then challenged him to nine holes and removed another two hundred dollars.

The Twelve Club A club at which members select twelve horses for the flat season and bet against each other on their selections; there are also good prizes for the winner, the member with most winners, etc. I joined when still in my thirties and found great friends like David Marchwood, Harry Beeby, Nick Robinson and Anthony Johnson were already members. There are two main functions a year, a dinner at the Turf Club on the first Friday of March, and a dinner dance two nights before the Derby, where the horses are auctioned. I used to go to both but now always attend the March dinner. I have got close to winning on a couple of occasions and have won the cup for the most individual winners.

The Derby Club I first went as a guest of David Montagu (later, David Swathling) and was fascinated by the sight of racing's establishment letting their hair down and behaving pretty badly. In those days the only drink at dinner was Bollinger champagne from magnums followed by vintage port. The Derby dinner always took place at the Savoy and was presided over by John Derby, who used to wave a baton rather ineffectively, calling for order. Eventually a group of us all became members and Robert Sangster, Charles Benson, Barry Hills and I had two guests at a table of twelve. The only time Charles Benson was absent was when he was the guest speaker and had to sit next to John Derby at the top table. He always said the audience was the most difficult in Britain to address and he started his speech by saying, 'I see in front of me several people who tried to bugger me at Eton.' This was met by gales of laughter and I wonder how it would have gone down in today's politically sensitive climate. The club has changed enormously and, though still enjoyable, in my view takes itself far too seriously. The climax came when for some inexplicable reason a minor ex-rugby international was chosen to make the main speech. He was twenty minutes into the same speech he had given at many rugby clubs and was boring anybody who was not interested in rugby rigid. Then three elderly members, all who had drunk too much, started heckling him. Teddy Derby was forced to intervene and the speaker, who showed no sense of humour, instead of making a joke of the three inebriates, refused to go on speaking. He received a standing ovation; the only two on our table who refused to get up were Barry Hills and myself. The dinner has been for the past years at the Park Lane and it will be interesting to see, when it returns to the Savoy, whether the enjoyment we all used to have and the quality of the food and drink returns with it.

The Portland Club A famous bridge club, which I joined through Toddy Hanbury and which is still nominally responsible for the rules of bridge; no conventions are allowed except for the strong two and a weak one no trump, showing twelve to fourteen points. The stakes have always been high, though the minimum of five pounds a hundred has only doubled to ten pounds now and the much larger stakes game, which could go up to a hundred pounds in the seventies, are now fifteen to twenty pounds and generally at one table only. The membership has always been mixed from dukes and politicians to self made tycoons, the common denominator being a liking for playing bridge for money. Some of the original membership who were there when I joined are still regulars – David Wolfson, Tommy Ricter and Jim Slater being three and Sonny Marlborough is still a member although he rarely plays. Another famous member was Lord Lucan, who played there a lot. In fact I saw him there four days before the famous incident when the Lucan nanny got killed by mistake. He looked terrible and had obviously been drinking to excess, his normally handsome face had become very dissipated. The photograph of him playing bridge with me is I believe the only photograph ever taken of him playing cards. Although the newspaper headline accompanying it talked about millions being lost under the green baize, the Portland members were in fact playing in a charity bridge tournament organised by Ladbrokes at the Ladbroke Club. They had enlisted the finest professional bridge players in the world to play with us and gave us a very good dinner with some excellent wine. The tournament was duplicate not rubber bridge and was the only time I ever played duplicate bridge. Partnered with one of the Dallas Aces, the combination of too much wine and duplicate for the first time produced a very poor performance. Lucan was to win the tournament although he was only an average player. Plainly the effects of the wine, which he was well used to had no effect on his performance! In the summer a golf weekend – Thursday to Sunday – takes place, which used to be often in Scotland but in recent years almost always in France, Deauville having been the most popular choice. Over forty years I have won three times, at Turnberry, Muirfield and finally, after a long gap, at Deauville. The handicapping system is the best I have come across and goes purely on results – a substantial cut if you are in the first four and an automatic extra shot if you are not in the first eight.

The club has changed a lot since I first joined. The afternoon game, during the week, which used to be well attended from four to eight, now struggles for regular attendances and the club is centred around the Monday club dinner and private members dinners, which take place throughout the year. No longer do games go on through the night until breakfast, as Christopher Soames, Salem Zilka, Jimmy Goldsmith and others were wont to do in the seventies. Drinking has become much less, and to me the sad thing is that chicargos (four hands of bridge and finish) are played non-stop and it is virtually impossible to persuade members to play 'normal' bridge, even if there are several tables operating.

The Turf Club A famous London club, which I joined almost by accident when they were short of members and Sam Vestey said, over a drink at the Cheltenham festival, that I should be a member. When I didn't immediately decline, I found a proposal form in the post the following Monday, with Sam Vestey as my proposer and three weeks later I was a member. Now it would take up to two years to go through the same process. I have thoroughly enjoyed the club which, when I first joined, had the best pre-lunch bar to drink in, in London. Unlike Whites, which has a much bigger membership, people make a real effort to talk to each other and I found a very convivial group of regulars. Sadly most are no longer with us and the mortality rate has been a lot higher than my friends in Whites. It has two golf days a year – early summer and autumn – and I usually play in the autumn event, which I did win once, mainly because I was playing with Edward Kitson, who told me what clubs to take throughout the round. I was actually two shots behind him at the last and got my only birdie, whilst he took his only bogey.

The club has a very strong presence at race meetings, particularly Cheltenham, where it has a very popular tent – which used to have Barry Copes fish, which was the best on the racecourse. Also Ascot and Goodwood but Newmarket has gone by the wayside.

Whites Club Whilst right wing and elitist, it is not really as much so as its critics make out and is an extremely comfortable, well run club, which I have enjoyed more and more as I have got older. I was put up for membership by Owen Lloyd George, my cousin, who was chairman at the time. The food is almost the best in London and, unlike the Turf Club, they have had a wine committee since way back, which includes some very knowledgeable and professional wine buffs. A meal in Whites will be the equivalent of a top class London restaurant at a third of the price. Also it has a thriving golf side and a major presence at Royal Ascot. The waiting list is considerable and it takes a few years to join.

The Jockey Club Probably one of the most exciting moments of my life was when Philip Leverhulme told me I was being put up for membership. The club was of course for centuries the ruling body of racing but in the last two decades it has voluntarily relinquished its powers over racing and has now become a club which is partly social but owns fourteen British racecourses, including Cheltenham, Aintree, Epsom, Sandown, Kempton and of course Newmarket, the headquarters of the club. I have to confess that the club I joined was far from what I expected. Having been used to trade federations, cricket and golf clubs, which had a definite structure and method, however imperfect, of electing its governing members, I was astonished to find absolutely no structure at all in the Jockey Club. When I expressed my astonishment to a senior member, I was told it was their greatest strength. After over thirty years I could not disagree more. Only now – far too late in the day – have sensible and progressive senior stewards like Julian Richmond Watson and Nicholas Wrigley started to build a proper structure and go back to having a chief executive. I still think that Lord Howard de Walden, who was the first when I joined, was the best of my time. He had a major and definite agenda, knew exactly what he was doing and achieved all his aims. Stoker Hartington was another who had a major agenda and started the dismantling of the club's powers over racing. He was absolutely right in my view to detach the political from the administrative side of racing and create a body which could talk to government. He also had a competent chief executive in Christopher Haines, who lost out to Tristan Ricketts for the new chief executive post of the British Horseracing Board and sadly left the Jockey Club – who were without a chief executive until Julian Richmond Watson appointed Simon Bazaglette. In the intervening period the club gave up all its administrative functions, against the wishes of many of its members and after decades of building them up. It now has a very able senior steward in Nicholas Wrigley, probably the best qualified in my period of membership, and one can only hope that a club I have tremendous affection for finds its new role as a major player in the racecourse world a satisfactory one. It is certainly not a role current members who have been with the club for sometime would have expected.

Annabel's I am not sure whether I was a founder member or whether I joined just after it opened. My friend there was George, the barman, who invited me for a drink three days before the opening. George had presided over many memorable sessions in Jules Bar in Jermyn Street, before being lured to Annabels. He took me for a tour of the empty building before opening a bottle of my then favourite champagne, Bollinger, and pouring two glasses, 'What do you think of it all, Bobby?' 'George it is far too lavish and you are going to have to charge far too much, I fear it might become a white elephant.' Just goes to show how totally wrong one could be. In fact the club took off and became the one place everybody wanted to go to after dinner. Robert Sangster took me there for a memorable cabaret by Neil Diamond in the early seventies and I found myself there more often then I wanted, as I was always after not too late a night. My opportunity came through my investment in Euan Hilleary's fish business, Minch, who were suppliers to the club. Annabels were always bad payers and Euan went down to talk to the secretary accountant and was extremely rude to her, little realising she was Mark Birley's latest mistress. Two days later a cheque and letter arrived from Birley informing Euan the account was closed and he was barred from the club. This was a dreadful blow to Euan and I wrote Birley a polite letter offering to take Euan's place. An equally polite letter came back from Birley, saying that he had no quarrel with me and hoped I would continue to use the club. Many memorable nights followed including several celebrations in the private room including the famous one after Robert's first Derby triumph. My last appearance in the club was equally memorable, as Angela and I had taken three children and their friends to a pre-Christmas dinner. After dinner there was a chorus of please take us to Annabels. I wasn't sure if I was still a member and when we got to the street door there was a queue outside. I told the young it was hopeless and was just about to move away when the doorman said, 'Go straight downstairs.' There to greet me was the successor to Louis, the famous club restaurateur, 'Mr Bobby, what are you doing amongst this rabble? We so miss you and Mr Sangster.' Despite there not being a table or chair available, within five minutes he had cleared a table and eight of us sat down. Never has my stock risen so fast with my children!

Mark's Club Another club started by Mark Birley which was purely for dining, though there was a nice bar upstairs. The subscription was £500 and I found myself only using the club two or three times a year, which meant that if you divided the subscription by two or three and added the result onto the dinner bills, the meals became very expensive.

Tarporley Hunt Club The oldest Hunt dining club still active in the country and the members used to be male representatives of Cheshire families with large houses and ties with hunting. In recent years the qualifications have become rather different and members who prefer shooting probably equal the hunting enthusiasts. The dress is a Hunt coat with green collar, trousers similar to plus fours with long green stockings and a green waistcoat. I was first asked as a guest by Evelyn Delves Broughton and marvelled at the excellent food and wine in those days, mainly vintage champagne and port. As the fifties progressed the current preference for Bordeaux led to a change in the club's drinking pattern, Bordeaux taking the place of port and brandy to some degree.

I was not elected a member until the year I bought Tilstone Lodge and John Barlow, who made a short speech of introduction, pointed out that the fell hounds at Llanarmon accounted for more foxes than the Cheshire and Wynnstay hunts combined. In my reply, I said I was delighted to become a member but, in a reference to my recent house purchase, said I did not realise how expensive the opening subscription was.

The club has a dinner after the opening meet of the Cheshire Hunt and a further one the next night at which there are speeches, with a lunch for members in between. It has its own room in the Swan Hotel in Tarporley, where hunt paintings are hung around the room and many of the panels have the names and coats of arms of all the presidents back to the eighteenth century. My own presidency took place in 2005 and my chief guest, who had to make the main speech, was Charles Moore, the former editor of the *Daily Telegraph*. A keen hunting man himself, he made an excellent speech.

Chapter 16

The Nineties and into the Next Century

My year as High Sheriff of Cheshire coincided nicely with my retirement from the family company. A High Sheriff is an ancient office with the Queen herself perusing the list and 'pricking' the candidates. Each High Sheriff is allowed to nominate somebody to follow on three years later and I had been nominated by David Stern. The uniform is quite exciting with a black frock coat with diamante buttons, breeches, ruffs, tights and black silk stockings, complete with ornate pointed shoes. You also have to have a sword and I was lucky to borrow the family sword which was in cousin Bill's possession. He was to become High Sheriff himself of Buckinghamshire a few years later.

I also borrowed the hat, which I can only describe as similar to admirals, in Nelson's time, and the rest I bought myself to wear, first at the swearing in ceremony in Chester in April 1994. My predecessor, Richard Gray, was extremely helpful and had asked me to two dinners for judges and explained my duties. The two main duties are to be present whenever a member of the Royal family is on an official visit to the county and to welcome and attend a High Court judge's first day in court and make sure his stay is comfortable and give at least one dinner party for him and expect to attend at least another at the Judges Lodgings. You can also expect to receive a host of invitations to company functions, Mayoral dinners, etc.

I was very fortunate that my first judge and first case was probably the most exciting of my twelve months. The judge was Ronald Waterhouse (later Lord Waterhouse), who had been junior counsel for Myra Hindley at their famous trial in the same courtroom. The defendant was accused of murdering the centre forward of Nantwich Town Football Club by luring him into a house and then setting fire to him, causing injuries from which he died a couple of days later. We met the judge in his lodgings, a house on the edge of Chester, adjacent to the Zoo. I had been warned to go easy on the coffee I was offered, as it was at least two hours in court and although the judge had a loo through the door behind him, I did not want to use it my first morning in court.

We were taken in a large Daimler car to court with two police on motorcycles in front and there were a large number of police inside the court, as there was a rumour the accused might try to escape. In fact this was the only time in several other murder cases and numerous lesser ones that large numbers of police were present. So it was an exciting opening day. During the morning the Q.C. for the defendant asked to see the judge in chambers and an argument ensued between the three barristers representing the prosecution and defence. At the end the judge announced he would give his decision in court and when the others had left, he turned to me and said, 'What do you make of all that, Bobby?' A very interesting first morning.

Although it is not automatic you can expect to be asked by the judge to lunch with him, and Angela and I went back to the lodgings for lunch. Whilst I always had a couple of glasses of wine, I noticed the judge drank little and this was the case throughout the year. They had to work and concentrate far too much during the day, whereas at dinner they could relax and enjoy the wine I provided – my cellar was to suffer major depletions, as two great Bordeaux years, '82 and '83, were ready for drinking and I'm afraid most of my stocks of those years were drunk at the numerous dinner parties I gave.

I attended another two days of the first trial. It was obvious that the accused would be convicted but the big question was murder or manslaughter? The difficulty was to prove he intended to kill the victim, rather than cause him serious injury. In the end the jury convicted him of the lesser charge and Waterhouse gave him a hefty sentence, which still didn't deter some of the media, who thought the original murder charge should have stuck.

The next major event on the High Sheriff calendar was the Mayoral dinner. Here, to my surprise, I ranked higher than Gerald Westminster and was on the right of the female City Sheriff, who was chatty and attractive and told me her draw at dinner was the ambition of a lifetime (I think she was wildly exaggerating). I then had a series of excellent judges and further murder trials – one much less interesting about a 'down and out', murdered on the banks of the Dee, close to the racecourse.

Two of the judges became friends: Richard Curtis had his own small vineyard near Hereford and was, like myself, immensely interested in wine. Michael Connell, a national hunt enthusiast, had been to Harrow and become a governor. A member of the Jockey Club, I still see him at meetings and social events. A slight drama occurred the first day I accompanied him to court when a young girl was giving evidence in a child molestation case. Because of her age, she was allowed to give her evidence on closed circuit television in a room away from the court. Michael turned his television on but could not get it to work. He turned to me and asked if I could work it; when I shook my head we had to have a recess to get the television fixed.

Although the eight murder trials were the highlights of the year, there were many other interesting cases. Apart from the case on Michael Connell's first day in court, there were two others where family members were accused of molesting children. Although I felt all three accused were probably guilty they were all acquitted; it is obviously difficult to get juries to convict in these cases.

I had been appointed at a time when High Sheriffs were still able to choose to some degree how much time they gave to their year. Some of my friends had been appointed when they quite young and working hard. A year or two after I handed over, the office became much more time consuming and anybody now accepting the role should expect to give a lot of time to it.

I did make my theme for the year 'drug abuse' and was amazed to find how widespread drug use was throughout Cheshire. Even Tarporley, our large village, had dealers and I was told they would meet the customers outside the chemist in the middle of the village after the shop had closed. As Bill Laurie, the chemist, was a friend of mine he was rather shocked to hear of meetings outside his shop to sell drugs very different from those he was prescribing inside.

I managed to get the whole of the Cheshire drug squad to a meeting at Northwich – forty-two officers were present – and I started the meeting by asking if anybody thought Cannabis should be legalised (it was a major press topic at the time). Not one hand went up and a senior officer, who analysed drugs, explained that there were nine or ten different strengths to Cannabis and whilst the lower end probably would not cause major problems, most users tried the higher strengths and then went on to use other hard drugs.

I was very lucky to have a chief constable, Mervyn Rees, who strongly supported the High Sheriff role and did everything to bring me into the mainstream. He even persuaded me to take on his driver,

Bob Messer, who had just retired at fifty with the words 'he has a better future with you than me'. Bob is still with me to this day.

I was very sad when the year finished. I went into the Portland and Isadore Kerman said, 'Here comes the Sheriff.' I told him I had just retired and he said, 'There's nothing so ex as an ex High Sheriff.' That was certainly true at the time but now High Sheriffs get involved with crime prevention to a degree that many carry on after their year finishes. My biggest regret is I hadn't spent more time in court. You get a unique opportunity to do so and court dramas have always fascinated me!

I still had plenty to do. At Chester and Bangor I was very occupied with helping Richard Thomas build up an extremely profitable business. The recruitment of Richard was certainly the best single move I made in my time as chairman of Chester. I handed over to Charles Lowther at Bangor when Chester bought the course. In the winter I was very occupied with Llanarmon, now becoming one of the premier shoots in the country. When we were one of eleven in Britain to gain five stars in *The Field* for quality of birds, I really felt a sense of achievement.

I also had a non-executive role at Hall Engineering, a successful, highly diversified, family company in steel stockholding, steel reinforcement and car accessories. It had overseas business in South Africa, Hong Kong and Singapore, so there was plenty to keep the directors occupied. Unfortunately this all came to an end in 1999, when an opportunist bid, when the shares were ludicrously low, brought on a management buy-out and all the non-executives left. Richard Hall had bought the steel stockholding before the bid and although everybody thought he had paid too much, it is now a thriving family business with both his sons doing most of the work of running it. Not so the original business, although the principals made themselves a lot of money when they refloated it, they then got into a lot of trouble and it is now worth next to nothing.

Unfortunately my private life went through a very difficult period. Jeremy Hindley had been the first to admit to an alcohol problem and had gone into a clinic in what was the old family home. His brother, Christopher, lived in a nice house nearby, farming the estate at Gisburn in Yorkshire. Jeremy emerged full of praise for Alcoholics Anonymous and became such an enthusiast that, when he moved, as a resident, to Cape Town, he founded a half-way house, where those coming out of clinics could acclimatise for a short while. Up to this point I was very dismissive of the 'Genes' therapy, firmly believing that a lot of people, including myself, drank too much at times and it was strength of mind which pushed one in either direction. A few years later I was to become far more knowledgeable on the subject and am now certain that most alcoholics are there because of their genes. As Jeremy Hindley once said to myself and Barry Hills – you drink too much, I am an alcoholic.

Angela was certainly an example of those who believed in the 'genes' therapy. Both her parents were enormous drinkers and although before and after the Second World War people did not get labelled alcoholics and few sought treatment, they would have been considered so today. It would also be easy to say that Angela's drinking problems stemmed from her terrible accident but I think, in honesty, they would have surfaced anyway.

I got increasingly worried about her and eventually her doctor and I persuaded her to go to the Priory and she was given an excellent counsellor, who had been, as he put it, to hell and back on the drinking front. Angela actually rather enjoyed her stay there, mixed in well with a wide circle of fellow inmates, and was extremely well advised by her counsellor, who saw her regularly afterwards. The Priory encourages you to be quite open with the problems and discuss them in groups, which works for most people. Angela is a very private person and although she went to AA meetings for some time afterwards, she was never really comfortable with them. Unfortunately she had also been told by a well-meaning friend, in a similar state, that she could have a drop of Angostura in her tonic water. Angostura is very alcoholic and one thing I learnt is that those in Angela's situation simply must not have a drop of anything alcoholic.

Angela's bout of drinking prior to her second spell at the Priory was far worse than anything before, as it was in secret and intense, but the second spell did do the trick and, again helped by the incomparable Richard, she has not touched a drop since the day she walked in for the second time.

I believe I am now quite an expert on the subject. I strongly believe in the genes situation, i.e. that most alcoholics are, sadly, born that way. Whilst there is a very thin line between heavy drinkers and alcoholics; anybody who wants to test themselves has only to go on the wagon and see if they crave alcohol during it. I go to a health farm once a year and for several days never miss it at all. In fact now, in old age, I feel the effects more and try and have a day or two a week with none. What I am quite sure of is that alcoholics must not touch a drop. I used to get furious with well-meaning friends of Angela who said 'one drink won't hurt her'. One drink is the equivalent of suicide, believe me!

Chapter 17

Obituaries

I got into writing freelance obituaries for the *Daily Telegraph* almost by accident. After Father's death I thought he should have an obituary and rang up my cousin, Miles Kington, who seemed the obvious person to do it, as he wrote for a national newspaper, the *Independent*, every day. Initially he agreed and I sent him some notes on Father but he rang back to say that he had a rule of only writing his own stuff and that as he didn't really know Father he would prefer not to write it. I assumed it would not get printed and nobody was more amazed than myself when my notes appeared almost verbatim in a full-scale obituary in the *Independent*, a few months later. Somebody I had never heard of put his name underneath.

I was astonished how good the piece actually looked and one day playing golf in Cape Town, with Jeremy Deedes, I told him about it. He suggested I might like to write freelance for the *Telegraph*, where he was managing director, and agreed to introduce me to Hugh Massingbird, the doyen of obituary writers. I was very intrigued, and rang Jeremy on my return to England, and a meeting and lunch was fixed up. Hugh Massingbird was very helpful, gave me a number of things to concentrate on, and we had lunch in the directors lunch room on the top floor, a great honour apparently. Hugh's female number two, who succeeded him, told me later that was the only time in her life she had been asked up there.

Shortly afterwards, Hugh rang me up to say that he would like me to write the obituary of Lloyd Kenyon, a local worthy who I knew well, with particular emphasis on his work as keeper of the Royal Manuscripts. This came as a complete surprise. Lloyd Kenyon and I were fellow directors and stewards at Bangor-on-Dee racecourse. I knew all about his breeding fine Welsh ponies but the Royal Manuscript part was news to me. I did my best but Hugh considerably embellished the piece, particularly on the manuscripts, but I still think the final combination of Hugh and myself produced one of the best I was paid for. I did receive the full, extremely modest, standard payment.

After that I was on my own and a stream of obituaries followed – the lady who followed him seemingly believed I knew a lot more city notables than I did. There were some interesting moments. Asked to do the obituary of Sir Cyril Kleinwort, who I had never met, I discovered that his son had married Bill Shand Kydd's daughter. I rang Bill up and suggested he could be very helpful. 'Indeed I could – he was a mean, pompous, precious, prick. Put that in your obituary, with my compliments.' Thank you Bill! I then rang up Kleinwort Benson and was put on to a public relations lady who was extremely suspicious. 'Look,' I said, 'all I want is to write a nice obituary but I am not getting good vibes.' Finally I was put through to Simon Robertson, who did help me and gave me the son's phone number. He was obviously keen to do his best for his father and gave me a deal of useful information. He never mentioned that, unknown to me, he was a friend of my second son, Christopher, and had been with him to Llanarmon. It's such a small world.

Another interesting one was Lord Mais, whom I never met, though I knew the large London building company, Trollope and Colls, where he had been chairman. I rang up his widow and in fact his son answered the phone, saying to his mother, 'A reporter from the *Telegraph* for you.' She was very cooperative, obviously anxious for a kind obituary and I then realised that Victor Matthews, who was in retirement, living in Jersey, could contribute, as he was running Trafalgar House, who had taken Mais's company over. I rang his Jersey number and Victor answered the phone. His response was typical of the man, 'Trollope and Colls, a complete steal, Mais was far too busy being an alderman to run the company properly' – and so on. Then, because he was bored, he asked after all his former construction friends. The whole conversation took forty-two minutes, as I was to find out when the bill from British Telecom arrived. For the only time, I rang Hugh Massingbird and asked for a little extra. The princely sum of twenty-five pounds duly arrived.

One of the most exciting parts of writing obituaries was to ring the copy department and have my copy typed for me and sent to the obituaries editor. I was able to act out the same role as a genuine reporter, which always gave me a bit of a thrill.

I had also been asked to do a series of 'advance' obituaries for well-known people still alive and I did about twenty of these. Unfortunately, I believe they all disappeared when the offices moved to Canary Wharf.

I was at least paid for them.

One I was able to do was Isadore Kerman, and I told him the *Telegraph* wanted me to do a 'profile'. We had a fascinating hour whilst he recounted his career, which was even more interesting than I expected. At the end of the meeting I was going through the door, when he shouted, 'When is the profile going to appear?' 'Not too soon, Isadore, I hope,' was my reply.

One of the more difficult obituaries was that of Frank Sanderson, who had actually caused terrible problems for me when he resigned suddenly from Alfred McAlpine's main board. Frank had not benefited from what, I am sure, was a decision at the time where he thought he was going to make a lot of money going on his own – and he died with major financial problems piling up for him. Nevertheless, I concentrated on the good periods in his life and particularly the way he had built up Bovis. Charles Robins, who had introduced us, rang me up afterwards to say that he didn't think I had it in me to be so nice about somebody who had done me so much damage.

Another obituaries editor, David Jones, came and went and it was when Christopher Howse succeeded him that my happy flow of obituaries began to get stemmed. I used to ring the office and ask for Christopher, who I have never actually met, and a gentleman called Twiston-Davies invariably answered the phone. Whilst Howse was always helpful and I still have a letter in his own handwriting, saying how pleased he was I was writing for him, his sentiments did not seem to be transferred to his staff.

I had by this time written nearly forty obituaries and whilst some had taken time to appear, there had been no question that they would appear. It was a considerable shock when I wrote an obituary for Charles Barnett's father, Ben, which was never published. Benjamin Barnett had briefly owned one of Britain's most attractive villages and estates, Glympton in Oxfordshire, but his chief claim to fame was that he was one of two British officers who were in the first official party to take control of Belsen concentration camp. I still have the manuscript I sent to the *Telegraph*. I enclose excerpts from this:

It took the battery commanded by Dick Taylor another two days before they reached the neutral zone and Taylor, Barnett and eight selected men met the German officers, who consisted of the Wehrmacht Senior Officer, Oberst Harries, Kramer – the SS Commander of the camp – and his second in command, Scmidt. Harries disclaimed any responsibility for the crimes, said he had never been inside it and was liable to be shot by the SS if he went too close.

The first thing to strike the small party was the appalling smell coming from the camp, where there were still shots being fired by the SS at the internees. Kramer was immediately given orders that his men were to stop firing. As the party walked down the main roadway into the camp they saw a large number of corpses lying around, in places quite large heaps of them. They were mostly naked and of both sexes. As they went further on they discovered the camp was divided into eight separate blocks, each block being separated from the other by a barbed wire fence with anything up to ten huts, some with bunks and some without, but it was quite impossible for all the internees to enter the huts allotted to them at the same time, so therefore many were living in the open.

As they pushed through the internees a remarkable thing happened, as a figure (and Barnett was to tell friends afterwards, he used the word 'figure' because it was quite impossible to tell males from females) pushed through the small group and ran up to Dick Taylor, saying, 'Mr Dick, Mr Dick, I am Anna Marie, do you remember me?' Of course he didn't remember her because she was a skeleton figure with a shaven head and most of her teeth knocked out. It transpired that this girl had been employed before the war by Dick Taylor's mother at their home in Northumberland and at the outbreak of war she had returned to her home in Paris, had then gone into the resistance in Paris, had eventually been picked up by the Gestapo, tortured, thrown into a concentration camp and fetched up at Belsen, where the first Englishman she saw was her employer's son! Earlier, very strict instructions had been given that not one person was to be allowed out of the camp, to avoid spreading diseases, but this girl was the exception to the rule, she was taken out of the camp and was one of the survivors from the inmates.

Belsen was the first concentration camp to be discovered by the Allied advance and there was no indication to those who were first in, of the full horrors to be uncovered. Barnett personally arrested Kramer and had him put in the cold store room in the Officers Mess, where he was to remain for 36 hours, with no clothes other than underpants.

I found the details so interesting that I could not believe the paper would not publish them. Worse was to follow as my next obituary on Eileen Bissell, who owned large tracts of land in Staffordshire and Stalybridge, near Manchester, and was a descendant of Lady Jane Grey, also failed to appear.

I was fortunate to have a mole in the obituaries department, in the shape of my eldest son Euan's brother-in-law, Phillip Ede. He was too tactful to tell me too much about what went on inside the paper but I understood that, for whatever reason, my writing was not popular with Twiston-Davies. I asked Jeremy Deedes for advice and he agreed to introduce me, at a lunch, to the new obituaries editor, Andrew McKee. The lunch went well but unfortunately the new editor proved even more difficult to contact than Howse had been and Twiston-Davies seemed to be effectively running the department. I managed to get two or three past him, including Charles Benson, which I still consider one of the best I wrote. The crunch came when I was told by Twiston-Davies that he had a writer lined up for Robert Sangster but he would put him on to me. We didn't get off to a good start when I asked him what he had on Charles Benson and he replied he had never heard of him. I told him he could not write an obituary on Robert without mentioning Charles and whilst the final obituary was perfectly adequate, it lacked the intimate family details I could have supplied.

I only tried once more, having done a major profile on David Swinton, which I was prepared to update. To my amazement, I was told he was unlikely to rate an obituary, which is when I retorted with the comment 'that it is easier to get a Russian juggler into the *Telegraph* than a great British landowner'. David was not just a landowner, he had been very active in local government particularly on the education front, he had been Commander of the Queen's Bodyguard and deputy chairman of the Conservative whips in the House of Lords. If anyone merited an obituary, I would have thought it was him. Surprisingly, *The Times* were also luke warm, although I did manage to get a brief summary in their 'Lives Remembered' column, but my words were cut from six hundred to four hundred.

Two or three years after I ceased writing for the *Daily Telegraph*, a large landowner in Cheshire died and his widow contacted me within hours to ask for an obituary. I gave her the advice not to mention my name but to find somebody with contacts at the *Daily Telegraph*. It took time but eventually a very nice obituary appeared. I was delighted as the friend concerned was a really nice, popular figure and although he had nothing like the career of David Swinton, he deserved it.

Chapter 18

Haynes, Hanson and Clark

I got into the wine trade entirely by accident. Peter Grubb was a cricketing friend, whose father, Jack, was a major local figure, chairman of the local magistrates bench and of the Nantwich Conservative party. Peter seemed the model younger son, who became the youngest area director of a large wine company, Grants of St. James. When he rang me to say that if I bought the lease of a small wine shop in Kensington Church Street, he would run it and we would both benefit from profits and cost price wine from the shop. I duly put the money down and for a couple of years all went well, until Peter parted from his wife and started living with a much livelier lady, who seemed to change Peter totally.

I began to find out just how much a small shop in London could lose once the manager took his eye off the ball. I had accepted an invitation from Dennis Haynes to go to a wine tasting at André Simon's main shop. Dennis was an old cricketing friend of Father and myself, had captained Staffordshire and the combined minor counties cricket sides and had a wine business in the Potteries, where Father had bought all his wine. He also had a marital bust-up and had sold the Staffordshire business and had moved to London, where, unlike Peter, his career had taken off. I told him of my woes and he suggested a meeting the following week as he felt he could help.

In fact he did much more than help, as he then proposed a full partnership with my putting in the lease of the Kensington shop plus some money and he matching it. 'I am sick of big business,' he said, 'and although Cadbury Schweppes, who took over André Simon, have offered me a directorship, I would much rather restart my own business.' He also told me he had two very promising assistants, Anthony Hanson and Nick Clark, who would come with him.

So the business of Haynes, Hanson and Clark was founded. One of the first meetings was to agree the name and after several attempts to incorporate McAlpine into it, I said that although I had a half stake, I was the sleeping partner and it was more important their three names stood out.

After a few years the shop at Kensington Church Street was too small and the working conditions appalling, so the decision was taken to move to Fulham, where there was ample office and warehouse storage space. Although the business worked well enough, the results were not startling and Dennis Haynes's health was a major worry, as he had a serious heart condition. In 1994 things came to a head and both Dennis and Anthony Hanson wanted to sell their shareholdings – Anthony and Nick having been given quarter shareholdings by Dennis and myself. A fair price was agreed and I went back to being a half owner with Nick as a partner. Anthony continued to write our wine catalogues and was invaluable on the expeditions to taste wine abroad and back at home.

In 1994 Nick and I made the decision to make a double move, from Fulham to Eccleston Street and at Stow-on-the-Wold into a shop in the middle of the town. These moves were very beneficial and the company thrived until the recession of 2007-8, when we had one particularly difficult year. A further move from Eccleston Street, which had become less profitable as changes to the road meant that customers could no longer park outside, to Ellyston Street in Chelsea has resulted in an excellent shop being established there. Two new directors, James Eustace and Charles Stanley-Evans, have both acquired shares from me so there are now four shareholders, with Nick Clark, the managing partner.

I cannot finish without mentioning the Haynes, Hanson and Clark race at Newbury on the Friday of the mid-September meeting. We have now sponsored for over thirty years and are the longest running sponsor at Newbury. The race is for two-year-olds, who are starting their careers on the racecourse and being over a mile attracts promising future classic three-year-olds. We have had three Derby winners including Shergar and other very good horses like Kings Theatre.

Chapter 19

My One Shot

'The day thou gavest Lord is ended,' is the first line of my favourite hymn and will, I hope, be played at my funeral. Approaching eighty, it certainly isn't all over but as one heads into the next ten years it is time for quiet reflection.

I was going to begin the chapter by saying that I was in wonderful health without serious illness since my jaundice in the mid-twenties, but unfortunately a few weeks before writing this I was hit by a small stroke. It came right out of the blue following two great days shooting at Llanarmon with my own guests, no tensions and, dare I say it, I shot better than I have for several years and even got a right and left at Stynog. I was intending to play golf on the Sunday, having missed it for two weeks because I felt three days consecutive shooting had earned me a couple of 'lie ins' on the Sunday. When I woke up I automatically looked at the clock by my bedside but this time the figures on the clock were dancing around and looking around the room I realised I had blurred vision. I woke Angela up and told her something was very wrong and she later told me my eyes were 'all over the place'. She went downstairs rang for an ambulance, came back and told me to lie still on the bed. Two paramedics duly arrived and took me to Leighton hospital. Angela followed by car.

Being a Sunday it took time to get seen and the doctor who examined me was plainly uncertain about the problem. He later told me he had made a phone call to a senior consultant, who told him it was most likely a stroke was the cause.

It was fortunate I had not seen a programme on the local news I was to see ten days later, giving the statistics for deaths at weekends. Leighton hospital was the worst locally, with an 11.4% increase in deaths on admission at weekends to weekdays.

I arrived at seven in the morning and it took until midday to gain admission to the stroke ward, a mixed ward with six beds, three with men and three with women. I should have been horrified to be in a mixed ward but I have to say none of us seemed to mind at all and the sense of camaraderie was considerable. We were a very mixed bunch, opposite me was a middle-aged lady who had no family but was well supported by a number of ladies, next to her a relatively young man, probably under forty, who had had a second stroke quickly after the first and plainly was finding his job as a driver very stressful. He was constantly on his mobile which couldn't have helped the condition and had a young wife and two small children. Apparently he got no money when not at work and I felt very sorry for him. Next to him was an old lady of ninety, who spent most of the time asleep, so we were, as I have said, a strange mixture.

As the first scan failed to pick up the problem and as my blood pressure was all over the place, I was not allowed out of bed for three days without help from the nurses. They were excellent, extremely helpful, as were the doctors, the main problem being that they seemed to change every two days and having established some rapport one had to start all over again with a fresh team. In five days I had four different ward sisters and three different doctors. The one regular was a doctor who had shot at Llanarmon and, though nothing to do with my case, he came to see me every day and was most helpful.

The second major scan, an MRI, established the cause of the problem, which was a small clot at the back of the head and as the major heart scan only detected a little 'wear and tear' I was allowed home on the following Thursday. Angela, who had been marvellously supportive, collected me and I breathed my first gulps of fresh air for five days and went home, where I woke up to my first breakfast in bed in twenty-six years of living there.

On the whole I would award Leighton quite high marks, seven or eight out of ten. The staff were very compassionate and there was none of the poor treatment you read about in the press. Even the food was fairly good. The worst thing, as I have already said, was with the shifts worked, you see constantly different staff but I suppose that is inevitable in a large hospital.

On the whole it has been a pretty good life with some very bad moments – my brother's death, Jane's terrible stroke and my last years in the family company being some of them. For the vast majority who have no involvement with a family firm, it is probably difficult to imagine how it takes over your life. There are of course tremendous advantages and for all but the last eight years I had the benefits of helping to build up a large, highly successful company. Our problem was that we became too large and complacent in an industry where it is essential to adapt to changing times and conditions. When you get to the top, worries about staff and family do get to you. By the end my worries about preserving the inheritance of twenty-nine young family beneficiaries of the family trusts probably outweighed anything else, as I and the older generation had already received our inheritance.

It would be easy to admit to making many mistakes but I only really made one crucial one, I should have brought in a chief executive some years before I was finally forced into it. Although it would have been a tremendous shock to all the staff who had been used to three decades of uninterrupted growth, anyone who could see where the industry was heading (and I was one who could see) would realise that a major shake-up was needed. It would have been very difficult for the staff to appreciate the problem. They had grown used to years of plenty and a job for life (there had been virtually no redundancies or sackings except for dishonesty in the past thirty years). Whilst it would have been difficult for a chief executive, I'm sure that had I been brave enough to go that route there were people around who could have got us through the difficult times. It is worth remembering that, out of our construction dining club of sixteen mainstream construction members, only Balfour Beatty, Sir Robert McAlpine, Carillion (formerly Tarmac Construction) and Costain survive in much the same form today. All the others have merged, been taken over or have gone into related activities – house building, quarrying or, in the case of Amec, oil related business.

Although my failure to maintain the family presence in Alfred McAlpine did my image with the construction press no good, I still believe I was a fairly competent businessman, as my time as a non-executive director with Hall Engineering and Aintree Racecourse and the chairmanship of Chester Race Company would prove. I have though to confess to some personal failings. I was very naïve on a number of fronts and I tended to believe people were both more competent and nicer than a number turned out to be. Robert Sangster, in his short business career, had a much more ruthless streak. I could have done with some of it.

Eighty years of existence has seen tremendous changes on a number of fronts. The barriers broken down on the social side are truly amazing and few of the young today can imagine how seriously social status was taken in the years I grew up. Nobody worries about people's backgrounds anymore, the important thing is how they carry on with other people. Nowhere is that better illustrated than on a Sunday morning at Delamere Golf Club, where David, Ricky, Stuart, Derek, Keith, William, Tom, Paul, Ellis and I meet. I haven't a clue about half of their backgrounds but we all happily throw the balls in the air, divide into groups and have a drink afterwards. It would not have happened sixty years ago.

The multi-racial society we now live in is certainly a far cry from the almost entirely white environment I started life in. I did spend a couple of evenings electioneering for Enoch Powell – though I never met him – when I lived in Wolverhampton. In fact the only time I met him was years later when he came to Carden after hunting with the Wynnstay. I did witness at first hand the passionate opposition of those who lived in Wolverhampton to the first influx of non-whites, mainly from the Caribbean, in search of a better life. The opposition was much more on economic grounds than actual dislike of the new arrivals. As one staff member of our Wolverhampton office put it, 'They only have to buy one house in a street for the rest to put theirs up for sale.' Certainly there was no city where his 'River of Blood' speech would have had a better reception and what they made of the subsequent invasion of Muslims from Africa and Asia I was not there to witness.

Money is of course important, particularly if you are lucky enough to have sufficient to lead the life you want. As I had to live on a comparatively modest salary until my late twenties, I was very much taught the value of it and whilst I can't claim to have spent entirely wisely, I at least had considerable enjoyment from it. Surprisingly some of my very rich friends have been far from the happiest – Robert Sangster was a classic example. As he became a leading racehorse owner he became the target of every bloodstock agent around. As his first wife, Christine, said to me on the weekend they broke up, 'They all arrive and treat Robert like a god, get a cheque out of him and then leave as soon as they can. It has simply gone to his head!' Very rich people are not treated like ordinary mortals and it needs great strength of character if they are to remain well balanced and content.

Neither of my parents was remotely religious so I was never subjected to that sort of pressure. In fact it was only when I became engaged to Jane that I had any real contact with the church. The decline in religious beliefs in the Christian part of our society had been truly amazing and whilst churches were not full when I started life, apart from Christmas and Easter, they are now almost empty. Three if my four children all started life as Catholics but none are practising Catholics today. I have to say I find the decline in belief rather sad. Whilst I have not always obeyed the Ten Commandments, I have certainly admired them and the general Christian way of life.

Perhaps the decline in belief also contributed to the sexual revolution of the sixties, which in general has been a good influence, as the young seem to have a much more relaxed attitude than they did when I grew up. I have always believed that the Gene system also applies to sexual activity. Both men and women are born with high libidos – or the opposite – and whilst men have always to some extent been able to tailor their desires, women have surely been the greater beneficiaries. No longer are they expected to go to the altar as virgins and the percentage that do so must be miniscule. Moreover they are taught to expect far more from their partners.

One area that has improved greatly is education for young people. I can't speak for state schools but private schools are like holiday camps compared to the rough old days I was brought up in. The standard of teaching has improved enormously and all my six grandchildren have been very happy at school. That is as it should be. The old axiom that schools are there to make a man (or woman) of you is totally discredited, and rightly so.

Sadly one area which has not gone the right way had been respect for a government and politicians, who now seem to be a target for the public, egged on by the media. I have long felt that members of parliament should be paid more and that if they were we would see a higher standard. We have had in recent years some exceptionally poor government, as money has been poured into welfare, education and health, much of it badly spent. Capital spending has been the greater sufferer and Germany and France have far better infrastructures than Britain. When I see Kenneth Clarke and government ministers trying to find reasons for lower sentences and floundering on television, I long to shout, 'Why don't you build better and bigger prisons.'

When you live for eighty years your friends inevitably change and sadly many great friends from the past are no longer with us. Of all my old Shropshire friends, only Michael Stoddart, Doug Graham, Hugh Meynell and Michael Mander are still living there, although Willy Jenks has taken the place of his father Brian. In Cheshire, David Stern and Cecil Jenkins are still going strong and younger friends like Ricky Roundell, Stuart and Adele Williams and Richard and Henrietta Thomas have taken the place of old stagers. David Marchwood, Panton Corbett, Richard Hall and Tim Kitson are from a great way back and I still see them regularly. The racing side had produced many strong friendships of which Barry and Penny Hills is the foremost. Jeremy Hindley lives in South Africa and John Edwards in Ireland. Dick Bonnycastle, who has been with us on many memorable holidays, sadly rarely comes to England. My brother-in-law, Peter Shaw, has had a major scare but is now fine as is my sister, Valerie. Friends are very important and I have been very lucky in this respect.

Finally, the big question, is there life after death? I remember my mother ruminating over this many times. Although not religious she was full of curiosity, right up to her final hours. As a cushion in the drawing room of a friend of mine stated 'life is not a rehearsal' and Professors Cox and Dawkins are impressive in their certain view that death really is the end. Have I any regrets? Yes, plenty, but the happy memories outweigh them. On the whole it's been a pretty good life – so far.

Index

Index

Index

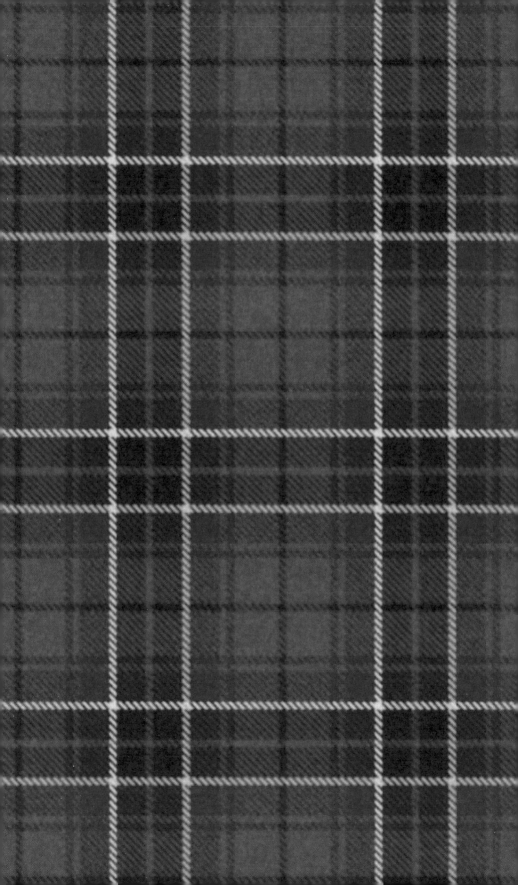